The Creative Self is a novel contribution to the c
and education. With narrative flair, wit and a
amining the promise and perils of the design
invites readers to take Winnicott to school. Imagine then, how our earliest
tional ties to the mother's care have a second chance in pedagogical relationships. Bibby's insightful analysis gives us the spirited thinking that, after all, with the provisions of pedagogy as creative relations, and with dedication to the ins and outs of well-being, education, too, can become 'good enough.'

Deborah Britzman, Distinguished Research Professor, York University Toronto, Canada.

THE CREATIVE SELF

The Creative Self engages with the work of the psychoanalyst D.W. Winnicott to develop alternative ways of thinking about key issues at the heart of pedagogy; specifically pedagogic relationships, creativity, defiance and compliance. These issues underpin the desires and defences of professionals located in educational institutions, such as the desire to know what is best, to know how to reach all learners, normalised expectations of behaviours and outcomes, and sometimes challenging engagements with students and the curriculum.

Each chapter provides both a theoretical focus and illustrative demonstrations of the ways in which Winnicott's theories may be relocated and used productively as tools for professional and academic reflexivity. By building extensively on Winnicott's understanding of the ways in which relationships facilitate (or hinder) the development of the self, this book extends his clinical focus on parental and analytical relationships to think about the ways in which the pedagogic relationship can provide an environment in which people may (or may fail to) develop as learners.

This approach provides powerful ways of thinking about pedagogy and pedagogic relationships that stand apart from the cognitive and rationalist tradition. This focus can be used constructively to support people working in educational settings to re-establish a sense of personal and professional autonomy in an environment recently typified by compliance. *The Creative Self* is an engaging and innovative read appealing to postgraduate students, teachers, researchers and academics with a desire for a new analytic lens through which to explore the educational experiences of both learners and teachers in schools, colleges and universities.

Tamara Bibby is an independent researcher and writer, previously at University College London, Institute of Education, UK.

Foundations and Futures of Education

Peter Aggleton, UNSW Australia
Sally Power, Cardiff University, UK
Michael Reiss, UCL Institute of Education, UK

Foundations and Futures of Education focuses on key emerging issues in education as well as continuing debates within the field. The series is inter-disciplinary, and includes historical, philosophical, sociological, psychological and comparative perspectives on three major themes: the purposes and nature of education; increasing interdisciplinarity within the subject; and the theory-practice divide.

The Creative Self
Psychoanalysis, Teaching and Learning in the Classroom
Tamara Bibby

Materialities and Mobilities in Education
Rachel Brooks and Johanna Waters

A Social History of Educational Studies and Research
Gary McCulloch and Steven Cowan

Teacher Education and the Political
The Power of Negative Thinking
Matthew Clarke and Anne Phelan

Questioning Leadership
New Directions for Educational Organisations
Gabriele Lakomski, Scott Eacott and Colin Evers

Teacher Subject Identity in Professional Practice
Teaching with a Professional Compass
Clare Brooks

Understanding the University
Ronald Barnett

Lifespan Transitions and Disability
A Holistic Perspective
Iva Strnadová and Therese Cumming

Religion in the Primary School
Ethos, Diversity, Citizenship
Peter J. Hemming

Discerning Critical Hope in Educational Practices
Vivienne Bozalek, Brenda Leibowitz, Ronelle Carolissen and Megan Boler

Education and Masculinities
Social, Cultural and Global Transformations
Chris Haywood and Mairtin Mac an Ghaill

THE CREATIVE SELF

Psychoanalysis, Teaching and Learning in the Classroom

Tamara Bibby

Routledge
Taylor & Francis Group
LONDON AND NEW YORK

First published 2018
by Routledge
2 Park Square, Milton Park, Abingdon, Oxon OX14 4RN

and by Routledge
711 Third Avenue, New York, NY 10017

Routledge is an imprint of the Taylor & Francis Group, an informa business

British Library Cataloguing-in-Publication Data
A catalogue record for this book is available from the British Library

Library of Congress Cataloging-in-Publication Data
Names: Bibby, Tamara, author.
Title: The creative self: psychoanalysis, teaching and learning in the classroom / Tamara Bibby.
Description: Abingdon, Oxon; New York, NY: Routledge, [2018] | Includes bibliographical references.
Identifiers: LCCN 2017014255 | ISBN 9780415716796 (hbk) | ISBN 9780415716802 (pbk) | ISBN 9781315876757 (ebk)
Subjects: LCSH: Psychoanalysis and education. | Reflective teaching. | Teachers—Psychology. | Learning, Psychology of. | Winnicott, D.W. (Donald Woods), 1896–1971—Influence.
Classification: LCC LB1092 .B52 2018 | DDC 370.15—dc23
LC record available at https://lccn.loc.gov/2017014255

ISBN: 978-0-415-71679-6 (hbk)
ISBN: 978-0-415-71680-2 (pbk)
ISBN: 978-1-315-87675-7 (ebk)

Typeset in Bembo
by codeMantra

CONTENTS

ACKNOWLEDGEMENTS

I would like to thank the many and various good enough (m)others who have helped me to think about and write this book. I would like to express my particular gratitude to Anne Murray, Elena Lopez, Helen Lucey, Lisa Farley, Meg Maguire, Peter Aggleton, Ros Sills and Zoe Loumis. I know I am a nuisance; my creativity, such as it is, is woven into my relationships with you. Thank you all for your many kindnesses, your patience and encouragement. Any remaining half-formed ideas, loose threads, dropped balls, holes in arguments and so forth are mine alone.

Thanks are also due to Laura Teague and Amir Lamouchi for their permission to use data from their original research work. Also to Charlotte for permission to reuse a vignette written as part of the 'Approaches to Disadvantage' seminar series.

Thank you too to the Economic and Social Research Council (ESRC) for funding the projects whose data I continue to use:

- *Children's learner-identities in mathematics at key stage 2* (RES-000-22-1272 with Alex Moore).
- *Bridging the structure/agency divide: Interdisciplinary approaches to disadvantage and education* (Seminar series with Ruth Lupton and Carlo Raffo).

1

INTRODUCTION

The writing of this book has been a drawn-out process. It has unintentionally spanned a hiatus in my own life, a hiatus that is interesting in terms of the subject matter I deal with here. As someone who has spent most of her life in educational institutions – as a pupil, as a student and as a teacher and lecturer – and as I leave that life and meet new people, the question of education takes on new hues, and I find myself wondering again about this business. What is this thing, this process we call education? What is it for? Is 'it' a singular thing or a plural thing? Should we talk rather of 'educations'? How does it/do they relate to 'schooling'? or 'training'? To what extent is education an event or a process? Is there a moment when we become 'educated'? What do we mean when we identify individuals as educated: 'He is an educated man'? or indeed, 'He is an uneducated man'?

An important, but often overlooked, question to ask when thinking about schools is 'what do we want education to achieve?' This is a complex question requiring complex answers. Part of an answer might include the idea that we want education to enable people to continue learning throughout their lives. Under current policy regimes in countries such as the UK, the USA and Australia, this idea is paid lip service, but it is not always clear whether 'lifelong learning' can mean any more than 'be prepared to do courses to facilitate changes of career in an unstable jobs market': we have to hope it can! If we aspire to continue learning and having more than a utilitarian meaning of 'education', then what might it be? And how can compulsory education hope to create the personal qualities and skills needed to enable people to keep themselves learning? Because not all learning takes place in formal contexts, this surely involves much more than attending schools, colleges and universities.

For some (like myself), the business of being a student seems never-ending. I have always liked learning new things. Well, some new things. I am currently learning to run, and I am not at all sure that I like that! But education is full of transition and exit points: new ages and new phases of education, new institutions, new expectations. Is education essentially the same or different after these transitions? And what about education in or after employment? What about 'lifelong learning'? The developmental story that accompanies education implies 'growing up' and differences – I am no longer 5 years old, how can education be the same when I am 15? Or 25? Or 55? Or 75? Yet, part of the purpose of this book is to challenge this storyline and to suggest that there is a timelessness to the business of learning about and learning to be. I want to notice and explore the effects of conflating education with growing up, or educatedness with maturity. Such conflations create many difficulties for schools and teachers at all phases, difficulties that lie at the heart of this book and will be explored in later chapters.

A nub of this book is that all learning is creative. All learning (beyond rote memorisation) requires a willingness to keep an open mind, a preparedness to keep being surprised, a capacity to hold onto curiosity and sense of wonder, a desire to keep asking questions. This goes far beyond utilitarian notions that we need to be prepared to keep learning so that we can pass exams or undertake professional development to retrain or develop our professional portfolios; we may indeed need to do all of those things, but there is far more at stake. The suggestion I want to make is that these qualities – of openness, wonder, curiosity, questing and their like – are central to mental health or well-being and that the contexts for learning expand far beyond the walls of the formal institution.

In an effort to define 'health', Winnicott said:

> Let us say that in health a man or woman is able *to reach towards an identification with society without too great a loss of individual or personal impulse.* ... [But] the life of a healthy individual is characterised by fears, conflicting feelings, doubts, frustrations, as much as by the positive features. The main thing is that the man or woman feels he or she is *living his or her own life*, taking responsibility for action or inaction, and able to take credit or blame for failure.
> *(1967, pp.26–27 emphasis in original)*

This statement may surprise. Winnicott suggests that 'health' (what we might now tend to call 'wellness') includes a capacity to tolerate emotional pain or discomfort. The idealisation of 'ease' and its conflation with wellness troubles much of our modern life, yet Winnicott removes the impossible expectation that if we are 'well', we are only and always happy. Dis-ease is part of health, life is not 'easy'. There is so much more to be learned than a mandated curriculum if we are to learn about and tolerate our own creativity, our own learning processes. I suggest that a capacity to engage in learning implies not only that we know what we need to do to progress through the education system or to further our careers, but also – and more importantly – that we can recognise and respond to our own desires. While we might expect that such recognition would be easy, it is often not: 'I want to write but feel I have nothing to say'; 'I want to travel but am not sure where I might go or what I would do there'. In a more practical vein, the difficulties some people have stepping aside from work at retirement or moving on from redundancy offer concrete examples of the very real difficulties that can be experienced when we try to locate our own desires and identify what we want – particularly after busy (compliant) working lives.

So, how do we come into being as subjects, as people able to know ourselves and (even some of) our desires? How do we learn to make contact with those desires and what might get in the way of that? What role does the environment (mother, home, teacher, classroom, school, society) play in our becomingness? The way Winnicott understood developmental processes was in terms of a movement in the infant from dependence to independence. Adam Phillips has highlighted the fact that we tend to operate with restricted, linear and concrete understandings of 'growing up'. He contrasts this limited sense with Winnicott's more generous understanding. Growing up, Phillips points out, has become a rush to rationality, independence and (self-) control ...

> [a] necessary flight from inarticulacy; from the less affectively ordered self, a self without its best behaviours to be on, a self that suffers and enjoys at a pitch that the grown-ups often find daunting. ... But if we describe development as not merely or simply the acquisition of linguistic – and therefore moral – competence, we may be better able to nurture in children the necessary to and fro between the inarticulate and the articulate selves: a to and fro that might be sustainable throughout life rather than having its last gasp during adolescence.
>
> *(Phillips, 1998, pp.48–49)*

Here, Phillips is hinting at a problem with the ideas of development and linear growth that schools take as a given. Schools are structured around 'growing up': children change year (and often teacher) annually; they move to primary school in latency and secondary schools at adolescence. Transitions from nursery to primary and again from primary to secondary schools are often talked of as moving to 'big school'. Similarly, graduation from compulsory education is taken as the beginning of adulthood; although the edges are blurry, within a year or two of leaving school young people begin to gain access to full membership of society and legal responsibilities: work, marriage, voting, joining the army, taxation, etc. These linear 'growning ups' sit alongside chronological time enabling our institutions to function smoothly but, do we really 'grow up' so smoothly? Teachers are often frustrated that children appear to 'forget everything over the long summer holidays', secondary school teachers complain that primary teachers 'don't teach children anything', and children leave school 'ill prepared for the world of work'. Clearly, all is not as smooth and straightforward as the developmental story would suggest. There is something looping and recursive about learning. Jerome Bruner's (1960) 'spiral curriculum' and the need to revisit topics come as a relief as we add caveats to complicate notions of development (perhaps to the point where the coherence of the story is lost). The difficulties with developmental narratives and linear growth are explored in a little more detail below and are a continuing theme of this book.

Teaching and education

This book begins from a belief that teaching – and therefore learning and education – is fundamentally about relationships: relationships with people, those who teach us, those we learn from, our families and peers; relationships with the knowledge they embody and share, their passions; and relationships with our own growing (or diminishing) sense of ourselves as knowers and not knowers. Elsewhere (Bibby, 2009) I have argued that how we come to know anything – from how to roast a chicken to reading and mathematics – is intimately bound to the contexts and particularly the people in which and with whom we do that learning. Even apparently independent learning is shaped by those we have internalised and who have helped us form our tastes, our passions, our ways of thinking and engaging with the world.

So, I begin from an acceptance that we are relational beings, that we are constituted in, and exist through, relationships: relationships with people, ideas and our surroundings. More than this, we are profoundly susceptible to others; they exert an uncanny influence upon us. For Freud, this is what it meant to be human.

> [P]sycho-analysis has taught us that the individual's emotional attitudes to other people, which are of such extreme importance to his later behaviour, are already established at an unexpectedly early age. The nature and quality of the human child's relations to people of his own and the opposite sex have already been laid down in the first six years of his life. He may afterwards develop and transform them in certain directions, but he can no longer get rid of them. The people to whom he is in this way fixed are his parents and his brothers and sisters. All those whom he gets to know later become substitute figures for these first objects of his feelings. (We should perhaps add to his parents any other people, such as nurses, who cared for him in his infancy.) [...] His later acquaintances are thus obliged to take over a kind of emotional heritage; they encounter sympathies and antipathies to the production of which they themselves have contributed little. All of his later choices of friendship and love follow upon the basis of the memory-traces left behind by these first prototypes.
>
> *(Freud, 1931, p.242)*

Here, Freud is pointing out that the unconscious ambivalence we feel towards our parents, our siblings and other members of our immediate family – our passionate, contradictory and mercurial loves and hates – are visited on others, just as theirs are visited upon us. This is not something we can wish away or completely control, it just is. As a primary school teacher, it was not unknown for children to call me 'Mum' or 'Gran' (depending on who they were living at home with) and, if they caught themselves, to be immediately embarrassed. Perhaps we have all had moments of having to remind ourselves that someone is not our father, not our mother, not our sister or brother, that we do not always have to respond – with anger, fury, depression, love, envy, however – *as if* they were.

We are not born blank; we bring instincts and needs to our first relationship, and as soon as we are born, those instincts, needs and reactions are being given back to us: they are named, tamed and shaped. These actions and reactions, needs, and desires and our understandings of how these are responded to, these are the building-blocks from which our sense of self is formed and sculpted. As we progress through life, that initial template shapes our later interactions. Our desires, our ways of being and ways of relating, develop, grow and shift over time, but any changes that are made are to that early template. While tastes and proclivities develop over time, making changes to these or to the shape of our fundamental desires is less easy, so while radical changes can perhaps be made, this is never an easy process. Our relationships to ourselves, to people in the past and present, to people in the world and people in our minds, and to knowledge are central to who we are. And, if we are teachers, relationships are central to our professional lives as well.

If we accept that relationships and relationality are central concerns of learning and teaching, then how best can we think about them? Which ideas and theories are the most productive when considering the relational nature of work in education contexts? How can I think about how I conduct myself as an educator and how I seek to engage – or perhaps to re-engage – people with the ideas, knowledge and ways of working that it is my business to share? Traditional advice to teachers on relationships has never felt very helpful: not smiling until Christmas, maintaining zero-tolerance policies with regard to non-compliance, leaving 'myself' at the school gates, following three-step escalations of punishment (or reward). In fact, such advice seems designed to minimise (or even deny) the need to recognise and think about the very relationships that are at the heart of learning and teaching: is selective relationality desirable or possible? And is it ever possible to engage people with ideas without fully engaging oneself?

For Winnicott, the self is forged in relationship with a primary carer. His focus in the first instance is on the last weeks of pregnancy and the first few weeks of infancy, and so he always talked about the primary carer as mother. His suggestion was that where the primary carer was the father (or someone else) at this stage, they are acting *as mother*. For Winnicott (1971), the 'father' cannot exist for the infant until it is able to recognise and tolerate the existence of not-me objects. His famous suggestion that 'there is no such thing as a baby' (1964) speaks to this understanding that the baby is always in relationship; part of a pair. We might wonder, is this also true for the learner? We might wonder: does a learner exist without a teacher? Even (or especially) if the teacher is in the mind? A teacher without a learner? This book uses the work of D.W. Winnicott and others to explore different ways of acknowledging and working with and within pedagogic relationships. The people whose work I will draw on are primarily psychoanalysts, which perhaps raises immediate questions: Why aren't I just drawing on 'regular' psychology? What has psychoanalysis got to do with teaching? What is psychoanalysis anyway? Is it okay to use these theories to think about classrooms?[1] And, why Winnicott?

Why not 'regular' psychology?

Traditional (cognitive) psychology is highly invested in its beginnings in science. There is typically a strong concern to follow scientific methods and to treat the human condition as susceptible to rational, scientific efforts. While there is much that this approach to the human mind and human behaviour can and does tell us, there is also much that it cannot. A common complaint against cognitive and rational beliefs about human life is that they treat people like other objects in the natural world: as knowable, measurable and predictable. But people cannot necessarily be measured in the same way as inanimate objects: Is IQ a fact of life or an artefact of our desire to measure intelligence as if it were a fixed and stable entity? Does measuring the density of granite affect its existence beyond that measurement in the way that measuring IQ affects a student's subsequent opportunities?

However that may be, 'regular' psychology, scientific psychology if you prefer, is very familiar to educators. Indeed, developmental psychology shapes much of what is done in schools and nurseries. It also sets limits on our idea of childhood, of what is 'normal' and of human development more broadly. All of the ideas that make up 'regular' and developmental psychology (see, for example, Moore, 2000) – from Piaget's stages of learning though Vygotsky's zone of proximal development, and on to the work of more recent theorists like Engstrom and Bruner – have come to be accepted as a kind of common sense. Developmental psychology's 'truths' about children and childhood have been annealed in the fires of custom and practice until they pass unnoticed as common sense.

Scientific psychology appeals to our adult desires for rationality, control, order and predictability, and in meeting those needs, the more familiar forms of psychology have been very successful. But we need to ask ourselves questions about this taken-for-granted status and to reveal what psychology can blind us to. Much has been written about the difficulties with developmental psychology, about the ways the discourses it mobilises come to produce the very child it seeks to enumerate and describe (see, for example, Walkerdine, 1984, 1986; Burman, 1994). It is not my intention to rehearse those critiques here, although I recommend them to anyone working in education. But I do want to notice some of the particular difficulties that developmentalism can bring: its tendencies to normalise and blind us (or make us intolerant) to difference, its linearity and its unidirectionality.

'Developmentalism' is a belief that developmental narratives are rational descriptions of something real, universal and timeless. Such an understanding relates to physical maturation and holds up adulthood as an endpoint, a culmination and an achievement; adulthood is the 'natural' outcome of childhood. The maturity of adulthood is seen as the polar opposite of immature childhood with the two embodying differences that appeal to our adult minds: rationality and experience are set against a certain animalism and innocence, completion and wholeness against incompleteness and unformedness, the simplicity of childhood signals our adult complexity and progress: See how far we have come (Silin, 1995). 'The child' comes to be created as less than adult, as male, as a work in progress, as a vessel for adult hopes and ambitions, as a fantasy of what our better selves might become. The monolithic 'child' of the developmental story keeps our adult desires safe by providing an 'other' into which we can project that which we would disavow in ourselves: our stumblings, our irrationality, our anxieties and disappointments. Such is one reading of developmentalism. These themes are a constant throughout this book, which might, on one level and ironically, be (mis)read as an entirely developmental story.

Turning to the tools of psychology, particularly the statistics of cohorts: scientific psychologies normalise some things and simultaneously render others abject. Through its habits of averaging and graphing, psychology effects a smoothing of the irregularities of life. When averaging (in whatever way), statistics shave off extremes and a 'normal' or an 'expectation' is created. Statements such as 'Six-year-olds can …' or 'The average 4-year-old is …' can create anxiety for parents and teachers alike. Anyone whose child is 'ahead' of the (normal distribution) curve may feel pride and delight, but what of those whose 6-year-old cannot or whose 4-year-old is not …? And what of the children themselves? What if they do not recognise themselves in the corresponding charts and categories? What are they to make of themselves? If one individual sits at an extreme of the cohort or is an outlier, if they do not fit the norms of growth and development, how are they to understand themselves? What are we to make of them? How do we deal with the more (or less) than normal? The diagnostics that accompany the statistics come with labels – euphemisms – for developmental abnormalities: withdrawn, autistic, special needs, slow reader, dyslexic, dyscalculic, ADHD, school phobic, short, tall, … I would not deny that some people struggle to learn, or perhaps struggle to fit into the rigid versions of education and learning that they are faced with in formal learning settings. Rather, I would want to notice how the labels are generated and how hard they are to shift once they have been given. And we might want to notice how those who fall outside the dominant frames of development[2] and who are therefore subject to pathologising diagnoses, require discipline and correction.

Finally, we can see how these narratives of development are linear and unidirectional. They provide ladders to climb and paths to be trod. We grow *up* not down or sideways, let alone off to a tangent, round in circles, or backwards (Stockton, 2004). I am starting here to point to other traditions, to critical psychologies, to queer theory and to psychoanalysis. To me, life and experience are far from straightforward, never simple and always full of regressions and recursions. We loop and judder through life, racing on and faltering – and rarely recognising each for what it is. We can spend hours, weeks, years retracing our steps, realising we have doubled back on ourselves or spent great effort describing an arc that brings us back to somewhere only too familiar that we thought we had left far behind. These thoughts – a rejection of linearity, a suspicion that reliable rationality is a fantasy, a desire to embrace my not-normal bits and to celebrate loopy learning – these are the things that led me to psychoanalysis.

What is psychoanalysis?

Psychoanalysis provides us with ways of thinking about the edges of experience, about our uncanny responses to others, about our loopy learning. The edges that scientific psychology would smooth away, the outliers it would delete, these are the bread and meat of psychoanalysis. Its aim is not to describe the general but to find a language with which to explore the particular. And through considerations of the particular we can come to recognise aspects of our own experience – sometimes directly, sometimes in negative. And we are reminded that we might deny and refuse hard-to-accept facts and emotions that cut too near the knuckle.

Psychoanalysis is a branch of psychology and, for some, it retains its links to science. Winnicott, in a talk given to the Oxford University Scientific Society, explored precisely this question and is generous to the two fields in both their 'pure' and applied forms:

> Psychoanalysis [...] extends scientific territory to cover the phenomena of human personality, human feeling and human conflict. It claims, therefore, that human nature can be examined; and [as with science] where ignorance is exposed, psychoanalysis can afford to wait and need not indulge in flight to superstitious formulations. One of the main contributions of science is the halt that it calls to hurry, fuss and bother; it gives time for a breather. We may play our game of bowls and beat the Spaniards too.
>
> *(Winnicott, 1961, p.14)*

Freud too was concerned to be scientific and the ideas and methods he developed as part of psychoanalysis aim to take account of the undoubtedly, and deliberately, subjective nature of the subject (Elliott, 2002). As Winnicott suggests, the focus in psychoanalysis is on the human condition and the experience of being and living in social contexts/society. The focus in psychoanalytic theory is on people's *experiences* of living their lives and the ways they account for these experiences. Making sense of these experiences and the patchy and contradictory accounts we offer to ourselves and others, is the stuff of psychoanalysis, which explores the ways our unconscious shapes and impacts our lived lives. Since Freud first began his work, others have taken up and adapted or radically altered and moved away from his first ideas; and Freud too developed his ideas and changed his mind over his long career. Despite these changes, there are core ideas that remain central to psychoanalysis, its theory and practice. Key amongst these is the notion of the unconscious as a dynamic force, our divided selves and our nature as defended subjects.

The divided mind

On a fairly familiar level, our non-unitary nature means that we occupy multiple and complex positions. As I sit and write this book, I take up the position of one who has something to say, someone who knows things others might feel are helpful (or choose to reject). However, I also train my dog and, when I go on training courses with him, I am someone with fragile knowledge and I can feel both vulnerable and stupid, guilty for the mistakes I have made, overwhelmed by the extent and depth of my ignorance. I also know I have never learned to play a musical instrument, faced with a guitar or a violin I barely know how to hold let alone play it. I am therefore simultaneously knowledgeable, learning and ignorant; confident, uncertain and lost: it depends on the context, but I have multiple states of being. As I traverse contexts, aspects of my identity remain relatively stable, but other aspects might be called into question. I can potentially be shown my ignorance or uncertainty by anyone of any age if I am open to that as a possibility, especially if I can tolerate the experience of discomfort or shame. I am also prepared to accept, in my states of ignorance, insecurity and confusion as I try to learn something new, that I have to allow myself, once again, to be vulnerable to and dependent on whoever I choose to trust to teach and nurture me. Fortunately, as an adult, this is generally a choice I can exercise; in this matter, children are less fortunate.

On another level, our divided nature extends to our minds. Alongside our conscious lives – those aspects of our selves that we know about – lies an unconscious, a profoundly unknown and unknowable part of our minds. Uncomfortably for some, this aspect of ourselves is, psychoanalysis suggests, what shapes and drives our conscious lives. As Frosh explains, 'what we are taught to see as "natural" in the human condition, the capacity to use *reason*, is only a small part of the story: behind every action is a wish, behind every thought is an unreasonable desire' (2002, p.17). This underscores the idea that we are not entirely in charge of ourselves, an idea that sits uncomfortably with beliefs in humanity as rational and ourselves as able to deliberately and consciously control and effect change in our lives, particularly change in who we are. But, as anyone who has ever tried to break a habit, or struggled to like a colleague who irritates them, will know, wishing our selves different (unfortunately) is not enough; it is never that simple.

The dynamic unconscious and the defended self

That the unconscious is unknowable is difficult to accept, although its emergence in slips of the tongue, in dreams and in our forgettings trips us into facing it. The unconscious may be easier to recognise in others, perhaps in those moments when what is said and how it is said fail to match (perhaps a note of anger that accompanies a protestation of love), when we catch a glimpse of a hidden desire putting truth where the conscious mind sought to hide it (perhaps a mis-naming that attributes some aspect of me to my sister) and so on. But how annoying is it to have such an inconsistency pointed out or to hear an unintended word slip out, and how quickly do we jump to deny or reassure? 'No, that's not what I meant!'

One suggestion for part of this unknowability is the origin of the unconscious in pre-verbal life; we have no way to speak our unconscious because it was formed perceptually before we had words to use (Klein, 1930). Another is the necessity for repression: some of what is unconscious is unconscious because it has been repressed, shut away as too dangerous (shameful, destructive, unacceptable) to know: our murderous rage, our greed and envy, our terrors of love and dependency and so forth. That is, we are constituted as *defended subjects*, always protecting ourselves and others from the presumed worst of our selves.

Another factor to take into account is the dynamic nature of the unconscious; it does not sit still waiting to be known but is constantly active. For every slip that perhaps provides some sense of the anger we are repressing, our changing contexts, our changing conscious awarenesses and new experiences mean the unconscious shifts to reorganise old affects to incorporate new understandings and new experiences. The unconscious is a dynamic, active process, and we need to be beware of making the unconscious sound wholly negative:

> [T]he concept of a *dynamic unconscious* is two fold: not only are unconscious ideas dynamic in the sense of having to be held back by an opposing force, but also in the sense of being *causal*. It is the unconscious that produces much of the warp and weft of psychic life, its richness and its confusion.
>
> *(Frosh, 2002, p.15)*

While the unconscious as an effect or an activity is undisputed, the ways in which it is thought about vary, with slightly different metaphors being applied to convey the imagined functions – charting these is a complex task beyond the scope of this book (but see, for example, Elliott, 2002; Frosh, 1999). Here, it is sufficient to note that, while Klein and Freud suggested that instincts were constitutive of the self, Adam Phillips (2007, p.9) reminds us that, for Winnicott, instincts serve the self. As others have explained,

> For Klein, with closer ties to [Freud], phantasy is primarily an internal phenomenon, generated by the drives and related to the world of real others only secondarily. In Winnicott's system the primacy of phantasy is preserved but the content is altered. "Fantasy is more primary than reality, and the enrichment of fantasy with the world's riches depends on the experience of illusion" (1945: 153). For him phantasy is oriented towards personalised reality from the start, manifesting itself in a readiness to develop illusions of control over what the real world actually provides. Through phantasy the infant is poised, at the "moment of illusion," for relational interchange with the outside world.
>
> *(Greenberg and Mitchell, 1983, p.203)*

This is a complex statement, which I will let sit for now. Its meaning will, I hope, become clearer as the book progresses and ideas beyond the unconscious are introduced and elaborated. But we see here the depth of Winnicott's commitment to ideas of relationality, his belief that the unconscious forms in relation to real people in the world, not just to part objects in phantasy (the Kleinian model). These are ideas that will be explained and elaborated throughout the rest of the book.

What has psychoanalysis got to do with teaching? And, is it okay to use these theories to think about education?

The central concern of psychoanalysis is our capacity to live in relationship, and, as I suggested above, teaching is similarly concerned with relationships. Beyond this simple statement of concern, it is helpful to distinguish two interrelated facets of psychoanalysis: (1) psychoanalysis as therapeutic alliance and (2) psychoanalytic theory as a set of tools that enable psychotherapists to think about their work with their clients – and non-clinicians to think about the relationships that are working in/with.

The most common understanding of psychoanalysis is of the therapeutic alliance intended to enable an individual to come to terms with living with themselves and others. An individual oppressed by their life, struggling with depression or a multitude of problems can choose a psychoanalyst whose work may be grounded in any of a number of approaches (Freudian, Lacanian, Jungian, Kleinian, Ego psychology, Object relations ... the list is long). The notion of 'the talking cure' has developed in many ways since Freud's original work, but importantly this is not the use of psychoanalysis this book employs. This book is emphatically *not* about teachers psychoanalysing themselves or their students; such actions would be irresponsible and unethical. It is instead about making use of a set of ideas that are essentially about relationships and re-casting these, re-contextualising them from the clinic to the classroom to think differently about schools and schooling, teaching and learning, teachers and students, schools (or colleges or universities) and teachers, knowledge and knowers.

This book is not a 'how to' manual for psychodynamic or any other form of teaching, although it might act as a 'what if' prompt for reflection. The aim of this book is to think again and think differently about what might happen in learning contexts and to ask: Can we think of these things in another way? And, if the answer is 'yes', what might we want to do with this new knowledge?

Why Winnicott?

So, given the number of psychoanalytic theorists and the range of their ideas, why focus on the work of one man, Donald Winnicott? The simple answer is that his absolute focus on relationships and the way in which these make possible (or constrain) development seems to hold the potential to be particularly productive for teachers. Initially a paediatrician, Winnicott trained as a psychoanalyst following his own analysis. Given his particular background, he developed his ideas about the business of becoming in relation to the ideas of his colleagues but remained an independent thinker, avoiding the divisions and internal politics of the British Psychoanalytic Society (see, for example, the early chapters in Britzman, 2003).

As an analyst Winnicott often wrote for and spoke to non-clinical audiences including parents (particularly mothers), teachers and social workers. In the public imagination, his work is often linked to ideas like the 'good enough mother' and 'transitional objects'. His concern with very young children has led to some unhelpful ideas about him. This book is not intended as a defence of Winnicott's work, but where criticisms are relevant, they will be included and engaged with. I have come across those who, registering his concern with babies, young children and 'good enough' mothers, either infuse his name with syrupy notions of love and unrealistic doting self-sacrifice or criticise him for holding up an ideal of motherhood that only the middle classes could afford to access. But, as Winnicott notes, it is possible simultaneously to be both physically present and emotionally absent. Being 'good enough' is never a matter of money; it is a matter of thought and intention, so many criticisms (whether dismissive or idealising) miss the mark and are profoundly unhelpful; his work is far from romantically inclined. As the chapters that follow will show, he was concerned with the full person: not only their loves, desires and generosities but also their hates, angers, furies and destructive urges (and actions). He sees signs of hope in 'delinquent' behaviour and despairs over quiet compliance. There is a steel hawser that wires his ideas together: the expectations he had of those taking on the position of adult in any relationship were high, but he is understanding of inevitable lapses. There is nothing syrupy about D.W. Winnicott. His ideas are not particularly easy, and as the chapters that follow demonstrate, thinking them through is not always comfortable. However, anyone who thinks that working with children or learning is a soft option or easy has clearly never engaged with either!

Despite his overt focus on very young children and mothers, Winnicott's work has relevance beyond the nursery. While Winnicott's ideas were developed initially in relation to his work as a paediatrician and his hours of professional observations of mothers and their babies in his consulting rooms, he went on to work with adults too. He was clear that processes of development, begun at birth, are never completed and that his ideas could be used to think about people of all ages:

> What we provide goes on being important as the child grows, and indeed never ceases, and joins up with the provisions that concern those who care for the aged. In other words, it will profit us to look at the needs of infants and then to translate those needs into language that is appropriate for all ages.
> *(Winnicott, 1962, p.69)*

This quote both reminds us of the timelessness of the unconscious and also highlights a central challenge to reading and using psychoanalytic theory to think outside the clinic, that is, the problem of language. If we step to one side to consider the ways in which we talk about ideas, projects, thoughts and thinking, we can, perhaps begin to see some parallels. We give birth to babies but also to ideas, we nurture children and also plants and projects, and we care for children but also for the outputs of our professional lives. Doctoral students, for example, often talk of feeling bereft once they have sent their manuscript to the binders; they have had to let their research and writing go out into the world and relinquish absolute control of the manuscript's life. If childbearing is a creative act, so too is writing a book, and developing a solution to a problem; goods as well as babies are delivered.

So, we need to extend the ways in which we read and understand the words of psychoanalysts. Mothers exist in literal and extended senses. Private schools often have 'house mothers' to take care of the pastoral needs of borders, teachers are *in loco parentis* (in the place of parents), a supervisor at the university or a form/class teacher in a school often takes on a mothering role. A (literal) mother is one who takes care of a baby – a vulnerable, developing infant—while an (extended) mother is also one who nurtures someone at a vulnerable or developing stage in their lives. So, whether the person in a state of dependency is 6 months or 6, 16 or 60 years old, if we are nurturing their growing independence, in whatever context and whether we are male or female, older or younger than them, we can be thought of as providing a mothering function.[3] Throughout the book, I refer to '(m)others' as a way of keeping the multiple possibilities for metaphorical mothering alive.

A first facilitating environment is by definition provided by a primary care-giver. A subsequent facilitating environment may be provided by a parent or other relative in the home, or by a teacher or lecturer in a classroom or seminar room. The literal and metaphorical holding of the first mother and later (m)others have parallels that are discussed in Chapter 2. A first transitional object provides a way for a baby to move towards the world beyond its mother's lap; subsequent transitional objects (and spaces) – including culture – enable us to move beyond familiar ways of thinking and being and to play with ideas and our selves. These are the ideas that form one dimension of the chapters to come.

Winnicott in relation to this book

Winnicott developed many ideas to enable him to conceptualise and describe his vision of the human condition: 'primary maternal preoccupation', 'the good enough mother', 'the facilitating environment', 'transitional object', 'the stage of I Am' and so on. His books, perhaps particularly *The child, the family, and the outside world* and *Playing and reality*, have received and continue to receive wide readership. It is not the intention of this book to describe his life's work; others have done that (most notably Adam Phillips, 2007). Rather, my goal is to take aspects of his work and, through describing and discussing these, think about issues that belong to education.

> In the master-plot of human development that he worked on for over forty years, Winnicott tried to explain how the individual grows, through dependence, towards a personal way of being, how he becomes at once ordinary and distinctive according to the sense he has of himself. Growth was this on-going task of psychosomatic integration. He was to stress the need for continuity of care – 'good enough mothering' – to sustain what he called the 'going on being', the 'life-line' of the infant at the earliest stages of his life. He would talk, enigmatically for a psychoanalyst, of instinctual life as a possible 'complication' in the individual's more fundamental needs for relationship.
>
> *(Phillips, 2007, p.2)*

For Winnicott, full health was relative and therefore dependent on stage of development: 'in terms of development … health means maturity according to the maturity that belongs to the age of the individual' (cited in Abraham, 2007, p.220). So, maturity is not some singular endpoint, nor is it something that comes with age; it is relative and multiple; perhaps we should think of developing maturities? In a talk whose topic was precisely an exploration of his understanding of health, Winnicott stated:

> Perhaps at one time psychoanalysts did tend *to think of health in terms of the absence of psychoneurotic disorder*, but this is no longer true. We now need more subtle criteria. We need not now throw away what we used formerly when we now think in terms of freedom within the personality, of capacity for trust and faith, of matters of reliability and object constancy, of freedom from self-deception, and also of something that has to do with richness rather than poverty as a quality of personal psychical reality.
>
> *(1967, p.26 emphasis in original)*

The process of development that Winnicott elaborates is one that moves from dependence to independence, and his focus is on the ways in which needs change as degrees of independence are reached. As non-unitary and defended beings, these developments are unlikely to be even across any one person's character or life-span, any aspect of development may be subject to getting stuck or reversals at different times and in different contexts. That is to say, we do not develop our independences evenly. For example, as we move through our education, across sites and years or even between teachers within a year, our levels of anxiety and dependency will vary with our familiarity and confidence with people, topics and tasks. Similarly, moving between professional roles or sites can strip us of our confidence in our knowledge and authority, temporarily regressing our relative independence as we look to colleagues for help and support. Winnicott's work explores degrees of (in)dependence: how they might be achieved, the kinds of environment that will facilitate (or hinder or distort) such changes. As a psychoanalyst, his work began in situations of 'environmental failure'. So, from ideal situations and environmental failure across the age range, Winnicott's work provides tools for thinking about the vicissitudes of being with ourselves and (single and multiple) others in relationship.

The creative self

This book uses Donald Winnicott's work to explore what it might mean to be creative in the classroom: creative as a learner, creative as a teacher, creative as a colleague and possibly even creative as an institution. This broad understanding of creativity is developed more fully in Chapter 5, but here we can say it concerns an attitude, a form of relationship with one's self and one's own interests and desires; and with the ideas and desires of others. Creativity is expressed in our attitude to curiosities (our own and other people's) and to demands on our time and attention. The creative life or response may not be artistic – it might be practical or scientific – and it may sit well or uncomfortably in professional contexts – that is a matter for personal reflection. The book as a whole has these tensions as its themes and is structured in three parts.

Part I of the book (Chapters 2–5) considers *Things that go right* and sets out the theoretical underpinnings of the rest of the chapters. It explores Winnicott's 'ideal situations', what things look like when they are going well. The meaning of wellness is expanded upon in Chapter 2. The nature and role of a 'facilitating environment' are also explored. The early importance of illusion is discussed along with the way behaving *as if* things were real can cause difficulties in adolescence. Chapter 3 turns to Winnicott's developmental narrative and the need to create a 'me' so that 'not me' can come to be noticed. The need to keep in mind literal *and* metaphorical readings of age-related terms is underlined in both of these chapters. The difficulties with Winnicott's developmental narrative is highlighted through the use of illustrative examples that relate to older children rather than to babies.

Chapter 4 explores the development of communications that manage, or fail to maintain, a to-and-fro quality. It begins by considering the way communication gets started and how we develop both verbal and non-verbal ways of communicating that are inter-personal and also intra-personal in nature. The nature of the relationships within which communication takes place (or fails to take place) and which profoundly influence our experiences of those relationships and what we might (or might not) learn within them are also discussed. The work of Jessica Benjamin is used to provide metaphors that perhaps sit more comfortably with more modern ways of talking but stay close to Winnicott's meaning.

Chapter 5 explores creativity, potential space and transitional objects – originally teddy bears but later people and cultural artefacts – the tools that enable us to think playfully. Of course, as teachers we are more often exercised by the things that go awry and tend to take for granted the 'going right'. The precariousness of play and the productive teetering that might characterise being able to make creative use of potential spaces are looked at in relation to life in classrooms.

Part II of the book explores *Things that go wrong* – which is often more familiar-feeling territory for teachers! Chapter 6 explores Winnicott's notions of a True and False Self Structure in greater detail. These are strange terms that I have failed to rename despite their unfortunate overtones. They describe our interior lives, the ways in which these can come to feel threatened and how we might defend ourselves. The balance we manage to maintain between these two aspects of self is part of how Winnicott defined health or wellness; they set out the extent and contact we have to our own desires and curiosities. The ways in which this balance, the to-and-fro between our inner lives and the world beyond, can go wrong are key to difficulties in educational life. Chapter 7 considers the perils of too great a concentration on demands from outside, on compliance. This is difficult for education. A student's False Self dominated by a compliant attitude makes a teacher's life much easier but comes at a great cost to the person 'being good'; the implications for this are explored here. More familiar and recognisable difficulties for education are the forms of non-compliance that Winnicott identified as 'antisocial tendencies', particularly nuisance and defiance. Despite education's current vilification of 'non-compliant' behaviours, these two forms of difficulty were, for Winnicott, signs of hope. The discussion in Chapter 8 suggests that we should perhaps be less quick to punish those who annoy us or break rules.

The final part of the book (Chapters 9 and 10) considers the challenges of *working through* some of the difficulties inherent in pedagogic relationships. These include teacher/student difficulties or student/knowledge difficulties. Chapter 9 maintains the classroom focus to explore the ways in which anger, hate and aggression may play out for both students and teachers; it asks whether these difficult emotions need to be banished from classrooms or given more careful thought. Is it only students who are aggressive? What if ordinary acts of hate and aggression are as much a part of being a passionate and engaged teacher as kindness? Finally, all this is turned around and the relationship between teacher and institution are considered in Chapter 10. How can we (can we?) think about the compliance, nuisance and defiance of teachers and institutions? What does it mean to suggest that aggression and hate come from teachers and institutions as much as they do from students?

Overall, the book asks more questions than it answers, but I hope it will provide you with some different ways of thinking about some entrenched problems – ways of thinking that have their roots in the work and writing of Donald Winnicott.

Notes

1 Throughout this book 'classroom' is used as shorthand for any learning context including schools and early-years settings, further or higher-education settings and so includes seminar rooms, lecture halls and supervision meetings.
2 With thanks to Lisa Farley for letting me read early drafts of writing about 'childhood beyond pathology'.
3 When writing about mothers in relation to children beyond the first few months of life and certainly once they have separated to some extent from their mothers (reached the stage of 'I am'), Winnicott adds in fathers, generally in parentheses.

This might be a function of the times in which he was writing (the middle of the 20th century), a time when gender roles were not seen with the complexity that we recognise today.

References

Bibby, T. 2009. How do children understand themselves as learners? Towards a learner-centered understanding of pedagogy. *Pedagogy, Culture and Society*, 17(1), 41–56.

Britzman, D.P. 2003. *After-education: Anna Freud, Melanie Klein, and psychoanalytic histories of learning*. Albany: State University of New York Press.

Bruner, J. 1960. *The process of education*. Cambridge, MA: Harvard University Press.

Burman, E. 1994. *Deconstructing developmental psychology*. London: Routledge.

Elliott, A. 2002. *Psychoanalytic theory: an introduction*. London: Palgrave.

Freud, S. 1931. Some reflections on Schoolboy Psychology. In *The standard edition of the complete psychological works of Sigmund Freud*, edited by J. Strachey (Vol. XIII, pp.241–244). London: Vintage.

Frosh, S. 1999. *The politics of psychoanalysis: an introduction to Freudian and post-Freudian theory* (2nd edition). London: MacMillan.

Frosh, S. 2002. *Key concepts in psychoanalysis*. London: The British Library.

Greenberg, J.R., and S.A. Mitchell. 1983. *Object relations in psychoanalytic theory*. Cambridge, MA and London: Harvard University Press.

Klein, M. 1930. The importance of symbol formation in the development of the ego. In *The selected writings of Melanie Klein*, edited by J. Mitchell (1991 edition, pp.95–111). Harmondsworth: Penguin.

Moore, A. 2000. *Teaching and learning: pedagogy, curriculum and culture*. London: RoutledgeFalmer.

Phillips, A. 1998. *The beast in the nursery*. London: Faber and Faber.

Phillips, A. 2007. *Winnicott*. London: Penguin.

Silin, J. 1995. *Sex, death, and the education of children: our passion for ignorance in the age of AIDS*. New York: Teachers College Press.

Stockton, K.B. 2004. Growing sideways, or versions of the queer child: the ghost, the homosexual, the Freudian, the innocent and the interval of animal. In *Curiouser: on the queerness of children*, edited by S. Bruhm and N. Hurley (pp.277–315). Minneapolis: University of Minnesota Press.

Walkerdine, V. 1984. Developmental psychology and the child-centred pedagogy: the insertion of Piaget into early education. In *Changing the subject: psychology, social regulation and subjectivity*, edited by J. Henriques, W. Holloway, C. Urwin, C. Venn and V. Walkerdine (pp.153–202). London: Methuen.

Walkerdine, V. 1986. Progressive education and political struggle. *Screen*, 27(5), 54–60.

Winnicott, D.W. 1962. Providing for the child in health and in crisis. In *The maturational processes and the facilitating environment*, edited by D.W. Winnicott (1965, 2007 edition, pp.64–72). London: Karnac.

Winnicott, D.W. 1964. *The child, the family and the outside world* (1991 edition). London: Penguin.

Winnicott, D.W. 1967. The concept of a healthy individual. In *Home is where we start from: essays by a psychoanalyst*, edited by C. Winnicott, R. Shepherd and M. Davis (1986 edition, pp.21–38). London: Penguin Books.

Winnicott, D.W. 1971. *Playing and reality* (2008, Routledge Classics edition). London: Tavistock Publications.

PART I

Things that go right

Chapters 2–5 make up Part I of the book. All of these chapters focus on aspects of a story of optimal development: what things could look like if all went as well as might be hoped.

2

THE ORIGINS AND MEANING OF WELLNESS

In this chapter, I explore what Donald Winnicott thought of as 'health'. As with much of his writing, we need to see through his (now) apparently dated language to make sense of him for our own times. His notion of health challenges current-day preoccupations with physical health and the ways in which educational institutions operate to maximise their own 'efficiency' – generally thought of in financial terms. The idea of health that Winnicott developed is the one that will underpin the arguments of this book, so it is worth making sure the complexity of his ideas are clear; in fact, his way of thinking about health – or wellness or coming into being – is the grounding for all that follows.

Put simply, Winnicotian health is a state of being in which the person is aware of themselves as a thinking and feeling individual. For Winnicott the healthy individual has a connection to their own desires and can tolerate the difficulties and challenges that arise as these desires meet – and are helped or resisted by – other peoples' reactions and our own sense of propriety. Such an individual is able to know herself well enough so that she can respond creatively to life. This is no small thing, since it requires that conditions for early trials at life be 'good enough' and that a 'facilitating environment' exists to support her when she later needs it – all ideas that are developed further below.

The idea of health then suggests a capacity to experience life in a way that is personally meaningful. How best can we unpack this rather platitudinous statement? Winnicott comes at it in a bewildering variety of ways. This is one of them:

> A large number of [experiences that feel real] form the basis for a life that has reality in it instead of futility. The individual who has developed the capacity to be alone is constantly able to rediscover the personal impulse, and the personal impulse is not wasted because the state of being alone

> is something which (although paradoxically) always implies that someone else is there.
>
> *(Winnicott, 1958, pp.33–34)*

What though does it mean for life *to have reality in it rather than futility*? What might 'reality' and 'futility' mean in this context? How can one be alone if someone else is there? Why should 'reality' and relationality matter so fundamentally to becoming a person? Our current sensibilities suggest that self-fulfilment is a personal and private state. Like all of Winnicott's ideas (indeed, like many psychoanalytic ideas) there is, as he himself suggests, something paradoxical at their heart.

Writing and thinking about paradoxes is difficult: Where does one start? And, in writing about paradoxes, is it possible to avoid engendering in the reader experiences of persecuting nihilism (perhaps especially if the reader is a professional used to doing and acting and to solving problems rather than 'sitting with' them)? Winnicott's suggestion (and it is a psychoanalytic suggestion) is that the best thing to do with paradoxes is to observe and think about them not to try to solve them (after all you will fail: That is what a paradox *is*). Part of the issue of coming into being as a person is precisely the difficulty of what to do about *doing*; an important part of *being* is *not doing*. This is particularly true if the doing is a manic activity that drowns out and defeats reflection. This is very much what tends to happen in schools, colleges and universities where progressing relentlessly through the curriculum has become the guiding principle. Gloriously, 'not doing' is not a passive waiting for something to happen; it is *an active not doing*. The paradoxical idea of *an active not doing* underlies this chapter and the next; in fact, it lies at the heart of the whole book. To begin to get a picture of active not doing, perhaps imagine a tightrope walker standing still on her high wire. She is not going anywhere – neither forwards nor backwards and we hope not down – yet her stillness is far from still, maintaining balance is an active process requiring huge concentration: an initial go at active not doing!

Current concerns about healthy living and healthy lifestyles focus on what Winnicott might have thought of as the soma, the body: the physical body's fitness, mobility, nutrition, exercise, etc. However, Winnicott's enduring focus was on the psyche: the affective experience of a life lived in a world structured by and saturated with relationships. His contention was that, being more concrete and visible, the soma, the body, could be taken care of more easily than the psyche. We recognise this today in the seemingly endless quest to take care of the mental health of ourselves and others; good intentions to manage a better work-life balance and to take some 'me time' are too easily drowned out by other, apparently endless, demands for our attention. As we know (but tend to forget), many difficulties of somatic living can be seen as externalisations of difficulties stemming from the psyche. Put crudely, for example, many problems of addiction or other personal neglect, the problems of overeating and type-2 diabetes, difficulties with maintaining a good 'work-life balance' can be seen as the emergence and expression of emotional difficulties in the physical world. This may be something recognised by the urgent use of CBT (Cognitive Behavioural Therapies) to try to help individuals overcome addictions (to food, drugs and alcohol and gambling and other behaviours), but there is something altogether more subtle about many of the more mundane difficulties we face in regulating our appetites. We often know what we 'should' do, but doing it still somehow eludes us.

So full, healthy living involves being able to tolerate the *psyche-soma* (the mind-body) as an ensemble.[1] It means feeling able to pay attention to feelings and intuitions as well as to rational plans; it means not exaggerating the value of the visible and easily controllable physical world to the detriment, or at the expense, of the affective experience. In this way, Winnicott's concern for a 'good enough' environment that meets both the objective (soma/body/physical) and subjective needs of the developing individual comes to have meaning. A good enough environment (initially a mother) will ensure that the baby can develop as a being as it transitions from the womb to the world, from merger towards gradual independence (first literally and later metaphorically: from womb to arms, lap and beyond). These transitions are facilitated by an environment that provides not only food, warmth and physical experiences of security (being held, a place to sleep and so forth), but also provision for the subjective needs of coming into being: a sense of control, of being visible, valued, loved and cared for within an appropriate relationship. While objective and subjective needs can be teased apart as part of an intellectual project, for Winnicott, as part of lived experience, they are inseparable. The rest of this chapter and the next explore what his vision of health and coming into being mean, how he suggests development can be facilitated to provide maximum opportunities for a 'healthy' life and what, in turn, accepting such a vision could mean for those helping people to learn.

Winnicott's coming into (healthy) being: reality and relationality

Chapter 3 focuses in detail on the developmental story that Winnicott the paediatrician describes, but we can imagine here the new-born baby's initial sense of fragmentation, of emerging from the womb to a new environment ill equipped to survive and utterly dependent on others. Yet, even in the earliest and most dependent days, being, Winnicott suggests, requires that we develop a capacity to be alone in the presence of someone else. This profoundly puzzling suggestion begins in his developmental story, a story we need to read both literally and metaphorically as being characterised by

> a special kind of relationship, that between the infant or small child who is alone, and the mother or mother-substitute who is in fact reliably present even if represented for the moment by a cot or a pram or the general atmosphere of the immediate environment.
>
> *(Winnicott, 1958, p.30)*

As an infant, initial experiences of fragmentation and the gradual process of integration suggest that a fear of falling into pieces will be experienced as terrifying; to fall into pieces implies annihilation: an end of being. To avoid the catastrophe of annihilation the infant needs, among other things, to experience *being* in the presence of someone who is not constantly making too many demands on them – that is, someone who is able to leave them to experience their own personal lives (impulses, ideas). The requirement is for a quiet presence, someone who is able to actively do nothing if nothing is required, yet who will still be there. Children often like to play in the same room as an adult occupied with some other task who nonetheless will look over to them and perhaps share a smile and, as adults, we may equally enjoy 'companionable silences'. On the other hand, if the literal or imagined safe presence is absent for too long and can no longer be imagined or is making demands, then difficult feelings and the fear of annihilation will need to be defended against. In this case, the difficult feelings that have been defended against cannot then be experienced resulting in a loss of contact with reality. The suggestion here is that the infant, supported by the good enough mother/environment, comes to have enough of a belief in the mother and the benign environment that they can, from time-to-time, let their guard down enough to experience their own impulses. These impulses may be sensations, desires or ideas that might be frightening or exciting; learning to recognise and name them will, eventually, become an important way to make them more manageable (Klein, 1930), but that form of social communication is not yet possible.

> When alone in the sense that I am using the term, and only when alone [i.e. neither forced to nor seeking to respond to external demands], the infant is able to do the equivalent of what in an adult world would be called relaxing. The infant is able to become unintegrated, to flounder, to be in a state in which there is no orientation, to be able to exist for a time without being either a reactor to an external impingement or an active person with a direction of interest or movement ... In this setting the sensation or impulse will feel real and be truly a personal experience.
>
> *(Winnicott, 1958, p.34)*

When, as adults, we are relaxed we are better able (sometimes) to play with the 'what ifs' that might terrify or excite us (What if the boiler blows up and I can't afford to replace it? What if I apply for that job and don't get it? What if I apply for that job and do get it?). These moments of thought and thinking are where we can begin to experiment, problem solve and learn: 'I wonder what would happen if ...?' The significance of this state of being and of play is considered further in Chapter 5.

If a mother can help her infant feel loved and recognised as a whole separate, worthwhile individual, then a virtuous cycle may be started in which the sense of self is gradually expanded and strengthened. This rapport between mother and infant (Winnicott calls this ego-relatedness) lies at the heart of the capacity to be alone and, Winnicott suggests, forms the basis of later friendships. Friendships provide a facilitating environment; they are relationships with people we trust and in whose company we feel supported. It is to friends we turn when we feel overwhelmed so that we can experience feeling safe enough to allow ourselves a short period of collapse in which to experience and learn from our excitement, pain or fear. Friendship is the (metaphorical) arms and lap we need when confusion and fear return us to our primal fears. We turn to people we trust when we are overwhelmed by confusion, hurt, betrayal, anger ... visceral sensations and unaccustomed or unexpected thoughts that we might struggle to name and understand. But to get to the trusted-other, we first have to be able to call on them, and this requires that we admit our lostness and vulnerability – neither of which is easy: Asking for help can be much harder than we might hope. The fear of our own vulnerability and dependency can feel dangerously exposing and 'friends' who fail to listen properly but instead rush to offer 'solutions' can magnify the difficulty of asking for help. Winnicott's suggestion is that in order to access the real person (the physical friend), the (m)other-in-the-mind must first be there. That is, we need to have some expectation that asking for help might result in us receiving the help we need (rather than the help someone wants to give). While sometimes the (m)other-in-the-mind will be enough to see us over difficult moments, we will also need others when we are not enough for ourselves.

We can perhaps begin to see the ways in which, in the sense offered here, a teacher needs to be available as an academic friend to her students to allow space for reflection and support for the terrors of not knowing and potential failure. A teacher who is able to be with a child while they struggle to make a connection, or to take a risk with a new form of writing or to spell an unfamiliar word, a teacher who can do these things without leaping in to make things easier, to tell, to provide a spelling or correct an error, such a one might be an academic friend to a learner.

Time and good enough experiences enable an individual to move from absolute dependence to relative independence although, as Winnicott repeatedly reminds us, 'independence is never absolute. The healthy individual does not become isolated but becomes related to the environment in such a way that the individual and the environment can be said to be interdependent' (Winnicott, 1963a, p.84). For Winnicott, a mature, healthy adult is one able to live creatively, actively taking up and contributing to life on their own account and in relation to wider society. They can listen and respond to their own impulses and are not overwhelmed by demands that come from outside (they are able to be alone). To exemplify this, Winnicott considers adolescence, initially a developmental stage coinciding with puberty. He cautions anyone working with adolescents against trying to 'cure' them of their adolescence suggesting that, however terrible this period of life may be, most young people 'are best able to find their own salvation'. He goes on:

> The passage of time has significance here. The adolescent is not to be cured as if ill. I think this is an important part of the statement of health. This is not to deny that there can be illness during this age period when adolescence is due.
>
> Some adolescents suffer greatly, so that it is almost cruel to offer no help. At fourteen they are commonly suicidal, and theirs is the task of tolerating the interaction of several disparate phenomena – their own immaturity, their own puberty changes, their own idea of what life is about, and their own ideals and aspirations; add to this their personal disillusionment about the world of grown-ups – which for them seems to be essentially a world of compromise, of false values, and of infinite distraction from the main theme. As they leave this stage, adolescent boys and girls are beginning to feel real, to have a sense of *self* and of *being*. This is health. From *being* comes *doing*, but there can be no *do* before *be*, and this is their message to us.
>
> *(Winnicott, 1967, pp.24–25)*

Reflecting on the issue of adolescence in relation to secondary schools (and also in relation to our own ongoing adolescences in relation to institutional life) we can begin to recognise some of the difficulties we experience. As Helene Deutsch (1967) points out: 'the adolescent lives his life … between two worlds: one that has thus far complied with his demands and one that now demands his compliance (in Britzman, 2012, p.274). Caught between self and other, impulse and compliance, we might begin to recognise the urgent preference for *doing* (perhaps growing up and taking responsibility) over *being* (tolerating conflict and the presence of the unreasonable other). This preference for doing over being is one that haunts the anxious adult as much as the young person. If only we could skip over or hurry the terrible turmoil of adolescence so that relationships based in reasonable, mutual adaptation (compromise) could be reached, how much easier professions such as teaching would be! Notice too how this denial of the necessity for living through adolescence idealises adulthood and draws on a fantasy of linear and singular development that enables us to disavow our own continuing immaturities. As suggested above, when things are hard for us we can feel the press of our vulnerabilities return. The desire to act as if we were invulnerable, as if we had all the answers, as if we knew what is best among all the choices we are faced with, this desire to skip lightly across the chasm that has opened up in front of us is a defence against the difficulty of living life. We hurry past the point of decision with social rules that are convenient – we do this to avoid having to be in the difficult place of uncertainty with its threat of error and shame. And as adults we often do take this leap as if we could fly. A clue here is the 'as if' – the make-believe of the omnipotent wish. This conundrum is one that we will return to throughout the book *as if*, by repetition, we might come to understand and so master it.

Watching adolescents living through the throes of coming into being can be acutely painful: not only may they appear to put themselves at risk and refuse our painfully won adult good sense, they also summon up all our own experiences of lost loves, of mistakes made, of opportunities discarded, of ingratitude, of humiliation and shame. No wonder being with adolescence (in whatever body) can be such torture! Adolescence will endure for as long as it endures; time (subjective and chronological) needs to be allowed to pass. Unfortunately being human means that responsibility will only ever be accepted on a context-by-context basis from moment to moment. Our fantasy of the development of the body – from conception to adulthood – with an apparently finite period of 'growing up' (and getting taller) – is linear and seems to have an end point (although only if we ignore the vicissitudes of old age and death). Development of the psyche is a perpetual process; there is no end point. Unity and maturity are never assured as we move endlessly between developmental stages. An ongoing psychical adolescence is present in all of us; development is neither linear nor permanent.

Coming to feel real and being, then, involve a capacity to hear and tolerate our inner/affective responses to the experiences of living. A capacity to hear and listen to our impulses implies a connection to our 'true selves' (discussed below and in Chapter 6). Experiences associated with living will only be tolerable, Winnicott suggests, if they take place in an environment that facilitates their acceptance. As we mature, we may become part of our own environment, although we can never be the whole of it. This toleration would stand in contrast to defending against feelings we experience as too difficult. Learning to live with, recognise and respond to our own internal affects is the task of all stages of development. Every experience requires processing; every new experience has the potential to be beyond us: too alien, too much – overwhelming. If our defences are strong then new experiences may be missed/overlooked as we pre-emptively deny their significance and fail to learn from them. If, as a student, I am angry and dismiss my teacher's advice (what does she know?), I do not have to experience the pain of not knowing and of failure or the frustrating need for more work. But nor can I take in and learn from those aspects of her advice that might have helped me feel less stupidly stuck. If, as a teacher, I am contemptuous and dismiss my students' feedback (what do they know?), I do not have to experience the pain of not knowing and of failure or the humiliation of having erred or having been found to be lacking. But nor can I take in and learn from those aspects of the feedback that might have been helpful to me in developing my professional practice. Learning made in the scorching moment of personal relevance will always be the most powerful and feel most real – even if it feels hardest. If the possibility of these moments is stripped from me by a well-meaning or authoritarian other, I am left with futility and am powerless. As Winnicott repeatedly reminds us, while health may stand in opposition to disease, health and ease are not synonymous. Life *is* difficult!

A facilitating environment: the good enough (m)other and home, teacher and classroom

Attaining a state of being, of what Winnicott calls 'I Am' (a first developmental milestone, a state of fusion created from the fragmentation), relies on the presence of a 'good enough' facilitating environment and then a capacity to repudiate that which is 'not me'.

> … the good enough environment starts with a high degree of adaptation to individual infant needs. Usually the mother is able to provide this because of the special state she is in, which I have called primary maternal preoccupation. … Adaptation decreases according to the baby's growing need to experience reactions to frustration. In health the mother is able to delay her function of failing to adapt, till the baby has become able to react with anger rather than be traumatized by her failures. Trauma means the breaking of continuity of the line of the individual's existence. It is only on a continuity of existence that the sense of self, of feeling real, and of being, can eventually be established as a feature of the individual personality.
>
> *(Winnicott, 1967, p.22)*

The school may (or may not) provide similar functions to those of a 'good enough' home environment and facilitate development in a way that is dynamic and appropriate to the individual at the present stage. Reflecting on the nature of an environment that facilitates development Winnicott notes that:

> We can say that the facilitating environment makes possible the steady progress of the maturational processes. But the environment does not make the child. At best it enables the child to realize potential. … In other words, a mother and father do not produce a baby as an artist produces a picture or a potter a pot. They have started up a developmental process which results in there being a lodger in the mother's body and then in her arms and then in the home provided by the parents, and what this lodger will turn out to be like is outside anyone's control.
>
> *(1963a, p.85)*

For schools and colleges, this suggestion that intention cannot 'make' the successful child is, in the current policy climate, perhaps anathema. As a result, uncertain development is often denied and over-ridden by the doingness of objectives and assessments that frantically measure and re-measure. But, even accepting Winnicott's premise does not mean there is nothing to do; there is much active not doing to be done, much 'being' before 'doing'. Despite the fact that aptitudes, desires and achievements cannot be controlled or predicted, parents (or schools and teachers) can provide – or fail to provide – appropriate support for the growing and developing academic and social individual.

An environment that facilitates optimal development will, ultimately, enable the individuals being cared for to grow into creative and expressive relationship with themselves, their own lives and the lives of others. Such a facilitating environment provides both the *holding* and *handling* that will enable the infant to survive the first period of extreme dependency (lasting only a few weeks) and to begin the process of gaining independence. This recognition of the complexity of the care given by the 'good enough' mother is an important one for teachers and others working in schools to consider: How can we provide an environment in which students can come to know things? What will our feeding look like? How can we provide access to 'things' that are tasty? And, how can we help make sure that learners remain able to access their own responses to those things (i.e. to their own subjective experiences of learning)?

It is worth noting here that, as part of repudiating and thereby creating the not-me, we need to deny and reject the very people we need. A repudiation of parents in adolescence, or of a teacher's teaching or parts of that teaching, is only to be expected as a normal (if hurtful) part of development, and recognising this is part of enabling others to develop as students and knowers:

> There is an intermediate stage in healthy development in which the patient's most important experience in relation to the good or potentially satisfying object is the refusal of it. The refusal is part of the process of creating it.
>
> *(1963b, p.182)*

The suggestion here is that, in moving from an assumed or desired merger with parents or teachers (that is, in placing them beyond our omnipotent control), we need to recognise parents or teachers as separate. As part of doing this, we inevitably need at some point to refuse them and deny their value and significance in our lives. Indeed it is through a repudiation of those we love that we can rediscover, love and appreciate those qualities that mean so much to us and accept those who we find more difficult to accept. This will be explored in greater detail in Chapter 7.

Structures of self: becoming a whole person and a rounded learner

While communication is dealt with in more detail later, it is worth pausing here to consider the ways in which, for Winnicott, the way the self is structured unconsciously shapes communication.

Winnicott suggests that the baby's first experiences of communication are with what he calls 'subjective objects'. That is, the world is fantasised into existence, and nothing exists beyond what is experienced or fantasised. With its attention taken up with its own affects and desires the infant comes to have a sense of itself as a unit (rather than as fragmented). There is always the danger that this first, monumental achievement can get lost in the telling of the developmental story, but for Winnicott, it is important. He names this move beyond only being aware of chaotic fragments 'I AM', and he repeatedly underlines the importance he places on managing to experience self as a unit for later intellectual growth (see for example Winnicott, 1968).

Once I AM has been achieved, 'me' and 'not-me' can emerge.

> In health, when the infant achieves fusion [I AM], the frustrating aspect of object behaviour has value in educating the infant in respect of the existence of a not-me world. Adaptation failures have value *in so far as the infant can hate the object*, that is to say, can retain the idea of the object as potentially satisfying while recognising its failure to behave satisfactorily. ... What is often neglected in statements of this detail of theory is the immense development that takes place in the infant for fusion to be achieved [for 'me' to be known], and for environmental failure therefore to play its positive part, enabling the infant to begin to know of a world that is repudiated [not-me]. I deliberately do not say external.
>
> *(1963b, pp.181–82 emphasis in original)*

The fact that the object (perhaps initially the nipple) does not always magically arrive, that it can be annoying or frustrating (as well as satisfying) impinges on the infant's state of 'going on being'. In this way the frustrating object draws attention away from an inward focus on self and towards its separate existence. The importance of the mother starting to expect her infant to 'wait a moment' to be fed is real; her small and deliberate maladaption enables the infant to start to look for the source of its frustration and to notice her. That this will generate hate may sound perverse, but hate is as important an affect as love. Also important is the recognition that this separation – this sense of ourselves as separate (or our desire to be magically omnipotent) – extends beyond infancy and can affect us throughout our lives.

The states of being have changed. There is now a remembered state of merger, a state in which what was needed was fantasised into existence, a state of unitary existence or of fusion (of 'I am') and a state in which self and other can both be recognised (me and 'not me'). Alongside these terms Winnicott also develops the idea of what he calls a 'True Self Structure' and a 'False' or 'Compliant Self Structure'. This split is another iteration of the dichotomised and defended self of psychoanalysis (Frosh, 2002) of conscious and unconscious, mind and body, inside and out, good and bad.

The so-called True Self is another name for the core, the 'I am'. It is the unconscious self, a self of subjective objects and affects, a place of omnipotent control, a self hallucinated into being in a world managed by a good enough facilitating environment (mother) so as not to impinge too soon or too violently on the nascent infant. Since this aspect of the self is very private, and full of difficult affects – including hate, anger, murderous violence and rages – it needs to be protected from the world and those things that would impinge on its growth, and the world needs protecting from it. In the next chapter the costs of having this most private self seen are considered in more detail, but here we just need to note that 'me' initially generates a False self to protect this True self from the impingements of 'not me'. The False self looks out to the world and, recognising the demands of 'not me' (whether cultural norms, taboos and other social conventions or the more specific demands of particular people – perhaps that we be 'good' girls and boys), gives it what it wants – is compliant – to ensure its own survival. This is entirely understandable and healthy. Chapters 6 and 7 will consider what happens when the impinging demands of the world are experienced as too much and the True self gets lost.

The normal travails of adolescence

Winnicott identifies some of the difficulties that can arise in childhood and especially in adolescence, most notably stealing and destructive behaviours. These two difficulties, beyond the 'normal' travails of adolescence, were, for him, signs of hope. Regular adolescent storms were, he felt, something to be endured: the only cure being the passage of time. Even 'good enough' homes suffer through this period of development with their adolescents and, in the end, most do achieve adult maturity, 'even if in the process they give their parents headaches'. These difficulties are discussed in much greater detail in Chapter 8, but it is perhaps worth signalling something of the difficulties of or with adolescence here.

Part of the difficulty of adolescence lies in its isolation. Winnicott likens it to the period when the infant is coming to know about self and other, me and not-me. This is developmental work that can be supported by a 'good enough' facilitating environment or hindered by failures in the environment. However it is managed, development cannot be done *for* the infant or the adolescent, or indeed the adult: it is a job to be completed for oneself. The struggle of the infant to learn to relate to objects that are outside of its (fantasised) magical control ends with the achievement of separation and the ability to relate to real whole-objects in the world. And it can be imagined that after the difficult work of finding and making sense of the world beyond the self, real relationships may come as a relief. For the adolescent too, coming to know 'who I am' is central to their development towards adulthood. Pointing to the aphorism 'to thine own self be true', Winnicott reminds us that 'the adolescent is trying to find the self to be true to' (1963c, p.125). And, like the infant's journey, this too is essentially a journey of self-discovery, although adolescents can make it in the company of peers. Also, like earlier developmental phases, the transition from childhood to adulthood is never finally achieved. Winnicott repeatedly reminds us that 'if we are talking about adolescence we are talking about adults because no adults are all the time adult' (1960, p.117). The best adults can do is to provide a good enough facilitating environment and remember that the difficulties of adolescence may be so very hard to watch because they continue to be our difficulties: As we go through life we are perpetually confronted with the need to rethink and adjust who we are in relation to new events and new people. The violence and immediate threat of adolescent storms may be assuaged by the passage of time, but they never entirely disappear.

Of course, a major difficulty for teachers is that schools ask young people *not* to be adolescents. We insist that they behave 'reasonably', that they master their furies, stay focused, maintain endless motivation even when the subject matter is not of interest to them, that they remain bright and interested while supressing their own interests. The next two chapters – and indeed the rest of this book – start to explore this impossible place in more detail while struggling to hold on to the paradox of continuing adolescences and a refusal to idealise adulthood as if it were a place that had left the difficulties of adolescence behind (Britzman, 2012)!

Note

1 Interestingly gastroenterologists working with gut flora are coming to recognise the mind-gut connection as more literal than we have previously appreciated. See for example, Giulia Enders' (2015) book *Gut: The inside story of our body's most underrated organ*.

References

Britzman, D.P. 2012. The adolescent teacher: a psychoanalytic note on regression in the professions. *Journal of Infant, Child and Adolescent Psychotherapy*, 11, 272–283.

Enders, G. 2015. *Gut: the inside story of our body's most underrated organ*. Translated by David Shaw. Vancouver: Greystone Books.

Frosh, S. 2002. *Key concepts in psychoanalysis*. London: The British Library.

Klein, M. 1930. The importance of symbol formation in the development of the ego. In *The selected writings of Melanie Klein*, edited by J. Mitchell (1991 edition, pp.95–111). Harmondsworth: Penguin.

Winnicott, D.W. 1958. The capacity to be alone. In *The maturational processes and the facilitating environment: studies in the theory of emotional development*, edited by D.W. Winnicott (1965, 2007 edition, pp.29–36). London: Karnac.

Winnicott, D.W. 1960. Aggression, guilt and reparation. In *Depravation and delinquency*, edited by C. Winnicott, R. Shepherd and M. Davis (2012 edition, pp.116–123). London: Routledge.

Winnicott, D.W. 1963a. From dependence towards independence in the development of the individual. In *The maturational processes and the facilitating environment: studies in the theory of emotional development*, edited by D.W. Winnicott (1965, 2007 edition, pp.83–92). London: Karnac.

Winnicott, D.W. 1963b. Communicating and not communicating leading to a study of certain opposites. In *The maturational processes and the facilitating environment: studies in the theory of emotional development*, edited by D.W. Winnicott (1965, 2007 edition, pp.179–192). London: Karnac.

Winnicott, D.W. 1963c. Struggling through the doldrums. In *Deprivation and delinquency*, edited by C. Winnicott, R. Shepherd and M. Davis (2012 edition, pp.124–133). London: Routledge.

Winnicott, D.W. 1967. The concept of a healthy individual. In *Home is where we start from: essays by a psychoanalyst*, edited by C. Winnicott, R. Shepherd and M. Davis (1986 edition, pp.21–38). London: Penguin Books.

Winnicott, D.W. 1968. Sum, I am. In *Home is where we start from: essays by a psychoanalyst*, edited by C. Winnicott, R. Shepherd and M. Davis (1986 edition, pp.55–64). Harmondsworth: Penguin.

3

BECOMING A PERSON

Winnicott's developmental story

For Winnicott, indeed for much psychoanalysis, our lives as social beings begin at birth. What we become depends on how we become: our insertion into the world, our families, relationships, language, culture all shape the ways in which we experience our selves. The possibilities for how we will make sense of those experiences and how they will shape our later responses to new experiences depend on this initial template, which although malleable remains powerfully important and resistant to change. Affective processes are unconscious; they will act upon our conscious lives in ways that may be helpful or counter-productive. Defences that worked admirably for us as small children may, if unmodified, become pathological later in life.

In this chapter, we take a journey with Winnicott through a 'normal' development from birth to the beginnings of independence and health. Winnicott, as a paediatrician, observed many mothers with their infants – some attaining what he called 'healthy living', others struggling with aspects of their new lives together. Throughout the chapter we need to bear in mind the timeless nature of the unconscious and the literal and metaphorical nature of Winnicott's developmental story. We are only (literally) born once, but we can be 'born' into new ideas, new situations and new experiences repeatedly throughout our lives. While at birth we are (literally) vitally dependent on our mothers, later 'births' will leave us dependent – to a greater or lesser degree – on new (m)others. It is important to remember that the story as it is set out in this chapter and the next is of 'normal' or 'healthy' development; as such it is a tool for thinking, a series of generalisations to use, not a set of measures with which to judge people. We need to guard against our own omnipotent desires to know, to be right and to be in control! For me, his interests in the ways in which development can go wrong and the thinking we need to do in such adverse circumstances is what can make Winnicott particularly powerful. But, to think about difficulties that can arise, we first need a clear picture of something closer to an ideal, some way of recognising difficulties when they present; that is the purpose of this chapter and indeed of all the chapters in this section.

Getting started

All psychoanalytic theories characterise the initial period of life as one of imagined merger: a baby does not initially know that there is a world separate from but surrounding it; it does not know there is a mother taking care of it, structuring its environment, ensuring its safety and continued existence. Instead, psychoanalysis suggests, it fantasises a state of continued merger and continues to do so until such time as it can begin to take in its immediate surroundings: its mother and the things she presents to it and then itself: its fingers and toes and on, expanding outwards.

Winnicott describes the first requirements in the very early stages of life:

> At this [initial] stage the infant needs and in fact usually gets an environmental provision which has certain characteristics:
>
> - It meets physiological needs. Here physiology and psychology have not yet become distinct, or are only in the process of doing so; and
> - It is reliable. But the environmental provision is not mechanically reliable. It is reliable in a way that implies the mother's empathy.
>
> *(1960b, p.48)*

Initial maternal care involves what Winnicott calls *primary maternal preoccupation.* This is a phase characterised by a mother's initial absorption in the care of her new baby as both learn to adapt to each other's rhythms.

It is not hard to imagine how, immediately after birth, an infant has yet to learn that there is a world that is 'not me'. An initial stage of continued merger has to be lived through while the notion of a world beyond 'me' is gradually accepted and things in that world are learned about. This is part of what Winnicott (above) means when he indicates that physiology and psychology start off undifferentiated: to begin with, for the infant, there is only the experience of *being.* And it is important for Winnicott that this sense of being is maintained since at this stage not to feel a continuity of being would generate a fear (an anxiety) of annihilation and be experienced as traumatic. To enable this sense of 'going on being', a mother has to protect her infant from anything that might impinge upon it; she must hold the world at bay and only let it in a little at a time as and when it can be managed. Like the literal feeds a mother provides, the presentation of the world must initially be in small, soft mouthfuls lest the infant choke. An impingement then might be anything that interrupts the 'going on being' of an infant, anything that draws attention to itself too forcefully and insists on some 'doing' (recognition, making sense, rejecting). In the first instance, for example, she holds time at bay by allowing herself to be available day and night[1] so that the clock and our modern social obligations are fended off; initially being expected to manage hunger is too much to expect, although with time, we can learn to wait for meal times (or perhaps sometimes we cannot). The issue of impingements is taken up again below but it is worth noticing here how time and fears about the future are commonly used to urge learners to greater effort. Perhaps we should consider more seriously the ways in which adult demands are allowed to impinge upon children's experiences of schooling.

Holding: from merger to self and other

There are, Winnicott suggests, three overlapping stages that characterise a developing care environment:

a Holding.
b Mother and infant living together, here the father's function (of dealing with the environment for the mother) is not known to the infant.
c Father, mother and infant, all three living together.

Winnicott continues:

> The term 'holding' is used here to denote not only the actual physical holding of the infant, but also the total environmental provision prior to the concept of *living with*. In other words, it refers to a three-dimensional or space relationship with time gradually added in. [...] During the holding phase other processes are initiated; the most important is the dawn of intelligence and the beginning of a mind as something distinct from the psyche. [...] The term 'living with' implies object relationships.
>
> *(1960a, pp.43–45 emphasis in original)*

On emerging from the womb an infant needs to first learn that there is a world that exists beyond its skin: an inside and an outside – a 'me' and a 'not-me' – first its mother, then the family and later the outside world. Further, it is hoped that it will learn that this is a world it might survive and even find pleasure in.

If we first imagine a baby being born we can think about how, in its first hours and days, it is confronted with an entirely new reality, one it initially has no strategies for processing and coming to terms with. Indeed, in the early days of life, its senses must register an environment that assaults it: noises and physical sensations from the outside, noises and sensations from the inside: the voices, traffic, television, radios and household appliances; the air movements and temperature fluctuations, wet and dry nappies, clothes, arms ... and also the pain of hunger and the satisfaction of a feed, the noise of its own crying, the blurring of the world through tears and sleep and sensations of urination and defecation. All this must inevitably initially be bewildering and will need help from someone if it is to be survived. That is, a mother needs to help her baby to process its entry into the world. Typically she does that through the ways in which she holds and speaks to her child, soothing with comforting sounds and movements that gradually become familiar.

The early days of holding seem very far from the experiences of the student in school, but the issue of how school (or college or university or any new situation or idea) will be met and managed depend to some extent on the experiences of this early stage, and so holding remains important throughout life. To reiterate, Winnicott proposes two forms of holding: objective and subjective to manage both the soma and the psyche. Holding that is objective takes care of the physical and literal needs for a safe, secure environment within which to experience oneself as continuing to exist: an infant's first developmental achievement. But managing to experience 'going on being' suggests that there is also a subjective holding that meets the psychical needs of development, a holding that provides a sense of control, of being visible, valued, loved and cared for within an appropriate relationship. So, a nice classroom with good heating, ventilation and resources is not enough: the teacher needs also to engage responsively with students as individuals. Similarly, being a kind and empathic teacher is not enough, the child/student also needs appropriate intellectual feeding: challenges with which to engage.

So Winnicott suggests a responsive holding environment manages the physical and the psychical holding of anxieties so that we can come to manage (from time to time) to hold our own anxieties, can survive moments of disintegration even as we move towards developing a reliable sense of self (ego-integration). In a learning context this could mean, for example, knowing how much challenge is challenging without being either boring or overwhelming and knowing when to intervene and when to leave to struggle. These 'knowings' are not magically divined but are a matter of communication (this is dealt with in more detail in the next chapter). So, an important question for educators is: How can I provide holding that meets the needs of my students? And managers might ask: How can I provide holding that meets the needs of those I manage? Answers to these questions are to be found in balances that need to be sought from moment to moment, not in prescriptions or rules to be followed.

From illusion to dis-illusion, adaptation to de-adaptation

The stages above signal a move, tied to the development of communication, from merger (there is only me) to recognition that there is a difference between 'me' and 'not-me' and then further refinements of what not-me might include – that is from a recognition of two people in the world, to a recognition of three people and then other constellations; the stage Winnicott (above) called 'living with'. Winnicott suggests that making this move requires that a child master (temporarily) its fears of annihilation or disintegration. Learning that survival is possible requires an infant to develop an illusion of coherence before it is gradually dis-illusioned through the good enough mother's gradual, appropriate failures as she 'presents the world in small doses'. That is, alongside the objective weaning that moves a baby off the breast and onto solid food, there is a contemporaneous subjective weaning that never ends, repeatedly helping us to move from illusion to reality.

As discussed above, in its first merged state a baby has no sense of self, no sense of anything outside of or beyond itself. Winnicott talks of a baby creating what it needs in a 'moment of illusion':

> The infant comes to the breast when excited, and ready to hallucinate something fit to be attacked. At that moment the actual nipple appears and he is able to feel it was that nipple that he hallucinated. So his ideas are enriched by actual details of sight, feel, smell, and next time this material is used in the hallucination. In this way he starts to build up a capacity to conjure up what is actually available. The mother has to go on giving the infant this type of experience.
>
> *(Cited in Greenberg and Mitchell, 1983, p.192)*

These repeated experiences of the environment 'magically' providing what is needed and/or desired fill the baby with a growing omnipotence (the breast arrives because they want it) and a sense of 'going on being' or personal continuity. As a baby develops an attunement or awareness of its own bodily functions and impulses, these begin to form the basis for a slowly evolving sense of self – a 'continuity of being' (Winnicott, 1960a, p.54).

This sense of omnipotence, of control and personal efficacy, while it can become pathological, is also important. It provides the place from which we might begin to trust our own thoughts and ideas, it enables us to value our own discoveries (rather than needing to rely on being told). When we are engaged with a new idea or an act of creativity we can develop a sense that what we are doing is entirely new, that we have invented or discovered something. I have seen this occur often when working with young children in maths lessons. A period of investigation or exploration can lead to them believing that they have invented algebra or some algorithm for a calculation. Of course, the discovery is not a new invention in the grander scheme of things, although in the context of the individual or class, it may indeed be a new and important revelation. The illusion or feeling of creation and discovery is important, enabling children to develop a sense of mastery (rather than dependency or annihilation) in new contexts.

> During the holding phase other processes are initiated; the most important is the dawn of intelligence and the beginning of a mind as something distinct from the psyche … and forms the basis for dreaming and for living relationships.
>
> *(Winnicott, 1960a, p.45)*

Winnicott suggests that the good enough mother seeing her infant through the initial stages of instinctual life by enabling it to maintain the illusion that it created what it needs allows it to develop a sense of omnipotent control from which cognitive awareness and 'an intellect' will develop. While the notion of a mother so absorbed in her baby has been criticised by feminists (see for example Chodorow, 1989, 1999) as an unreasonable expectation, the brevity of this phase and the necessary failures to come perhaps redeem it somewhat. The reliability required is a quality felt in her attention rather than her intention – so the social class or economic situation of the mother is of less relevance for these early stages of development than her attention to the baby as baby (rather than as projection of her fantasies). That is a dense statement: What does it mean to suggest that a child might be a projection of an adult's fantasies rather than the person they actually are? As one example of this, we can think of parents whose desire for their child to be something – perhaps the same as them or something they were denied an opportunity to be – leads them to impose activities on their child and to read behaviours in a way that suits the story they have created for that child ahead of time. In a similar way, schools can come to believe that the list of performance indicators for children's academic progress tells a real story about how children learn rather than being a fairly arbitrary and politically influenced list of aspirations. An easy assumption is that middle-class mothers with their greater access to resources are more likely to be 'good enough' when in fact there is no such guarantee. Emotional resources are not purchased but a matter of the mother's own capacities to remain (subjectively) *with* her infant. While Winnicott suggests this state of being is instinctive, he also recognises that it is not easy:

> In the natural state (by which I mean when the two human beings involved are healthy [not depressed or physically unwell]) techniques and quantities and timing can be left to nature. This means, in practice, that the mother can allow the infant to decide what it is in his power to decide, because she is easily able to decide and provide what it is in her job to give in the way of management, as well as in the form of actual milk....
>
> The main trouble is that people easily feel overwhelmed by the responsibility of having a baby at all, and they only too readily welcome the rule and the regulation and the precept, which makes life less risky even if a trifle boring.
>
> *(Winnicott, 1964, pp.32–33)*

This suggestion, that it may feel easier to relinquish the onerous responsibility for making decisions to some external authority, is also familiar to teachers and (initial and continuing) teacher trainers who are often exhorted to 'just tell me how to do it'. Our desire for a manual telling us how to circumvent the difficult and time-consuming process of thinking about what to do and the attendant risk of getting things 'wrong' (and the risks of getting it right) can feel overwhelming so that teachers also need holding so that they can undertake such work when it feels dangerous (Britzman, 2011, 2012).

Managing impingements

Gradually, over time and in the reliable presence of someone holding their objective and subjective needs 'well enough', an infant (anyone) can have repeated experiences of itself 'going on being'. This requires not only the holding and managing of what is there, but also the warding off of that which is outside and beyond. As mentioned above, Winnicott labels things that are 'outside' and 'too much', *impingements*. Events and experiences impinge on an individual when they threaten or actually overwhelm and lead to an experience of annihilation in which the individual's sense of continuity – of 'going on being' – is disrupted. So 'beyond' refers to experiences that are not only beyond in the sense of outside and alien but, more importantly, beyond in the sense that they are too much and so cannot be thought about.

Winnicott warns us about time; it is an infant's first impingement and goes on being something that intrudes and threatens our sense of being. We gradually let time in, first to order night and day, sleep and wakefulness, then the pattern of meal times expecting children to gradually adapt themselves to the linear chronologies that shape our social lives. Later, children will become accustomed to the school timetable, but we continue to hold some of the implications of time at bay only gradually expecting them to plan for what they will be doing later in the day or week. Planning for future careers is at first a matter for creative play – for fanciful explorations of what it might be like to be an astronaut or a ballet dancer, a Viking or a farmer – only later can thinking about independence be properly explored. The compliant recitation of the idea that we learn so we can get a good job hints at the lack of connection many children and indeed many adults (some of whom who still seek for meaning in their having learned Pythagoras' Theorem) have to this idea. Unfortunately, this is often where teachers can become unreliable.

The use of an unknown and unknowable future to motivate (scare) children to work harder is experienced as an impingement by many and can have adverse results. After the UK government's introduction of standardised testing at ages 7, 11 and 14, Diane Reay and Dylan Wiliam conducted research with 10- to 11-year-olds as they prepared for their tests (SATs). The following extract from an interview Diane conducted with 10-year-old Hannah provides a case in point:

HANNAH: I'm really scared about the SATs [standard assessment tasks]. Mrs O'Brien [a teacher at the school] came and talked to us about our spelling and I'm no good at spelling and David [the class teacher] is giving us times tables tests every morning and I'm hopeless at times tables so I'm frightened I'll do the SATs and I'll be a nothing.

DIANE: I don't understand Hannah. You can't be a nothing.

HANNAH: Yes, you can 'cause you have to get a level like a level 4 or a level 5 and if you're no good at spellings and times tables you don't get those levels and so you're a nothing.

DIANE: I'm sure that's not right
HANNAH: Yes it is 'cause that's what Mrs O'Brien was saying.

(Reay and Wiliam, 1999, p.345)

Here, the way the future is allowed to make demands on the present is writ large and the adults' failure to hold time and the world at bay is beyond Hannah's capacities; the teachers' use of impingements interrupt her 'going on being'. Annihilated as a learner, Hannah is unable to think and, in a painful move, erases her future: 'I'll be a nothing'. The expectation that young children should be worrying about their career prospects (rather than playing with fantasy careers) is certainly more than it is reasonable to expect them to take on at this age. The way time and uncertainty were played on in this example was relentless.

It is easy to criticise teachers for making comments like these: the remarks made are crass and insensitive and hard to reconcile with our image of caring teachers. But we have to recognise the way that demands from outside, from the government and the media and perhaps also parents in response to league tables, impinge upon teachers. Teachers are judged by the performance of their students, and the judgements are made in very personal terms: *your* teaching, and by implication *you* may be judged unsatisfactory – a potentially mortal professional wound. If not managed well (held) by a line manager or an institution, these external demands or even the fear of them, can equally impinge upon teachers' creativity and result in their failing to maintain the facilitating potential of their classroom environment for the students in their care.

So, at every stage, a developing individual needs opportunities to come into a sense of themselves appropriate to the psychical stage they are at. For this to happen, the environment (mother, family, teacher, school) needs to simultaneously ward off impingements and provide challenges that feel manageable (neither entirely removed or too easy, nor overwhelming). Someone consistently able to provide the space within which 'going on being' can be managed is experienced as *reliable*; however, environmental provision cannot be 'mechanically reliable. It must be reliable in a way that implies the (m)other's empathy' (Winnicott, 1960a, p.48). Adam Phillips highlights the distinction that needs to be made:

> The impulsive gesture must be met, but the infant needs in a mother a collaborator – at once sufficiently other and sufficiently identified with him – but not an accomplice.
>
> *(Phillips, 1998, p.112)*

This may seem a curious distinction. Phillips' suggestion is that, just as an absent (m)other is existentially threatening, so is one who is over-identified with her charge and is therefore unable to afford it the space it needs to grow into. When one person is over-identified with another they fail to provide room for the other to explore different possibilities: if we are the same, there can be no different possibilities. Sufficient identification is required of a mother in the earliest stages of the child's life because initially it has few ways to communicate (tears, cries, physical movements) and the mother must use her imagination and knowledge of human suffering to infer meaning. She will get better at this with practice, and this is what Winnicott is referring to when he talks of empathy and attunement. Later, a degree of identification needs to remain so that we can, for example, recognise distress in another and take the trouble to ask about it.

Over-identification would enable a teacher to say to herself – without troubling to have a conversation – 'I can see that Jamie is upset, I found division hard too. I'll rephrase the question'. But this would be a transferential error; Jamie and the teacher are not the same; without actually asking, she cannot intuitively *know* Jamie's distress. In this way, a teacher can become the accomplice Phillips warns against. Student complaints that work is 'too hard' are too easily met by rewording and rephrasing until the answer is practically (or actually) provided by the teacher so that the student need only repeat it, or a child is placed in a 'lower set' so they need never risk failure again. This actually happens and is one reason girls are often over-represented in lower maths and science sets (Stobart, Bibby and Goldstein, 2005; Brown, Brown and Bibby, 2008). Collusion with real or imagined demands and needs does not help the child to grow: An accomplice colludes with our desire not to have to learn and leaves us stuck where we are, we need appropriate challenge to develop and to be helped into places of manageable uncertainty. The teacher, the (m)other, needs to be able to actively do nothing to allow students to be and become.

These ideas are developed further in the next chapter, and potential outcomes of collusion, compliance and defiance are subjects for later chapters. For the moment, the need for a non-mechanical, reliable presence continues throughout life. Teachers, and the role of an institution in managing their professional lives, are given further consideration in the final chapter.

Ways of being: a True and a False Self

This chapter has been about the development, or achievement of a sense of self, about getting to the developmental stage of 'I Am'. This capacity to pay attention to, to 'be' and to recognise our own impulses is what Winnicott identifies as health. The two ideas he puts in to help us think more about health are the notion of a 'True Self', which stands in contrast to a 'False' or 'care-taker' Self Structure. These are very unfortunate terms. Not only do they sound monolithic (do I only have one self?) but they also sound judgemental: Is my False self a lie? Am I somehow inauthentic if I have a False Self Structure? First of all, both True and False Self Structures are unconscious responses to the experiences of living life in the world. Since the True Self is an expression of our unconscious wishes it is of necessity defended to a greater or lesser extent and so is always (more or less) unavailable to us. Defending the True Self from the vicissitudes of life is the False Self. At its best and least intrusive ('in health') Winnicott describes the operation of the False Self in these terms:

> In health: the False Self is represented by the whole organization of the polite and mannered social attitude, a 'not wearing the heart on the sleeve', as might be said. Much has gone to the individual's ability to forgo omnipotence and the primary processes in general, the gain being the place in society which can never be attained or maintained by the True Self alone.
> *(1960b, p.143)*

Difficulties can arise, however, when the False Self takes over, and the True Self becomes so hidden that the individual loses connection to it. It is under these conditions that a life can come to feel empty, unreal or futile.

Here, I want to draw on some writing by Amir Lamouchi,[2] a student I taught a few years ago. Reflecting on some of the ideas in this chapter, Amir wrote about three of his Year 4 students (aged 8 to 9 years) and their responses to a mathematics activity. I have chosen to reproduce two of his vignettes here: descriptions of Uman's and Tina's responses to a mathematics lesson. Uman seems to exemplify a student able to listen to and respond to his own impulses and so to have contact with that aspect of himself that Winnicott labels a True Self. Tina, on the other hand, highlights the difficulty that a defended False Self Structure can incur to learning but also why this defensive structure is perhaps sometimes enjoyed by schools. The vignettes are reproduced in full and are discussed below. The descriptions in the indented text are Amir's; other analysis and discussion are mine.

> ***Uman*** is numerate and able to think conceptually in Maths. For example, he has not yet learned the column method for multiplication, however when faced with the sum 18 × 32 in the investigation, he used his knowledge of related number facts and doubling and halving to come to the correct answer. ... A further example that springs to mind happened during a class discussion about learning. The question we discussed was: Why do we have to learn? It was clear that hardly anyone could move away from the first argument posed, which was that we learn to get a good job later on in life. Other children repeated this answer repetitively, whereas, towards the end of the session, Uman explained that learning makes him feel good, which spurs him on to do more. Here the unit personality is part of a wider concept of wholeness which soon will be part of a social life of an ever widening kind (Winnicott, 1968). He had already acquired an inner confidence which enabled him to act creatively when faced with something he could not achieve at first. When I asked him how he deals with his own limits of comprehension he answered:
>
> *First I think deeply to see if I can do it, but if I can't then I just ask my friend. I can also ask you. Maybe I can tell my parents about it, they always help me at home.*
>
> There is no need for him to fail, as there is always the option to get unstuck. He is secure within himself: he feels safe when dependent on others and he has reliable sources to deal with queries. This allows him to establish a sense of achievement, which in his own words motivates him to do more.

It seems here that Uman has internalised repeated experiences of feeling himself to be whole, separate, real and loved. By implication, then, he received subjective handling, which has enabled him to experience, survive and recover from repeated manageable moments of fragmentation. From the reading of Winnicott (above) we can infer that this might mean that, in the context of a maths lesson, he can allow himself to trust himself and his environment enough to risk new thoughts. This ability to recognise and respond to a spontaneous gesture or impulse stands in contrast to Tina's presentation in maths lessons (although we need to bear in mind the possibility that in other contexts she can appear more like Uman).

> ***Tina*** has learnt tricks to solve complex number problems. She is home tutored which has enabled her to consolidate the four number operations. She has learned methods to perform calculations, but when asked why these methods work, she is unable to elaborate. Not only that, she is adamant that in maths only the answer matters.
>
> I challenged this by asking her to tell me what she knows about 3 × 8. She immediately told me that the answer is 18. But when I probed further and asked her to show me what that looks like, she struggled to make sense of the question and replied: "Well, one and eight of course." Moreover, when she completed the first [parts of the] task more quickly than anyone else, during the morning session, she did this out of a sense of 'duty'. I could not detect a personal sense of gratification for the completion. The learning was not owned. [...]. Tina can tackle problems in only one way, which is her security. As soon as her modes of thinking are pushed to the boundaries, she gets angry. This is what happened during the second part of the morning.
>
> Tina had reached a point where she had to interpret a word problem in order for her to use her methods. This interpreting of information became more conceptual as the task progressed. She got stuck and uttered phrases like, "What's the point" or "I can't be bothered" and "I just don't get it, can I do something else?" When she was challenged the first time, she felt inclined to give up. Interestingly, this did affect her. She soon began to feel frustrated especially when I encouraged her to try it differently.
>
> We sat down together and discussed the meaning of the question. Praise calmed her down, which helped her to engage with the problem once again. When left by herself though, she firstly distracted other children in her group, then started to wander around before finally bursting out that "This lesson is so stupid!" She sat herself on a separate table and began to colour a picture. [...] Tina's inability to try and solve a maths problem reflected her sense of insecurity. The recognition that she did not know was intensely uncomfortable and perhaps emotionally painful for her (Pitt and Brushwood, 2007). She could not yet think of a creative way of coping with challenges. This resulted in her distracting the class's learning. I let her colour her picture.

Tina's predicament is painfully common and is familiar to me as both a teacher and lecturer. Something has happened to this bright girl that has resulted in her not being able to use her intelligence flexibly to develop her learning. In much of his writing, Winnicott warns mothers and teachers about the dangers of a clever child using their intellect to manage anxieties rather than relying on their (m)other (this is explored in greater detail in Chapters 6 and 7). And mothers and teachers are generally very happy to collude with this process and encourage a child's precocity as it makes their task easier. Winnicott explains that the baby 'well endowed' with intelligence ...

> ... soon gets to know from 'noises off' that a feed is being prepared. Without verbalization the baby talks to himself and says: 'those noises allow me to predict a feed, so, hang on! And the chances are all will be well.' ... Can you see that the intellect helps in the toleration of frustration? From this one can go on to see that a mother can exploit a baby's intellectual functions in order to get free from the tie that comes from a baby's dependence. All this is quite normal, but if you give the baby an intellectual equipment that is well above average, the baby and the mother may collude in exploitation of the intellect which becomes split off – split off, that is from the psyche of psychosomatic existence and living ... then the baby begins to develop a false self in terms of a life in the split-off mind, the true self being psychosomatic, hidden, and perhaps lost; so that while higher mathematics gets a boost, the child fails to know what to do with one penny.
>
> *(1968, p.59)*

In the vignettes above, Tina appears to have split off her intellect. Her family, keen to push this clever child ahead and to help gain her advantages in school, appear to have provided home tutoring that has accelerated her academic learning such that it has outstripped her development more broadly. This means that, in the context of maths lessons, she has lost her capacity to listen to and hear her own desires and anxieties; they are drowned out by the demands of others, which impinge on her ability to 'relax' and to hear her own responses. Like the baby recognising the signs that dinner is on the way and using these to manage its own anxiety, the somatic signs (signs that might be recognised by listening to the body and being responded to by a reliable, good enough mother) come to be meaningless and no longer worth listening to. Listening for and paying attention to signs from outside come to be experienced as more rewarding if this is praised and encouraged so progressively less attention is given to the personal impulses/signs. As listening and responding to the external signals are increasingly rewarded, the collusion grows. But internal voices do not go away; they just are not listened to and so get buried. Tina's protests are adult protests: This is not worthwhile; 'can I do something else?' She is unable to contemplate the idea that 3 × 8 might not equal 18. The invitation to think differently, rather than rely on faulty knowledge, leads to a descent into concrete thinking. This fact exists in isolation so there is no recognition that, if $2 \times 8 = 16$ or $2 \times 19 = 18$ then the answer she has makes no sense. In these ways, learning, and knowledge can become defences against anxieties: although we celebrate the bright over-achiever, the lack of attention that this gives to the rest of the child's development is worrying in terms of their future lives (within or beyond any 'good job'), although Rachael Peltz explains the payoff:

> Precocity is often an adaptation to trauma. Children prematurely take over their parent's caretaking functions and then hold this capacity in an unrealistic light, feeling contempt for their needful states. In a culture in which dependency is scorned, where people in need of assistance are considered freeloaders, is it any wonder that parents, insecure about their own ability to protect and provide for their children's futures, would promote precocity in their children?
>
> *(Peltz, 2006, p.75)*

The next chapter explores this issue further in relation to communication, and Chapter 7 explores compliance in greater depth.

Notes

1 The mother may equally send in a substitute. If the father takes a bottle to a baby in these earliest days, Winnicott suggests, the infant is unaware of the presence of another person (there is still no one outside – no 'not me') so maternal care can also be provided by a father or someone else.

2 These vignettes are taken from an essay Amir wrote that drew on Winnicott's 1968 talk to the Association for Teachers of Mathematics, 'Sum, I Am'. I am grateful to Amir for his permission to reproduce and use these here.

References

Britzman, D.P. 2011. *Freud and education.* London: Routledge.

Britzman, D.P. 2012. The adolescent teacher: a psychoanalytic note on regression in the professions. *Journal of Infant, Child and Adolescent Psychotherapy*, 11, 272–283.

Brown, M., P. Brown, and T. Bibby. 2008. "I would rather die": reasons given by 16-year-olds for not continuing their study of mathematics. *Research in Mathematics Education*, 10(1), 3–18.

Chodorow, N. 1989. *Feminism and psychoanalytic theory.* Cambridge: Polity Press in association with Blackwell.

Chodorow, N. 1999. *The reproduction of mothering: psychoanalysis and the sociology of gender.* Berkeley: University of California Press.

Greenberg, J.R., and S.A. Mitchell. 1983. *Object relations in psychoanalytic theory.* Cambridge, MA and London: Harvard University Press.

Peltz, R. 2006. The manic society. In *Psychoanalysis, class and politics: encounters in the clinical setting*, edited by L. Layton, N.C. Hollander and S. Gutwill (pp.65–80). Hove: Routledge.

Phillips, A. 1998. *The beast in the nursery.* London: Faber and Faber.

Pitt, A.J., and C. Brushwood Rose. 2007. The significance of emotions in teaching and learning: on making emotional significance. *International Journal of Leadership in Education,* 10(4), 327–337.

Reay, D., and D. Wiliam. 1999. 'I'll be a nothing': structure, agency and the construction of identity through assessment. *British Educational Research Journal,* 25(3), 343–354.

Stobart, G., T. Bibby, and H. Goldstein. 2005. *Moving to two-tier GCSE mathematics examinations: an independent evaluation of the 2005 GCSE pilot and trial. Final report.* University of London, Institute of Education.

Winnicott, D.W. 1960a. The theory of the parent-infant relationship. In *The maturational processes and the facilitating environment: studies in the theory of emotional development,* edited by D.W. Winnicott (1965, 2007 edition, pp.37–55). London: Karnac.

Winnicott, D.W. 1960b. Ego distortion in terms of true and false self. In *The maturational processes and the facilitating environment: studies in the theory of emotional development,* edited by D.W. Winnicott (1965, 2007 edition, pp.140–152). London: Karnac.

Winnicott, D.W. 1964. *The child, the family and the outside world* (1991 edition). London: Penguin.

Winnicott, D.W. 1968. Sum, I am. In *Home is where we start from: essays by a psychoanalyst,* edited by C. Winnicott, R. Shepherd and M. Davis (1986 edition, pp.55–64). Harmondsworth: Penguin.

4

COMMUNICATION. MAYBE

> The single biggest problem in communication is the illusion that it has taken place.
>
> —George Bernard Shaw

As George Bernard Shaw suggests, communication is never as reliably straightforward as we might wish. The importance of communication in education is underscored by the central place that language (or 'English') occupies in the curriculum. Speaking and listening, reading and writing are core activities in classrooms and are increasingly taken for granted as students get older. This chapter, and indeed, this book, take as an article of faith the fact that communication happens in many ways: sometimes with spoken or written words, sometimes not. Even where a language is apparently shared and words are assumed to mean the same things miscommunication happens more often than we might like to think. Communication is not entirely about conscious, rational intention; the unconscious also has a role to play, not least (as the famous Freudian slip suggests) 'when you say one thing but mean your mother'. All that and no mention of facial expressions or body language! One place to start thinking about this might be to wonder what other forms of communication may be overshadowed by the more overt and obvious aspects of inter-personal communication. This chapter begins by considering the way communication gets started and how we develop both verbal and non-verbal ways of communicating that are inter-personal and also intra-personal; forms of communication over which executive functions such as intention and rational planning may have some control, and others where the unconscious *is* the 'talk'. It will also explore the nature of the relationships within which communication takes place (or fails to take place) and which profoundly influence our experiences of those relationships and what we might (or might not) learn within them.

A Winnicotian take on the emergence of language

As discussed in the previous chapters, for Winnicott an 'ordinary devoted mother', in a state of primary maternal preoccupation, is well enough attuned to her new-born infant to be able to make sense of and respond appropriately to its first communications: its facial expressions, the sounds it makes and its thrashings, grabbings and wrigglings. Through her looking at and responding to these subjective communications, Winnicott suggests she is able to provide the infant with the illusion that it is alive and creating what it needs. Free from impingements, the infant initially has no need to feel gratitude or to wonder about anything; in a state of primary omnipotence, it hallucinates the objects it needs into being. This act of hallucination is important – it is crucial that the baby has control over this process – if it is forced too quickly to notice that it is being given what it needs then, for Winnicott, this breaks its state of creating itself as a unit and without this initial sense of self-as-whole the rest cannot grow. Importantly, over time, a mother does gradually let the world impinge upon the infant, drawing its attention out beyond itself and, in this way, prompts it to distinguish self and other; having created 'me' one can notice 'not me'.

The developmental moves that Winnicott proposes chart progress from a state of merger to one of separation. In a merged state the individual is able only to register its own experiences and is unable to distinguish itself from its surroundings. Winnicott calls the objects it relates to 'subjective objects': things hallucinated or dreamed into being, things created in reverie and out of need. On one level, beyond early infancy, this state of being is our imagination, our fantasy life. It can be a place of relaxation and a way of communicating with ourselves about our own experiences; it *is* thinking. As far as the world that is not-me is concerned, this is a place of non-communication; this may not be a problem as long as it is about one's own dreams and desires. It may become a problem if I start to behave *as if* my fantasy life were a way to operate in the world; omnipotence and a denial of reality might be fun to play with but they do not typically go down well with others!

An early stage of separation is characterised by the individual beginning to recognise aspects of the other; Winnicott calls this 'object relating' – a form of relating that remains partial and incomplete. In infancy object relating means that the breast has a separate existence from the mother; this enables the breast (an object) to be hated as frustrating when it fails to deliver food even as the mother (another object) is loved. To consider the ways in which object relating persists later in life, consider a student who sees their teacher only as the person who gives endless work. The realities of the teacher's own life and job do not enter this student's mind and they experience her as persecuting. There is a lot of omnipotence at play in this scenario – in the student's partial view of his teacher, the teacher's world is believed to be centred entirely on the student; she thinks of nothing but how to make his life a misery. It is a final, more difficult move to recognise, not only separation, but also the complex and different subjectivity of the other person: I may not like the way my teacher behaves towards me, but I have some understanding of why she does. I may try to discuss my difficulties with her and to search for a compromise. A final important step then is the acknowledgement that the other person is not only separate but that they also have a separate sense of being, a complex internal life with affective responses and knowledges different from mine.

To develop these ideas more fully I draw additionally on the work of Jessica Benjamin whose slightly different metaphors can help clarify Winnicott's ideas and make them easier to translate to education contexts. Like Winnicott, Benjamin (2004) highlights the difficulty of maintaining a belief that 'the object of our feelings, needs, actions, and thoughts, is actually another subject, an equivalent centre of being' (p.5). To distinguish different ways of relating and communicating, Benjamin draws on the metaphor of traffic in streets: Developing Winnicott's description of it as 'cul-de-sac communication' (1963), Benjamin typifies both merged (non)communication and object relating as one-way streets, while communicating inter-subjectively, she suggests, has the characteristics of a two-way street. Communication as a one-way street, she says, assumes *complementarity*. That is, it signals a breakdown in communication, a collapse into each party assuming that both are the same (a state we might think of as akin to merger, which Benjamin calls one-ness) or irrevocably different (which she calls two-ness and relates to Winnicott's object-relating). In either case, there is no space for the other to be held in mind and thought about; the result is a persecuting reactivity in which both parties will feel 'done to'. In states of merger/one-ness and object-relating/two-ness complementarity holds sway:

> The idea of complementary relations aims to describe those push-me/pull-you, doer/done-to dynamics that we find in most impasses, which generally appear to be one-way – that is, each person feels done to, and not like an agent helping to co-create reality.
>
> *(2004, p.9)*

It is so very easy to fall into the patterns of identification that ease light social interactions and enable us to not make the space to consider the position of the other. Walking behind two teachers as they left their school at the end of the day, I overheard an apparently innocuous comment: 'I'm exhausted, half-term can't come soon enough'. Here the teacher talking and the teacher listening perhaps identified with each other as professionals both involved in demanding jobs. They might both have assumed their exhaustion was equally onerous and that the holiday would provide equal respite, but there seemed to be a lot of assumptions being made. For example, a teacher exhausted by the overwhelming demands for care-giving at home is unlikely to feel the same about a week at home as a teacher who has no such responsibilities. A teacher using manic levels of engagement at work to blot out the pain of loneliness at home is unlikely to feel the same about a week away from work as someone suffering work-place bullying. These are somewhat obvious examples, but 'easy' communication relies to some extent on such over-identifications; the costs are rarely considered. And if the cauldron of miscommunication can bubble so hotly between two people for something as apparently neutral as a holiday, what might it be like magnified by the multiple, cross-cutting relationships in a classroom? How much is lost between a teacher who assumes her class hate maths because she did, those who delight in a shared and collusive opportunity to avoid the maths, and those others who experience maths as an interesting and challenging subject and are quite enjoying it …?

One-ness: merger and relating to subjective objects

When we communicate, it is easy to slip into an assumption that what the other person is feeling or experiencing is what we ourselves would feel or experience in a similar situation. This slip into an imagined merger is unconscious; it protects us from the difficulties of relating: of exposing our own feelings to others, and ourselves to the feelings of others. Such unconscious reacting can be seen in a form of 'empathy' that presumes to know the difficulty of, and solution to, someone else's situation without checking. Even the kindest of intentions under these conditions is likely to be experienced as persecuting by the person being 'empathised' with, and the perceived lack of gratitude can similarly persecute the 'helpful' friend.

Winnicott talks about communication with subjective objects as being a 'cul-de-sac communication'. The subjective object (the hallucinated, dreamed or fantasised object) is incapable of responding, so despite the fact that these communications enable us to feel real, the state of withdrawal that characterises them can be a trap. Yet, for Winnicott, this 'silent or secret communication with subjective objects, carrying a sense of real, must periodically take over to restore balance …. [Part of our selves] communicates silently [dreams, day-dreams, thinks about etc.] with subjective objects. There is', he says, 'room for the idea that significant relating and communicating is silent' (1963, p.184). It is through a connection to our inner worlds that we maintain a sense of ourselves as real. Too often, he suggests, the world impinges on our reveries too abruptly and calls us out from ourselves before we are ready. As a defence against the difficulty of this intrusion he says we develop a 'False' or compliant self; that is, a self that buries what *it* wants to satisfy the demands of the other perhaps eventually behaving 'as if' what the other wants is what the self wants. The 'false' or compliant self does not feel real since it circumvents the core or 'true self'. These unfortunately named ideas, which emerge in relation to these early forms of communication and their implications for education are explored further in later chapters.

Despite the difficulties raised here, Winnicott believes there is value in the apparently 'cul-de-sac communication' characteristic of merger, of one-ness. To illustrate the idea of a 'secret self' that he is trying to develop, Winnicott reports an incident from his clinical work. In analysis, a woman reported that when she was about 9 years old, she had

> stolen a school book in which she had collected poems and sayings, and she wrote on it "My private book". On the front page she wrote: "what a man thinketh in his heart, so is he." In fact her mother had asked her: "Where did you get this saying from?" This was bad because it meant the mother must have read the book.
>
> *(1963, p.186)*

As Winnicott suggests, had the mother read the book and said nothing the child/analysand would never have known and could have continued collecting words and phrases that touched her and whose tone and sense were helping her construct a picture for her of who she was and what she was like. The 'private book' was an intensely personal site of shaping and getting to know her developing self. The sense of violation, of having had her private-self exposed and questioned, was experienced as intensely traumatic, and we might imagine her feelings of humiliation, shame and rage at her mother's intrusion. Winnicott goes on to summarise:

> I suggest that in health there is a core to the personality that corresponds to the true self of the split personality[1]; I suggest that this core never communicates with the world of perceived objects, and that the individual person knows that it must never be communicated with or be influenced by external reality. ... Although healthy persons communicate and enjoy communicating, the other fact is equally true, that *each individual is an isolate, permanently non-communicating, permanently unknown, in fact, unfound.*
>
> *(1963, p.187 emphasis in original)*

This is a central tenet of all psychoanalytic theories, that there is always and inevitably a part of ourselves, a kernel, that we cannot know and that no one else can know either. This is the unconscious – paradoxically both socially and culturally constituted – and forever dynamic and unknowable. Winnicott is signalling that unconscious aspects of the self are precious and need protecting. If we so desire, we may be able to explore the parts that present themselves to us in dreams, as half-thoughts, as attractions to ideas, images or quotations, as identifications with particular people and so forth. But these nascent thoughts (and the ones we continue to repress) are potentially too exposing and dangerous so we protect them, and that is normal and healthy; a degree of defendedness is required to be a functioning person. This kernel is what he calls the 'True Self'.

Having this privacy challenged or invaded can be experienced as a gross insult to our sense of self. Winnicott (1963) likens this to a 'sophisticated game of hide-and-seek in which *it is a joy to be hidden but a disaster not to be found*' and expresses his lack of surprise that so many people 'hate psychoanalysis which has penetrated a long way into the human personality, and which provides a threat to the human individual in his need to be secretly isolated'. The problem we are faced with, a question also posed by Freud (1931), is: 'how to be isolated without having to be insulated?' (p.187). Before we can begin to explore that question, though, we need to consider the other form of defended communication characterised by complementarity.

Two-ness: self and other in object relating

A failure to hold the other person in mind – to remember that *they* are not *I* – has implications, not only for how we communicate with them, but also how we experience ourselves. In discussing some of these difficulties, Winnicott describes an analysis he undertook with a woman. Part of his description contains the following excerpt from a time when she was discussing her dreams. Winnicott recounts:

> A male pupil at the school where she teaches may decide to leave and get a job. She pointed out that here again was cause for grief; it was like losing a child. [...] The children she was teaching, especially if talented, represented herself, so that their achievements were hers, and if they left the school it was an utter disaster. Unsympathetic treatment of these pupils who represented herself, especially those who were boys, made her feel herself insulted.
>
> *(1971, p.179)*

This level of (over)identification is unconscious, and psychoanalysis calls it 'projective identification'; aspects of the self are 'projected' into someone else for safe keeping. In this woman's case her academic abilities and her own masculine (and therefore, to her, worthy) qualities were not something it was possible for her to own at that time. This misrecognition, this behaviour towards someone else 'as if' our good (or bad) qualities were theirs places a burden upon them requiring as it does that they succeed for our benefit rather than for their own. This is an example of object relating that can cause immense difficulties – as well as be used positively. While object relating is needed by the infant to survive, its continued use can become problematic. Such object relating can be seen in children's (and students') refusal to see teachers as fully human. A common fantasy among young children is that teachers live in the school building, that their only interests are in what they teach and that their only relationships are with each other. This fantasy simultaneously enables children to deal with these new adults in their lives with their range of demands and denies teachers their complex relationships and experiences beyond their professional lives; their part-existence here reduces them to object status: they are helpers, teachers, work-presenters, not whole people.

When discipline collapses in the classroom a teacher can feel persecuted/done-to by the class's lack of respect and disruptive behaviour (their refusal of her role as a teacher and the knowledge she embodies). Simultaneously, and with as much justification, the class can feel persecuted/done-to by the teacher's overbearing demeanour and shouting and her dull (or overly difficult) lessons. Neither party feels seen as whole and, without something significant changing, there can be no possibility for negotiating a workable classroom in which learning might take place. These 'bad' people (bad teacher, bad students) are subjective objects: they are parts of a whole that cannot be recognised; they are experienced (and hence subjective) as unreasonable and therefore threatening. In one response – the creation of a 'False' or compliant Self – the self defends by burying its own needs and acting to assuage the apparently unreasonable other's anger. The unreasonableness is transferred from the other to the self: 'my teacher would not call me lazy if I wasn't, I think I am working hard but obviously it isn't hard enough. I must work harder to please her'. A false or compliant self buries the lack of understanding or the boredom and tries to become the self that the other person wants. In the second scenario the self withdraws in fury and a sense of righteous indignation may develop to keep 'me' safely right and the other safely wrong and rejected. Any complicity I may have in the situation can thus be ignored leaving me to enjoy my subjective experience (and righteous indignation) alone.

Third-ness: self, other and intersubjective relating

In the previous section, I defined object relating and suggested that, while this is generally a very common form of relating, we might want to hold on to the possibility of relating to others, and of being related to by others, as whole subjects. This brings us again to Winnicott's 'sophisticated game of hide and seek' – a game in which we take personal pleasure in our dreams and desires but object to being ignored or not looked for – and to the question of how to be isolated without having to be insulated, how to protect our integrity without cutting our selves off from others. Is it possible to relate subject-to-subject without feeling shame or disgust? Why might we slide back to object relating with such apparent ease? These questions go to the heart of the difficulties of interpersonal communication.

In contrast to a 'doer-done to' dynamic, Benjamin suggests the possibility of creating a place of 'third-ness', a place which is neither mine nor yours, but a psychical space to which we each surrender ourselves and from which we might think about ourselves and each other. It is important not to idealise or reify this way of being. It is, she reminds us repeatedly, a temporary moment of seeing not a permanent state of being. Life is too complex and difficult for us to be able to maintain the balancing act of third-ness easily or for extended periods.

Her suggestion is that, from a position of third-ness, rather than having to choose between 'submission or resistance to the other's demand', we might be able to relate inter-subjectively. However, 'the recovery of subjectivity requires the recognition of our own participation. Crucially, this usually involves surrendering our resistance to responsibility, a resistance arising from reactivity to blame' (2004, p.11). Think again of the class that is beyond the control of their teacher. For order to be restored by mutual consent (rather than oppression) not only would each party have to accept and forgive the 'bad behaviour' of the other but they would also have to recognise and own their own complicity; they would need to be able to say (and mean) 'I share the blame for this situation'. This is a monumental step but both would need to be able to participate in taking it since 'the only useable third is, by definition, one that is shared' (p.13). Each would need to take responsibility for the difficult feelings the other evoked in them: fear, uncertainty, shame, anger, vulnerability. What does it mean to be a teacher who gets things so wrong? Why have my lessons been so boring? Why do my explanations mean nothing? What does it mean to have been part of a class mob? Why do I hate this subject so much? What do I need to say so that this teacher can help me? The suggestion here is difficult: that in a mutual relationship there can, from time to time, be sufficient trust that both participants feel able to let go of their need to bolster their own defences and to let the other in. And letting the other in means owning our responses to them – which may not be pretty.

To explore the idea of what this 'third' might be, Benjamin returns to a developmental story familiar from Winnicott and distinguishes two ways in which a third, intersubjective, space might arise: from a 'principle of accommodation' and from a 'principle of differentiation'.

> I have suggested that, while it is crucial for the mother to identify with the baby's need—for instance, in adjusting the feeding rhythm—there is the inevitable moment when two-ness arises in the form of the mother's need for sleep, for the claims of her own separate existence. [...] Here the function of the third is to help transcend two-ness not by self-abnegation, not by fostering the illusion that mother and baby are one; rather, at this point, the principle of asymmetrical accommodation should arise from the sense of surrender to necessity, rather than from submission to another person's tyrannical demand or an overwhelming task.
>
> A mother's pride in how overworked and self-denying she is undermines knowledge of her own limits and the ability to distinguish necessary asymmetry from masochism. Likewise, the mother needs to hold in mind the knowledge that much infant distress is natural and ephemeral, in order for her to be able to soothe her child's distress without dissolving into anxious oneness with it.
>
> *(2004, p.17)*

The idea of a necessary asymmetry is interesting when we think about teaching. Teachers who take pride in the extent to which the demands on their time – the planning, marking, being in classrooms and meetings – consume their lives can seem to take masochistic delight in their self-abnegation, leaving guilt to haunt any time they do take for themselves. The significant relationship here is between the teacher and her professional identity, a relationship from which real students have effectively been excluded. How can students be with such martyrs? The sense of having nothing worthwhile to put into such (enjoyably) mutually consuming relationships as that between a teacher and her professional-identity can silence students, leaving them outside and abjected. More realistically, teachers give of themselves and need time and space to replenish their reserves so they can continue to give in an inevitably asymmetric work-place. A teacher masochistically wrapped up in being consumed by their professional life is liable to burn out and, in a very concrete sense, no longer 'be there' for their students.

To develop her theme, Benjamin quotes a passage from a book by Stephen Mitchell in which he talks about his experience of being with his young daughter:

> When my older daughter was about two or so, I remember my excitement at the prospect of taking walks with her, given her new ambulatory skills and her intense interest in being outdoors. However, I soon found these walks agonizingly slow. My idea of a walk entailed brisk movement along a road or path. Her idea was quite different. The implications of this difference hit me one day when we encountered a fallen tree on the side of the road.... The rest of the "walk" was spent exploring the fungal and insect life on, under, and around the tree. I remember my sudden realization that these walks would be no fun for me, merely a parental duty, if I held onto my idea of walks. As I was able to give that up and surrender to my daughter's rhythm and focus, a different type of experience opened up to me.... If I had simply restrained myself out of duty, I would have experienced the walk as a compliance. But I was able to become my daughter's version of a good companion and to find in that another way for me to be that took on great personal meaning for me.
>
> *(cited in Benjamin, 2004, pp.25–26)*

In this account of learning to walk with his daughter, Mitchell realises that he has first to recognise and acknowledge his familiar adult self: a man who walks alone or with other adults who can match his pace, and who enjoys the physicality of movement and the sense of travel, of covering ground. However, he realises he simultaneously has to give space to a less familiar man: the new father who walks with his toddler to enjoy her discovery of new sights and sounds and so to have these sights and sounds renewed for himself. It is important, as he says, for this father to learn a new way of being developed with, and in response to, his daughter and not to be a dutifully compliant automaton-adult hobbled and frustrated by a 2-year-old who walked slowly and wanted to explore a fallen tree in minute detail. As a teacher, this story reminds me of the tyranny of a rigid lesson plan and the importance of staying open to learners' ideas – their seemingly frustrating peregrinations around my well-structured topic.

In considering the difference between surrender and submission, Mitchell reflects that submitting to his daughter's pace would have allowed him to hold onto his old sense of self and ways of being, but in doing this he would have needed to repress or deny his own desires. Such a submission would have subjected him to a very long hell of waiting for her to grow up and become what she was not yet able to be so that *she* could fulfil *his* desire for a daughter who might accompany him on his (adult) walks. In his surrender to his daughter's pace and interests, Mitchell reports finding a new sense of self. In his surrender he found that his new self did not destroy his old self; indeed, it left it intact giving him the parallel possibility of taking adult walks alone or with others who could participate with him.

As a teacher, I find this story both touching and interesting. It makes me wonder about the nature and qualities of the pedagogic relationships I have tried to foster over many years and in different contexts. While I never taught 2-year-olds, the sense of wonder that new learning can engender does not necessarily diminish with age. The need to go slowly and to savour new ideas, exploring their implications in the contexts that seem important, can slow teaching almost unbearably. Like Mitchell's initial desire for a daughter who could walk with him, as a teacher I can want students to be my peers, to know what I know so that they can engage with the ideas that excite and interest me. Such a picture is seductive: what a brilliant teacher I would be! How disappointing is it when students' interests are not the same as mine? And how much more frustrating it is to allow people the time they need to take in, learn from and grow into their own interests?

Teaching at all levels faces a tension between the need to cover the curriculum and to force-feed facts and to accept students' rhythms. How we manage this tension is the asymmetry inherent in teaching; it is part of what can make ours an 'impossible profession' (Bibby, 2011). As the 'adult' in this asymmetric relationship, teachers need to be able to hold their own frustration so that they can 'hold in mind the knowledge that much [student] distress is natural and ephemeral, [and] be able to soothe [her student's] distress without dissolving into anxious oneness with it'. And similarly, 'to hold in mind the knowledge that much [professional] distress is natural and ephemeral, in order for her to be able to soothe [her own] distress' without becoming paralysed by it.

Benjamin draws on the work of Britton to explore the way that, in an analytic relationship, 'the complementary opposition of my reality and your reality gets activated' (p.30). To translate the argument across to teaching, we can think about being in a state of two-ness (we are separate and different) in which

> ... both partners experience the impossibility of acknowledging the other's reality without abandoning one's own. The [teacher] may also be overwhelmed by how destructive the [student's] image of her is to her own sense of self. For instance, when the [student's] reality is that "You are toxic and have made me [wrong], [stupid] and unable to [think]," the [teacher] will typically find it nearly impossible to take that in without losing her own reality.
>
> *(2004, p.30)*

How can a teacher maintain a sense of herself as a teacher if she is someone who makes others feel wrong, stupid and unable to think? Similarly, how can a student maintain a sense of himself as student if his teacher's reality suggests to him 'you are toxic and make me ignorant, powerless and unable to teach'? How might we predict a teacher having such feelings would behave towards her student? And how might we predict a student having such feelings would behave towards her teacher?

Benjamin's suggestion is that the dynamic illustrated here allows for only one reality at a time to be 'real'. In the context of psychoanalysis, she suggests that to move beyond this situation analysts have to be able 'to find a different way to regulate [them]selves, one in which [they] accept loss, failure, mistakes and [their] own vulnerability'. Such a move, she says, requires that the analyst change

> from knowing what is right to a more 'intersubjective' view of the analyst as a 'responsible participant' able to 'acknowledge our own struggles. ... The analyst who can acknowledge missing or failing, who can feel and express regret, helps create a system based on acknowledgement of what has been missing, both in the past and the present'.
>
> *(2004, p.32)*

It is interesting, in the light of this suggestion, to consider the teacher who finds claims of ignorance a useful pedagogic tool: 'I don't know, let's find out' – ignorance feigned as pedagogic trope. A key question would be, can the statement really be true? And what happens when learning takes an unexpected turn? Can real ignorance be tolerated? For example, having presented the rule: *to divide fractions, turn the second one upside-down and multiply*, can the question 'why does that work?' be explored, or does it work 'because it does!'? What would we need to become aware of if we were to acknowledge what we had missed, failed in our pedagogic relations or what we regretted? And even then, Benjamin warns us, 'disclosure is not panacea, ... the [teacher's] acknowledgement of responsibility can only take place by working through deep anguish around feelings of destructiveness and loss' (p.40).

Under the threat of violent and invasive judgements from tests, examinations and external scrutiny of teaching, can the shame of ignorance, or the shame of being a disappointing teacher who *really does not know* and perhaps also does not know how to find out, be admitted and survived? Or would any such possibility need to be closed down and denied? It is on such points, and 'the acceptance of inevitable breakdown and repair', that opportunities for tolerating inter-subjectivity and the possibilities for communication rest. The implications of this are explored in the rest of this book; they are the hard questions that always lurk at the heart of pedagogy.

An example to play with

Throughout this chapter I have explored Winnicott's psychoanalytic explanation for the ways in which communication might begin. I have considered the instantiation and difficulties associated with communicating with ourselves: of dreaming and thinking and maintaining the integrity of our unconscious lives. I have also explored one way to think about communication that is experienced as persecuting and another that might have space in which we can hold each other in mind – a place of inter-subjective third-ness. In the final section, I want to explore a story that I find somewhat paradoxical – a story of both communication and breakdown.

Charlie and the mobile phone

This vignette was written by Charlotte, immediately after a workshop she attended for teachers working in schools in disadvantaged areas in England. This was part of a wider project 'Bridging the structure/agency divide: Interdisciplinary approaches to disadvantage and education'.[2] The incident reproduced below is particular but of a type familiar in most secondary schools in the UK. I have selected it to begin to highlight some of the difficulties associated with 'communication' in schools. The confused tenses (which I have left) suggest that the incident remained very much alive for Charlotte and that she was still thinking through its implications as she reflected on and wrote about it.

> Charlie is in form time when his phone rings. He takes it out of his bag and answers. The school rules state that students are not allowed phones on the premises at all. The form tutor (FT) asks Charlie to hand over the phone. He refused and instead decided to leave the room and began to walk out of school. FT followed Charlie and found him at the school gates with his mother. There was a heated conversation where the mother made it clear that Charlie would not be handing over his phone despite the fact he had very clearly broken the school rules. The head teacher noticed the situation and came over to Charlie, the FT and his mother. The head also stated that the boy needed to hand over the phone to the FT. There followed a conversation about whether that was necessary considering he had by then left the school grounds. The head teacher stated that the head of year would sort it out in the morning. The boy and mother left the school and as they did the mother turned to her son, winked and said 'Good boy'. The reinforcement of not following school rules and the excessive undermining of the hierarchy at school made it extremely difficult for us to modify Charlie's behaviour at school. Progress could be made but it was always back to square one when he came back from any extended period of time at home. This made externally excluding him a very difficult option.

How best can we think about the role the phone is playing here and what might that mean for schools?

The mobile phone appears to act like an umbilical cord, stretched through the ether, connecting a boy to his mother/home (and the mother/home to her son). But the school demand is for separation from home: for *no phone*. If a parent needs to contact a child during the school day the expectation is generally that they will comply with institutional regulations and that this contact will be indirect and mediated by the school office. Put another way, the school demand is for merger with (and compliance to) school and the teachers – and separation from home – an either/or construction that of itself is likely to generate difficulties. In the wink and joining at the school gates both mother and son – read by the teacher as *undermining the authority of the school* – are also reconfirming their own connection, a connection that may otherwise feel and/or be tenuous or threatened. The wireless connection between son and home/mother is paradoxically real and virtual; an umbilical cord that the school may fear bypasses school, rendering it invisible.

What might the school's furious rejection of the mobile phone really defend against? What piece of 'unbearable knowledge' does the phone embody? The non-centrality of the school in the lives of young people? The importance of other relationships and knowledges? If, like a real umbilical cord, this wireless connection enables the mother to feed the son, how can the school also feed him? How does a fear of its own obsolescence affect a school? If, as Benjamin suggests, creating a third space, a place of intersubjective possibility, requires surrender taking responsibility for our own concerns, are we even aware of what these concerns and mistakes might be? At a time when 'student voice' is valorised, how can real students actually be enabled to come into being enough to find and learn to express those voices?

The apparent dangerousness of the mother in this situation seems to attest to an otherness that the rational, ordered school stands in contrast to. The list of disadvantages that Charlie, as a white, working-class boy living in poverty, was felt to face certainly pointed to the school's fantasy of its primacy as the only possible source of learning; particularly learning to follow instructions. Clear from the larger vignette and the discussions that surrounded it (discussed further in Bibby, Lupton and Raffo, 2017), Charlie's disadvantages were portrayed as emanating from his apparently chaotic home life and a series of 'out there' issues that effectively blamed the family, the child, the previous school etc. No 'blame' was placed on current education policies (apart from over-long summer holidays that remove the child from the school's good influence), no consideration was given to the way the school located and interacted with families and there was little or no thought that any of this might be different.

At its roots, a struggle seems to be taking place in this vignette over the 'ownership' of Charlie, a tug of war. The mobile phone is perhaps a surrogate for the rope that the two teams traditionally pull on, Charlie the flag that signals its mid-point. In this form of (non)communication, both the school and his mother seem to want to claim Charlie; any thought that he could identify with both is apparently unthinkable. The demand that he submit to one (and repudiate the other) seems grossly unfair: What costs would either decision incur? And what would happen to the other aspects of his identity based on which 'parent' he submitted to? Might there be a way for the school to listen to and think about his need for connection to the world beyond school? A blanket 'no phones' rule – like all zero tolerance rules – ensures that the school need never think about his needs and what the phone means within his family. It also means that the school/teachers need never consider their own difficult feelings evoked by the bodies of the students: anger that they do not 'own' the children (despite talk of 'my class' and 'our children'), that they are not loved as they feel they should be (despite being *in loco parentis*) …?

I am sure the teachers would have had their mobile phones in school – a state of two-ness therefore exists: As an adult I can have my phone because I am different; I have to be able to be in contact with my partner/child, but you are different. A persecuting doer/done to relation has been set up between Charlie and the school – one has to be concerned about how this impasse might play out. Because his communication was inexpert and/or because he was trying to say something the school might not want to hear, we are left not knowing what Charlie might have been trying to communicate.

Before moving on to the next chapter I want to return to Winnicott to explore a little further the idea of the mobile phone acting like an umbilical cord. In *Playing and reality* (1971) he describes his contact, over many years, with one family and in particular with the mother and her son. On playing the squiggle game together when the boy was 2 years old Winnicott noticed that nearly every squiggle he offered the boy turned into something made of string: a lasso, a whip, a yo-yo string, a string in a knot. On mentioning this to the boy's mother she reported:

> That the boy had become obsessed with everything to do with string, and in fact whenever they went into a room they were liable to find that he had joined together chairs and tables; and they might find a cushion, for instance, with a string joining it to the fireplace.. They said that the boy's preoccupation with string was gradually developing a new feature, one that worried them instead of causing ordinary concern. He had recently tied a string around his sister's neck (the sister whose birth had provided the first separation of this boy from his mother).
>
> *(pp.22–23)*

There follows a discussion of Winnicott's suggestion and later confirmation that the string was symbolising the boy's anxiety about the separation he was experiencing from his mother: separation occasioned not only by the birth of the little sister, but also by the mother's depression and consequent unavailability (due to her preoccupation with her own worries). He goes on to reflect that:

> String can be looked upon as an extension of other techniques of communication. String joins, just as it also helps in the wrapping up of objects and in the holding of unintegrated material. In this respect string has a symbolic meaning for everyone; an exaggeration of the use of string can easily belong to the beginnings of a sense of insecurity or the idea of a lack of communication.
>
> *(p.26)*

Thinking about children bringing prohibited items like mobile phones into school – with their invisible strings to home or a parent or some other contact – starts to take on new significance. The layers of communication and relationship at stake in every interaction start to reveal their complexities.

The next chapter considers another of Winnicott's stories of hope: of play and creativity.

Notes

1 Split personality here refers to the defensive dichotomising that we all develop to deal with things that are too much for us and that generate anxiety. This defensive splitting is characterised by either/or concrete thinking and is typical of the object relating in the next section. It was also, for Winnicott, typified by the True and False Self Structures that mark the unconscious and the mind's attempts to defend it from the world.

2 The project, 'Bridging the structure/agency divide: Interdisciplinary approaches to education and disadvantage' was funded by the Economic and Social Research Council (ESRC) to run between 2013 and 2016. The website can be accessed at https://bridgingdisadvantageeducation.wordpress.com/. I am grateful to Charlotte and the project team for their permission to reuse this vignette here.

References

Benjamin, J. 2004. Beyond doer and done-to: an intersubjective view of thirdness. *Psychoanalytic Quarterly*, 73, 5–46.

Bibby, T. 2011. *Education – an 'impossible profession'? Psychoanalytic explorations of learning and classrooms*. London: Routledge.

Bibby, T., R. Lupton, and C. Raffo (Eds). 2017. *Responding to poverty and disadvantage in schools: a reader for teachers*. London: Palgrave MacMillan.

Freud, S. 1931. Some reflections on schoolboy psychology. In *The standard edition of the complete psychological works of Sigmund Freud*, edited by J. Strachey (Vol. XIII, pp.241–244). London: Vintage.

Winnicott, D.W. 1963. Communicating and not communicating leading to a study of certain opposites. In *The maturational processes and the facilitating environment: studies in the theory of emotional development*, edited by D.W. Winnicott (1965, 2007 edition, pp.179–192). London: Karnac.

Winnicott, D.W. 1971. *Playing and reality* (2008, Routledge Classics edition). London: Tavistock Publications.

5

CREATIVITY AND PLAY

Listening to oneself

In today's over-pressured, over-surveilled environments, play is typically relegated to the margins of life: to the early years, to times not designated as 'work' and to spaces that are less watched (holidays, play times, coffee breaks and cafes). In these ways, play has become a private indulgence away from public duties. In reducing work to 'not-play' (and play to 'not-work'), we have however created a split that restricts what each can be; we have denuded play (and work) of much of its potential meaning. A large part of turning to Winnicott as an analytical lens for educators is precisely his refusal to violate the idea of play in this way. For him play is a richly nuanced word and, as an activity, it is central to healthy being.

In *Playing and reality*, Winnicott famously wrote:

> Psychotherapy takes place in the overlap of two areas of playing, that of the patient and that of the therapist. Psychotherapy has to do with two people playing together. The corollary of this is that where playing is not possible then the work done by the therapist is directed towards bringing the patient from a state of not being able to play into a state of being able to play'.
>
> *(1971, p.37)*

In this context, play is the intensely serious business of living life creatively (i.e. engaging with life with curiosity and passion, bringing the self to it). For me, in relation to this comment, some important questions might be: Is it possible to use Winnicott and to think 'teacher' for 'therapist'? In what ways might these be similar projects? And, what would this project look like? So, to rephrase Winnicott: Pedagogy [or perhaps learning] takes place in the overlap of two areas of playing, that of the learner/student and that of the teacher. Pedagogy has to do with two people playing together. The corollary of this is that where playing is not possible then the work done by the teacher is directed towards bringing the student from a state of not being able to play [think, investigate, explore] into a state of being able to play. To me, this feels like a productive way of thinking about pedagogy, so this is the idea taken up here through a consideration of transitional phenomena, play and creativity. Previous chapters have begun to develop a narrative around *being* and *communicating* that suggests a close but hard-to-understand relationship between what is subjective (dreamed, hallucinated) and what is objective (perceived), between inner and outer, between self and other. This chapter focuses on that space in between, a space that Winnicott called a *potential space* and that, in later life, is also *cultural experience*.

Potential space is a 'hypothetical area that exists (but cannot exist) between the baby and the object (mother or part of mother) during the phase of repudiation of the object as not-me, that is, at the end of being merged with the object' (1971, p.144). For Winnicott, the potential that this space holds is the potential for living; that is, for play, for creativity and for relating. That sounds so simple, yet apparently it is not. If we stop and think, we know that entering and crossing apparently empty spaces – spaces with *potential* – can be difficult: Who or what is on the other side? Can I be sure that what I think or hope I can expect on the other side is what is really there? Will the bridge that spans the space stay up (it looks rickety and the drop seems long)? Is the road straight? How long will it take? What will happen if I cross the space? What will happen if I don't?

Any journey contains an element of uncertainty; we have to be able to travel hopefully if we are to take the risks and enjoy the process. As a psychoanalyst, Winnicott focussed particularly on the journey clients took to self-knowledge and a life more richly lived. As a teacher, my particular focus is on journeys to knowledge and knowing. And, because many of the journeys that teachers like myself bear witness to and accompany are not chosen (i.e. are compulsory) I believe I (or should this be we?) also have a responsibility to think about the personal lives developing in school every bit as much as we think about the growing intellects: the development of self- and social knowledge as well as curricular knowledge.

In *Playing and reality* Winnicott (1971) reminds us of his understanding of human nature as having three constituents: an inner psychic reality, an external reality and an intermediate area of experience. External reality is the world that exists beyond me, its continuation might be influenced by me, but it will go on without me and it is knowable by others apart from me. Inner psychic reality he describes as 'the personal property of each individual in so far as a degree of mature integration has been reached' (p.143). This reality is subjective, relational and has aspects that are knowable and aspects that are unknowable, conscious and unconscious.

> Of every individual who has reached the stage of being a unit with a living membrane and an outside and an inside, it can be said that there is an *inner reality* to that individual, an inner world that can be rich or poor and can be at peace or in a state of war.
>
> *(1971, p.3)*

These statements move us some way towards an understanding of human nature, but they do not tell the whole story. For Winnicott there is a 'third part of the life of a human being', a part characterised by cultural experience and creative playing, which also needs to be considered. This is the …

> intermediate area of *experiencing*, to which inner reality and external life both contribute. It is an area that is not challenged, because no claim is made on its behalf except that it shall exist as a resting-place for the individual engaged in the perpetual human task of keeping inner and outer reality separate yet interrelated.
>
> *(1971, p.3 emphasis in original)*

> [This area of experiencing] is extremely variable between individuals. This is because this third area is a product of the *experiences of the individual person* (baby, child, adolescent, adult) in the environment that obtains.
>
> *(p.144 emphasis in original)*

There are at least two important points here. The first is that the process of 'keeping inner and outer reality separate yet interrelated' is 'perpetual'; it is a task that is never complete, so while the matter of transitions and transitional phenomena and objects is started in, and most familiar from, childhood, it never ends. The second is that when we *experience* an event or a moment both our objective observations and our subjective responses contribute to that experience. Such an observation can be a blow to rationalist expectations that, for example, a scientist can be purely objective. The argument here would be that even where measurements are objective, the choice of what to study, what to measure, which problem was selected and how the initial question was formulated – the new questions that arise for this scientist (rather than that one) – all of these will be shaped by the individual scientist's rich *experiences* of living in the world and with their work.

We may recognise moments in our experiencing when we move from subjective to objective relating, when we test our fantasies against reality or dreamily let our perceptions of reality wander over less probable territories: What would happen if …? These movements between dreaming and wakefulness mark 'a process of becoming able to accept difference and similarity' (1971, p.8). So, when we sit up and engage with the world, are we able to hold onto the capacity for playful, creative thought? When is a call from outside too loud and insistent (when does it form an impingement)? What questions do such ruminations raise for our pedagogies?

Getting started

One of Winnicott's best known ideas is that of the 'transitional object' (the thumb, a soft or hard toy, a rag – and occasionally the mother), work that led him to comment on Charles Schulz's drawings of Linus sucking his thumb and holding a blanket to the side of his face, and A.A. Milne's Winnie the Pooh. Winnicott's suggestion was that, to enable its self to move from subjective knowing to the world beyond, a child might adopt a concrete object to act as a defence against the uncertainty that would inevitably accompany such explorations. The object and the way it is handled enable a child to comfort itself – perhaps through sucking, stroking and making sounds (transitional phenomena). The object and its handling help the infant to pass back and forth between the subjective and the objective. This transitional object is, he suggests, the first not-me possession (and the first use of a symbol), but importantly:

> It is not the object ... that is transitional. The object represents the infant's transition from a state of being merged with the mother to a state of being in relation with the mother as something outside and separate.
>
> *(1971, p.15)*

Like a handrail, an object enables the infant to move between states or places, but it is the person who does the moving, not the handrail. An important quality of this relating concerns dependence. Key to developing the capacity to move between the inner and the outer is the presence of the good enough (m)other. To quote Winnicott and to reiterate,

> The good enough 'mother' (not necessarily the infant's own mother) is one who makes adaption to the infant's needs, an active adaptation that gradually lessens, according to the infant's growing ability to account for failure of adaptation and to tolerate the results of frustration.
>
> *(1971, pp.13–14)*

The transitional object has to be alive to the child and therefore must be found and created by him. Winnicott lists the special qualities in the relationship between the infant and his object:

1. The infant assumes rights over the object, and we agree to this assumption. Nevertheless, some abrogation of omnipotence is a feature from the start.
2. The object is affectionately cuddled as well as excitedly loved and mutilated.
3. It must never change, unless changed by the infant.
4. It must survive instinctual loving, and also hating and, if it be a feature, pure aggression.
5. Yet it must seem to the infant to give warmth, or to move, or to have texture, or to do something that seems to show it has vitality or reality of its own.
6. It comes from without from our point of view, but not so from the point of view of the baby. Neither does it come from within; it is not a hallucination.
7. Its fate is to be gradually allowed to be decathected, so that in the course of years it becomes not so much forgotten as relegated to limbo. By this I mean that in health the transitional object does not 'go inside' nor does the

> feeling about it necessarily undergo repression. It is not forgotten and it is not mourned. It loses meaning, and this is because the transitional phenomena have become diffused, they become spread out over the whole intermediate territory between 'inner psychic reality' and 'the external world as perceived by two persons in common', that is to say, over the whole cultural field.
>
> *(1971, p.7)*

These qualities are important and, while teachers and ideas may at first not appear to be transitional objects in the sense that Winnicott originally meant, they may undergo similar stages. In his theoretical statement about transitional objects and phenomena, he goes on to mention different aspects of life that perhaps lend support to the move I make here. 'At this point', he says, 'my subject widens out into that of play, and of artistic creativity and appreciation, and of religious feeling, and of dreaming, and also of fetishism, lying and stealing, the origin and loss of affectionate feeling, drug addiction, the talisman of obsessional rituals, etc.' (1971, p.7). The need for the object, in this example the teacher or idea, to be able to withstand the extremes of their students' affects and to maintain her own vitality are explored more fully in Chapters 8 and 9 so they are passed over here, but we can note that, in the case of ideas, we may have met students who have hung onto familiar or loved ideas for longer than we might have expected. Ideas that outgrow their usefulness can include the rhythms and expectations of a previous class; it is not unusual for children to protest loudly that the way things were with a previous teacher still have relevance or that easy 'rules of thumb' that worked in previous classes are still true (the idea that 'multiplication makes bigger' has caused much trouble down the years!). More familiar to those who watch classrooms is the loss of animation that can occur when an ill-timed comment or onerous assessment robs a child or student of an idea they were enjoying playing with.

This idea of a potential space that exists between the mother and the baby, between the analyst and the patient (between the teacher and the student) seems particularly powerful to me. It is the idea from which (I think) Benjamin (2004) developed the third she used to think about communication that is mutually engaging (discussed in Chapter 4). It is a space that exists in between – in between the internal and external realities, in between people. Returning to Winnicott, we can now perhaps re-introduce and explore some of the richness of his original ideas.

In setting out his theory of play, Winnicott highlights four developmental phases. At first, a baby knows only subjective objects 'and the mother is oriented towards the making actual of what the baby is ready to find'. That is, she is sufficiently attuned to present what is needed or wanted so that it can be found (in the first instance, her nipple). This is followed by the object being 'repudiated, reaccepted, and perceived objectively', a process that is dependent on there being someone present 'to participate and to give back what is handed out'. As well as the baby who pushes or turns away from the breast, we can think of a small child's repetitive game of throwing a toy out of their pram, being delighted to have it returned and throwing it out again. In both of these phases, 'the mother (or part of mother) is in a "to-and-fro" communication between that which a baby has a capacity to find and (alternatively) being herself waiting to be found' (1971, p.63). This idea of play, and later cultural life, as a movement that initially requires someone else who is reliable and in whom trust can develop, underlines the precarious nature of play, of which more below.

A third phase of play is 'being alone in the presence of someone. The child is now playing on the basis of the assumption that the person who loves and who is therefore reliable is available and continues to be available when remembered after being forgotten' (1971, p.64). Here, we can think about the student who seems able to work in class but who might struggle to complete homework: are they 'just lazy' or 'badly organised'? Or might the physical presence of the teacher, the friend, or the props of the classroom, matter more than we like to acknowledge (perhaps since it interrupts our fantasies of – and relief at – independent learners)? If the reliable (m)other is away for too long, that is, for longer than their goodness, care and helpfulness can be kept alive in the mind of the infant, then, Winnicott suggests, their loss may be experienced as traumatic, pushing relative independence further away. This suggests that just piling on more, punitive homework for a child who is not completing theirs may exacerbate rather than address the problem – only further investigation will enable one to know.

Finally, in the last stage of play, the child is able 'to allow and to enjoy an overlap in two play areas [...] Thus the way is paved for playing together in a relationship' (1971, p.64), that is, for communicating, learning and teaching. Winnicott spells out his conclusion as it relates to psychotherapeutic work, but we can translate this to teaching. The work, he says, needs to:

> ... afford opportunities for formless experience and for creative impulses, motor and sensory, which are the stuff of playing. And on the basis of playing is built the whole of man's experiential existence. No longer are we either introvert or extrovert. We experience life in the area of transitional phenomena, in the exciting interweave of subjectivity and objective observation; and in an area that is intermediate between inner reality of the individual and the shared reality of the world that is external to individuals.
>
> *(p.86)*

This idea of precariousness gives us an indication of why play can be so hard to find in classrooms. The precariousness suggested is not so much a brittle fragility (although it is also fragile) as a delicate balance, one too easily impinged upon, too easily disturbed by interruptions, by calls for attention, by insistences on compliance. A disturbed balance tips one back onto the self or out into the world. To what extent can classrooms tolerate teetering without rushing in to support or prop up students? What does propping up stop? And (oh dear) when is support necessary? How can we ever learn to recognise productive teetering?

Can we anticipate or tell the difference between help that is welcome and help that hinders?

The paradox, trust and creativity

There is, Winnicott insists, a paradox at the heart of transitional phenomena that relates to their status as created or found. This paradox is most often stated in relation to the mother, who must never ask her infant: *did you create that [transitional object], or did you find it*? so that, as he says 'an essential feature of transitional phenomena and objects is a quality in our attitude when we observe them' (1971, p.130). The challenge (*did you create that, or did you find it*?) would deny the place of transitional phenomena in the potential space *between* subjective experience and objective reality (perhaps it was both found *and* created). An either/or answer forces the restriction, through rationalisation, of a less bounded, unconscious thought or link. The very demand implies that 'it' has a singular status, that there is no ambivalence or multiplicity in 'its' nature or purposes or existence, that I can even know what 'that' or 'it' refers to (what is my comfort blanket to me?).

Rather than consider this paradoxical quality in relation to blankets and teddy bears, which might enable our preferred adult denials of the relevance of these ideas to life beyond childhood, it might be more useful to consider them in relation to what he says about originality and cultural life. Winnicott (1971) is clear that, 'in any cultural field it is not possible to be original except on the basis of tradition'. The interplay between 'originality and the acceptance of tradition as the basis for inventiveness' is, he says, 'an example of the interplay between separation and union' (p.134). So, what I create in my cultural life will emerge between aspects of things that have gone before (that already have an existence 'out there' and so are part of objective reality) and originality (subjective experience that can only be mine). Of course, what is new to me may not be new to you, and here is the paradox and point of danger, perhaps particularly for teachers. To challenge the originality of an idea felt to be new and that the student wishes to play with is to break faith with the paradox: it is to demand an answer to the unanswerable question 'Did you create that or find it lying about?' When a student 'discovers' something we already know, can we allow them the pleasure of their discovery? Or do we need to point out that this is nothing new? Do the world and the canon need to be given or can they be rediscovered, reinvented, recreated? Or can both happen? Let us explore this in relation to a moment in a maths lesson. Actually, this is a moment I have observed on several occasions in different primary school classrooms, usually with children aged between 8 and 10 years. I present it here in fictional form with the two sets of responses I have seen given sequentially; the most common first, the less common second. The classes and teachers are working through a subtraction problem together. The calculation under consideration is $183 - 28 = ?$ In the first version, the teacher takes the class through the steps of a traditional algorithm:

Ms Smith: 3 take-away 8. You can't do it so you borrow one from the eight. Now you have 13 take-away 8, which is 5. Now there are 7 left here so, 7 take-away two is 5. And the one is left ....

$$\begin{array}{r} 1\ {}^{7}\not{8}\,{}^{1}3 \\ -\quad 2\ 8 \\ \hline 1\ 5\ 5 \\ \hline \end{array}$$

The answer 155 has been distilled from the numbers somewhat magically. You will notice that there is little opportunity for a child to contribute here beyond answering some closed questions. They are being led through the steps of a 'dance', the brevity of recording provides few places to gain purchase. I have only rarely seen a child challenge the assertion that 3 − 8 has no solution although many, if not most, will know that it does. Typically, those I saw risk the challenge were ignored or, on one occasion, told 'we are not doing negative numbers today'.

In the second version, in Ms Jones' class however, that suggestion was taken up and used:

MS J: 3 − 8 is ...?
CH: −5
MS J: (*writes up*) −5. And 80 − 20 is ...?
CH: 60
MS J: (*writes up*) 60. And then 100 − zero is ...?
CH: 100
MS J: (*writes up so the board now shows*)

$$183 - 28 = -5 + 60 + 100 \qquad \textit{and} \qquad \begin{array}{r} 183 \\ \underline{-28} \\ -5 \\ 60 \\ 100 \end{array}$$

So what is the answer?
CH: 155

Now, we might want to criticise Ms Jones for leading the class down the primrose path, but she has used a child's original suggestion and has played with a response made. This was typical of this teacher's practice; she took ideas and ran with them; this idea is not a new one, but it is played with *as if* it is new (it is certainly new to this class). This meant, most importantly, that children in her class often risked voicing their original ideas. On another occasion, considering 327 − 84, she took a child's suggestion that the 2 and 8 be swapped over to get over any difficulty associated with trying to take a large number from a smaller one (so: 327 − 84 became 387 − 24) and with the class worked and discussed the differences in the calculations that ensued. In this way, she worked *with* the class on a common misconception. No child was left to make this mistake on their own; no one had to feel the shame of an individual error and the reason it is a mistake was shared and developed together. In the general to-and-fro that typified her teaching, Ms Jones did not dismiss the 'to'; she did not drop the ball. In this regard, the contrast between the two teachers' responses seems stark and brings us to the issue of trust. Can I risk making an idiot of myself here? Is a teacher who ignores difficulties trustworthy? Does Ms Smith, even though she was trying to make life 'easier' by avoiding the thought of difficulties, stop them occurring? Do children just given the steps of the dance always perform that dance correctly? There is plenty of evidence that they don't (see for example Plunket, 1979) and, of course, the children with Ms Smith have been denied an opportunity to explore, experience and play with other ways of approaching the problem. In fact, more worryingly, they are learning that mathematics is not a subject to be engaged with thoughtfully and creatively.

In everything that has been presented so far in this book, the issue of the reliability of the facilitating environment/(m)other has been stated and restated. Here it is stated again:

> Potential space happens only in relation to a feeling of confidence on the part of the baby, that is, confidence relating to the dependability of the mother-figure or environmental elements, confidence being the evidence of dependability that is becoming introjected.
>
> In order to study play and then the cultural life of the individual one must study the fate of the potential space between any one baby and the human (and therefore fallible) mother-figure who is essentially adaptive because of love.
>
> *(Winnicott, 1971, p.135)*

The teacher who repeatedly and reliably plays with ideas in different ways, who does not 'drop' the playful idea tossed out, who can judge when to provide new ideas and who reliably responds to requests for help earns her students' trust. This is a teacher that can safely and profitably be taken in (to one's mind) and internalised (introjected), adding her voice to other voices that can be called upon when alone to help one get over moments of uncertainty. Confidence and reliability enable trust to grow and stabilise. And the play that happens in the potential space can here also be thought of as thinking and, therefore, potentially also as learning.

If this mathematical example provides an illustration of trust developing, what happens when it is missing? How can we think about what might be happening in the first teacher's classroom? In order to think about teaching and learning, and the way in which an individual comes to approach learning, one must 'study the fate of the potential space between any one [student] and the human (and therefore fallible) [teacher] who, we have to hope, is essentially adaptive because of love' (Winnicott, 1971, p.135).

Trust found and lost

Winnicott repeatedly emphasises that trust develops in slow and secret ways but can be stolen in a flash. For the therapist, a moment of trust-testing typically centres on the giving (or not) of an interpretation, and a mistimed interpretation can, he suggests, set a client back years. We can infer that the mistimed interpretation of the analyst has its equivalent in the classroom; the mistimed comment or assessment, the judgement – probably generalised to a point of meaninglessness – that cannot be processed: you do not work hard enough, you are a level 3, this story is not what I asked for. The difficulty of a mistimed interpretation is that it is more about the needs of the analyst (or teacher) than the needs of the client (or student). The development of the individual depends upon their experiencing a continuity of existence, a going on being, and the mistimed comment impinges upon this.

To experience going on being, the baby (client, student – the one developing in this context) needs impingements to be kept at bay. An impingement, as discussed earlier, is anything that it is beyond (too much or too difficult for) the individual to accommodate in the moment it is experienced. So, an interpretation that demonstrates the cleverness of the analyst but that the client cannot accommodate/understand is an impingement, and it will disrupt the client's sense of going on being and hinder development. The mistimed interpretation calls the client out of their reverie, forcing their attention onto the unwelcome statement and its giver. An impingement 'steals' a piece of the self that had been put into the potential space for exploration.

> In the relaxation that belongs to trust and to acceptance of the professional reliability of the therapeutic setting (be it analytic, psychotherapeutic, social work, architectural, etc.), there is room for the idea of unrelated thought sequences which the analyst will do well to accept as such, not assuming the existence of a significant thread. … According to this theory, free association that reveals a coherent theme is already affected by anxiety, and the cohesion of ideas is a defence organisation. … The patient has been unable to rest because of a failure in the environmental provision, which undid the sense of trust. The therapist has, without knowing it, abandoned the professional role, and has done so by bending over backwards to be a clever analyst, and to see order in chaos.
>
> *(1971, pp.74–75)*

Similarly, a comment that demonstrates the cleverness of the teacher but that the student cannot accommodate or understand is an impingement and will disrupt their sense of going on being and hinder learning. A demand to follow a series of algorithmic steps ('you do it like this because this is how you do it') is an indication of a teacher's anxiety and so is an example of an impingement: It puts into the potential space more than the learner can take in; it is too much; it is beyond. Free association, listening to one's own subjective experiences and allowing them to brush alongside objective reality, watching objective reality as it is touched by dreams, playing with ideas, these are examples of creative living. In the classroom, the putting out of ideas – often in blurts – might be one way a student starts to play with and experience ideas creatively.

Creativity

For Winnicott, creativity is conceived very broadly; it is about 'a colouring of the whole attitude to external reality' (p.87). He laments a tendency, when talking about creativity, to limit the consideration to art, drama, dance, literature, music and so on; that is, creative activities with obvious outcomes. So, psychoanalysts (and we might add social scientists and educators), have a tendency to focus on 'some outstanding personality in the creative arts' and to apply a secondary analysis to their outputs. It is as if, he says, 'the creation stands between the observer and the artist's creativity' obscuring our view of the 'creative impulse' (p.93). And it is this impulse to creativity, the impulse to engage with transitional phenomena in a potential space – to allow subjective and objective reality to rub along – that is of interest to him, and to me. The following example is taken from field notes that record an observation in a Year 5 literacy lesson observed as part of the learner-identities project:

> They are going to be doing 'instructions'. The class teacher asks the class what instructions are and they make some suggestions which she writes up:
>
> - *It tells you what to do*
> - *Tells you how to make things*
> - *You follow them*
> - *You do things in a certain order*
>
> this is followed by [the teacher] saying "there is a literacy word for that – does anyone know what it is?" – after a few suggestions that are greeted with 'no' someone says 'chronological order' which is what she has been waiting for. She says this is signalled by words such as 'first, next, then'. She also says there is a special literacy word for words like these and H provides 'connectives' which she praises fulsomely.
>
> - *Directions*
> - *Like a recipe*
> - *Instructions you get in a game (the teacher writes up: rules)*
> - *Working in a hospital*
>
> This comment about the hospital is also valued highly. She explains that in hospital you might have drugs and procedures that you need to follow exactly or someone might get hurt. The next few suggestions continue this theme presumably in an attempt to win more, similar approval but, although the suggestions are accepted, they are not elaborated.
>
> - *When you cut someone's stomach and get something …*
> - *What to do in an emergency*
> - *Ransom instructions if someone has been kidnapped*
>
> The next suggestions become more playful – as in the ransom demand. However, elaborate ideas are not listened to. One boy starts to explain

> that if you were new on a building site and someone had explained how to build a house and then left you alone … this was cut off. I got the feeling he was working up to what would happen if instructions were not understood or forgotten but we'll never know. This feels like part of [the teacher] listening but only for the answers she wants and a select few being able/allowed to break through this selective deafness. She curtails the growing playfulness with her own example of instructions on an exam booklet. This ends the playfulness.
>
> *(Field notes)*

As the children start to free-associate to her theme of 'instructions', the teacher appears to become anxious and impatient. She insists on sticking to her own 'coherent theme', the pre-determined 'significant thread' that is the lesson's objective. The children are unable to relax into the game 'because of a failure in the environmental provision' that has undone 'the sense of trust' that some of them began to display through their playfulness. She has insisted on spinning her own order from the apparent (feared?) chaos of 30 ten-year-old minds. In her panic about failing to meet the objective of the lesson and the accountability regimes in place within and beyond the school, the teacher calls the children away from play and creativity and towards compliance.

Premature failure of environmental reliability

'The potential space between baby and mother, between child and family, between individual and society or world, depends on experience which leads to trust' (Winnicott, 1971, p.139). While timely failure, as part of the (m)other's adaptation to the infant, is part of healthy development enabling the discovery of both me and not-me, untimely failure is altogether more problematic. Such untimely failure might relate to the absence of anyone, or a lack of other objects within the potential space: a child tries to enter the space and finds a desert, either because they bring nothing themselves or because there is no one to think about and place suitable objects there to be found. Or, it might relate to a filling of the potential space with other people's ideas, perhaps premature interpretations from an anxious psychoanalyst or demands for compliance to other ideas from a teacher (for example, ideas about what 'instructions' might be). There is a danger that such material, pressed in from outside, might be experienced as persecutory, leaving the client/child/student with no way to repudiate it. As an interruption to going-on-being that cannot be refused, an impingement cannot be processed at all. It sits like an undigested lump in the stomach causing discomfort and drawing painful attention to itself. In this unprocessed state, the impinging material cannot be introjected (accepted as part of 'me') or repudiated (designated as 'not me'): It cannot be thought about, used or learned from. We can see this in the silence of the children in the first maths example or in the comment from the researcher towards the end of the field notes on the literacy lesson that 'the next few suggestions continue this theme presumably in an attempt to win more, similar, approval'. The persecuted response might be thought of as: How can I reject or ignore your suggestions/creative outputs since, in having had them foisted upon me, I have lost access to my own sense of self and my subjective responses? What contribution can I possibly make now that you have reduced 'instructions' to what we get on an examination booklet?

If transitional phenomena exist in a potential space between subjective experience and external reality, then we might imagine that there are two ways one could defend against the risk of play, of separation, of experiencing life: unable to stay in a space of play and creativity, one might either flee inwards or outwards.

Introversion

We call a turning in introversion. Introversion signals a return to subjective experience. However, subjective experiencing that has no connection to the outside world, that admits only itself as a point of reference is, for Winnicott, a cul-de-sac experience, and it enables little more than the gratification of instincts:

> instinctual gratifications [...] become *seductions* unless based in a well-established capacity in the individual person for total experience, and for experience in the area of transitional phenomena. It is the self that must precede the self's use of instinct; the rider must ride the horse, not be run away with.
>
> *(1971, p.133)*

The implication here is that instinctual gratification (subjective living), which cuts us off from the outside, can become a seduction allowing us the considerable (illusory though temporary) comfort of behaving *as if* we were independent, omnipotent, omniscient. Unless we are able to modulate our moves to and from subjective living – towards and away from being merged with some real or imagined other – then this state of being keeps us in a dream-world of unreal fantasies, cut off from any possibility of reality-testing in the world. Instinctual gratification, an exclusive valuing of the internal voice, enables us to deny our relatedness, it allows us to dismiss any experience that does not fit with ours as irrelevant without troubling to think about how it might connect with us, or we with it.

Implacable insistence on personal voice can be a difficulty of teaching young people (of whatever age) who demand that everything have personal value to them (see also Gilligan, 1982; Benjamin, 1998). Our attempts to answer this subjective demand help neither our teaching nor their learning. The answer to the question 'Why do I have to learn Pythagoras' theorem?' lies not in collusion ('Don't worry, we can ignore that bit of the curriculum'), nor in appeals to some imagined future (exam success, jobs), but rather in mathematics. Since no teacher can know the subjective reality of the complaining student (and, indeed nor can the complaining student), an appeal from that place is unanswerable, the only possible response is either no response or a call to the reality of the topic.

Allowing students to stay with their subjective responses at the point at which these are being used as a defence against the pain of change and of learning strengthens the seductive allure of a self cut off from contacts with the world outside the self. Life that becomes only about narcissistic desires is an isolated and lonely place: Denying connectedness and ultimate vulnerability leaves no space for the other. So, appealing to mathematics, we study Pythagoras because it is interesting. Does the rule only work for right-angled triangles? What happens if that angle becomes greater or less than 90°? Come into an area of play that has triangles in it, and we can imagine other triangles while we are here. Perhaps there are some triangles that even the least mathematical 14-year-old can enjoy!

Contact with the world teaches us that we are not independent, omnipotent or omniscient, but this is only true if we can tolerate the challenging experiences and learn the lessons. Transitional phenomena and objects (cultural experiences) could enable us to experience the lessons and therefore learn from them, so a turn in (or indeed out) that becomes stuck precludes this possibility. An overvaluation of the internal response/denial of other realities can become pathological; such an eventuality is discussed in Chapter 8. While withdrawal or the dissociation of introversion is one form of defence, the other involves fleeing in the opposite direction.

Extroversion

If turning in and denying the value of the world is one defence against a failure of the facilitating environment to allow for transitional phenomena, turning out to the world and severing contact with subjective experience is another. A turn to the demands of the outside is a move to compliance, and the compliant self is the subject of Chapters 6 and 7: the development of, and over-reliance on, a False Self Structure. This is perhaps a more common defence than the shut-down withdrawal of introversion and indeed, is a defence institutions appear to encourage.

Pedagogy and potential space

The places in which we play and our cultural experiences are part of who we are; we are formed from our experiences in the world and our responses to the world as it touches us. What more compelling underlining of the importance of education can there be? School has the potential to be a place where this rubbing along can be challenged, be experienced as safe, explored and learned from. Not that it is the only place where this will happen, but it happens with our peers in ways that are not possible in family units. And not that we can take for granted what will be learned or experienced in school, learning objectives are tidy statements of someone's conscious intentions – actual learning is far less predictable or certain! While schools necessarily plan for learning, assessment does not guarantee it.

This talk of cultural elements and experiences does not necessarily mean trips to art galleries or the opera! For Winnicott, and so for me in the context of this book, cultural experiences and elements imply *everything* that has been (or is being) generated by people in the world: ideas, artefacts, others' lives, architecture, stories, wars – everything that has taken place between, and emerged out of, objective realties and subjective responses to these, subjective experiences expressed into the objective world.

To return to the recast quotation near the beginning of this chapter:

> Pedagogy [or perhaps learning] takes place in the overlap of two areas of playing, that of the student/learner and that of the teacher. Pedagogy has to do with two people playing together. The corollary of this is that where playing is not possible then the work done by the teacher is directed towards bringing the student from a state of not being able to play [think, investigate, explore] into a state of being able to play.
>
> *(adapted from Winnicott, 1971, p.37)*

Play for Winnicott is not a wild or formless event; it is intensely serious, and it requires a facilitating environment and a good enough (m)other to develop. We can think of adult dismissals of play as childish and to be kept separate from the 'serious' business of 'work' as a defensive move. There are many things that a denial of the importance of play – and a concomitant idealisation of 'work' – might defend against: the difficulty of having to take responsibility, the pain and vulnerability of growing up, the fragility of knowledge, the uncertainty of learning amongst others, the danger of new thoughts (see also Bibby, 2011).

Play is a mode of communication, something that takes place between the wild formlessness of my subjective experiences and the reality of the world beyond me. My suggestion is that those who are learning – are developing within a new (for them) context – will need feeding, and the adults in that context (those with greater experience, more familiarity) have a responsibility to nurture those coming along behind. Winnicott warns us here about the difficulties of play:

> The baby's confidence in the mother's reliability, and therefore in that of other people and things, makes possible a separating-out of the not-me from the me. … There is in many a failure in confidence which cramps the person's play capacity because of the limitations of the potential space; likewise there is for many a poverty of play and cultural life because, although the person had a place for erudition, there was a relative failure on the part of those who constitute the child's world of persons to introduce cultural elements at the appropriate phases of the person's personality development.
>
> *(1971, p.147)*

Limitations of the potential space may come from introversion or extroversion; they may also come from a failure of others to feed into the process, to take care of their end of the communication. A common concern about children's play in schooling contexts is the place of the adult and of adult intervention in that play.

Children's play is seen by some as sacrosanct (Rogers, 2011), but this is the other side of the idealisation of work: an idealisation of play that denies its broader meanings. Certainly play that is exciting and an escape is also important, as is play that enables peers to develop, explore, cement and abandon friendships, but there is more. The broader notion of play that Winnicott proposes might usefully be used to reconsider pedagogy as a relational endeavour. Thinking again about the example from the maths lesson above: Do we have to wait for children to 'discover' or 'rediscover' everything? Or, to put it another way, is all teaching an impingement? The reverse concern is also expressed, though less directly, in relation to the learning of older children and adults: Do they even need to play at all? Surely they can learn from being told and just 'get on with it'. We behave *as if* this were true when we lecture students without giving them (and structuring) space to discuss amongst themselves. Winnicott's ideas, and this chapter, suggest the vital role of the (m)other in play and in cultural life, in the to-and-fro of experience. While for more experienced players, the (m)other might have been internalised, the implication of these ideas is that the newer and therefore less familiar the context or ideas, the more necessary a concrete (m)other is likely to be. Development, playing and creativity have to be found and re-found repeatedly. As with the infant, the pace of disillusionment (or weaning) needs to proceed at a rate the developing individual can tolerate; judging this rate is what sensitive teaching is about; it requires active not doing (being) as well as doing.

There still has to be teaching. Development requires feeding: The good enough (m)other does not allow her baby to starve; ideas must be offered (placed into the potential space) for experiencing, for 'consumption' and digestion. The possibility of repudiation or rejection must be kept alive. Communication that is valued has a two-way quality; if play is a communication, it cannot be about not engaging. Children who are playing still need to be engaged with even if only (or perhaps especially) through a look that says 'I am still here; I can see you playing, and I am here if you need me'. Once play and creativity are operating there is a need: 'for those who have care of children of all ages to be ready to put each child in touch with appropriate elements of the cultural heritage, according to the individual child's capacity and emotional age and developmental phase' (p.148). The difficult question is what to say or do, and when?

> Summation or reverberation depends on there being a certain quantity of reflecting back to the individual on the part of the trusted therapist (or friend) who has taken the (indirect) communication. In these highly specialised conditions the individual can come together and exist as a unit, not as a defence against anxiety but as an expression of I AM, I am alive, I am myself. From this position, everything is creative.
>
> *(pp.75–76)*

The chapters in Part II consider what might happen when this fails to occur.

References

Benjamin, J. 1998. *Shadow of the other: intersubjectivity and gender in psychoanalysis.* New York and London: Routledge.

Benjamin, J. 2004. Beyond doer and done-to: an intersubjective view of thirdness. *Psychoanalytic Quarterly*, 73, 5–46.

Bibby, T. 2011. *Education – an 'impossible profession'? Psychoanalytic explorations of learning and classrooms.* London: Routledge.

Gilligan, C. 1982. *In a different voice: psychological theory and women's development* (1993 edition). Cambridge, MA and London: Harvard University Press.

Plunkett, S. 1979. Decomposition and all that rot. *Mathematics in School*, 8(3), 2–5.

Rogers, S. 2011. *Rethinking play and pedagogy in early choldhood education: concepts, contexts and cultures.* London: Routledge.

Winnicott, D.W. 1971. *Playing and reality* (2008, Routledge Classics edition). London: Tavistock Publications.

PART II

Things that go wrong

Chapters 6–8 pick up on the difficulties that have been hinted at in the chapters of Part I. What happens when an environment cannot be trusted? When a relationship is experienced as unreliable? When communication is felt to be persecutory? Ideas introduced in Part I are expanded upon here.

6

THE ROOTS OF COMPLIANCE AND NON-COMPLIANCE

True and False Self Structures revisited

I have something of an aversion to the terms True and False Self Structures. One difficulty inheres in the language and the split it generates; it would be very easy to fall into a simple dichotomy and to equate 'true' with 'good' or perhaps 'authentic' and, by implication, 'false' with 'bad', 'fraudulent' or 'lying'. I constantly need to remind myself that an idealisation of the 'True' self structure – like all idealisations – would be a defence against having to think, against the necessity of engaging with complexity that creates uncertainty. In fact, as suggested earlier, the idea of True and False Selves is not so as simple as this, not least because these are not unitary states. For Winnicott, in a condition of health, I will have both True and False Selves operating: there is no dichotomy, no either/or, but rather degrees and extents. The two ideas are not opposites or 'ends of a spectrum'; they are related but need thinking about differently.

For Winnicott, central to an understanding of health is a capacity to live between our internal realities and life 'out there'. This intermediate area is a place of thoughtful experiencing and playful creativity 'between the dream and the reality' he called 'the cultural life' (1960, p.87). Culture is a made expression of the internal world and its experience of life and reality. He called this 'creative apperception' – the mind's awareness of its own life, a reflexive urge. Here, Winnicott is not only thinking of what we tend to refer to as 'culture' writ large but also to more generally communicative endeavours that try to share the lived experience of the transitional space, the space of experience between internal and external worlds whether through written or spoken language, gesture, play or any of the 'bigger' arts. Culture, the lived and expressed experience of life, is what we are immersed in, if we can only focus on it.

> It is creative apperception more than anything else that makes the individual feel that life is worth living. Contrasted with this is a relationship

> to external reality which is one of compliance, the world and its details being recognized but only as something to be fitted in with or demanding adaptation. Compliance carries with it a sense of futility for the individual and is associated with the idea that nothing matters and that life is not worth living. … they [live] uncreatively, as if caught up in the creativity of someone else, or of a machine.
>
> *(1960, p.87)*

This chapter sets the stage for a more detailed exploration of compliance, for Winnicott the antithesis of creative living, and non-compliance. In it we move beyond the work explored in the first section of the book and the positive picture of what we might hope life to be like; the conditions and maximal outcomes of a 'good enough' facilitating environment, of a responsive enough (m)other, that would enable the developing individual to come into a sense of themselves as coherent and loveable. To recap: a reliable environment enables trust to develop; in this way the risks that enable learning and development to take place can be chanced, but what if the environment is not experienced as reliable? Two-way communication enables self and (m)other to learn about themselves and each other in mutual relationships, but what if the relationships turn out not to be mutual but rather one-sided? A sense of movement between my inner world (my psychic reality, my affective responses to the world) and the world beyond me enables me to live creatively through my experiences, but what if the demands from outside are so insistent that I can no longer pay attention to my own responses? In discussing these issues, I set the stage for Chapters 7 and 8, which turn to the difficulties that inevitably arise during these processes. I say inevitably because, even at its best – or perhaps especially at its best – 'good enough' mothering will fail an infant; it is through managed and manageable failures of adaptation that the outside world is found. Like all failures (and successes) we are talking here of degrees: the warmth of sunshine on my face is a pleasure but a fire pressed onto my face will damage, perhaps even kill, me.

Earlier descriptions of a good enough facilitating environment have inevitably touched on the question of failure and so Winnicott's proposal of True and False Self Structures needs again to be addressed including the idea that a False Self Structure, characterised by compliance, is a defence against annihilation. This chapter looks at these ideas in more detail and begins to consider the implications of such a position for schools and classrooms at all levels. The suggestion will be made that, while educational institutions expend a great deal of energy on non-compliance, they play with compliance (students' False Self Structures) and that this might be a game that should be played with great (much greater) care.

True Self Structure: an internal voice

Winnicott had relatively little to say about the True Self, suggesting that really it was only useful as an idea as far as it enabled thinking about the False Self. He said:

> There is but little point in formulating a True Self idea except for the purpose of trying to understand the False Self, because it does no more than collect together the details of the experience of aliveness.
>
> *(1960, p.148)*

So, the True Self is not a readily accessible idea: It is a collection of experiences of aliveness, a place of affect, and so is central to our dreaming – our imagination and our capacity to think creatively – and as such it shapes and colours our subsequent experiences. As Adam Phillips (2007) puts it, the difficulty of trying to define or encapsulate the idea of a True Self is that it 'covers what is distinctive and original about each person. It is simply a category for the idiosyncratic' (p.135). But, to complicate the picture, and as discussed in previous chapters, while 'only the true self can feel real, ... the true self must never be affected by external reality, it must never comply' (Winnicott, 1960, p.133). In Winnicott's world, for the true self (inner reality) to be affected by external reality, the psychical 'membrane' that keeps the inner and outer worlds separate would need to rip or collapse, a traumatic and catastrophic event that would signal the annihilation of the true self/personal life and a serious loss of health. Phillips goes on to summarise what can be culled from across Winnicott's writing: the True Self can be characterised, he says, in the following ways:

1. At first it is 'the theoretical position from which comes the spontaneous gesture and the personal idea. The spontaneous gesture is the True Self in action.'
2. The True Self is the source of what is authentic in a person. 'Only the True Self can be creative', Winnicott insists, 'and only the True Self can feel real.'
3. The True Self is bound up with bodily aliveness. It is 'little more than the summation of sensory-motor aliveness'. In fact it 'comes from the aliveness of the body-tissues and the working of body-functions, including the heart's action and breathing'.
4. As it is what is original about a person that derives from 'inherited potential', it is 'at the beginning, essentially not reactive to external stimuli, but primary'.
5. The True Self is the body as creative (2007, p.135).

This True Self then is perhaps similar to the unconscious of other psychoanalytic theories, although Winnicott never explicitly made that link. His desire to respond to and write about his own ideas in his own way, rather than trying to stitch his ideas into the canon, means it is difficult to know the extent to which these two ideas are the same or different. But there is enough of the unconscious here to assume at least some overlap – the True Self has something to do with an individual's inner reality, which will be more or less unavailable for direct knowing. It is the self of playful thinking and dreaming. The creativity of the True Self fuels our dreams, the ability to free-associate, to have ideas, to make plans, to formulate new questions.

The True Self for Winnicott is strengthened by every period of development and every impingement it survives. He wrote:

> Every new period of living in which the True Self has not been seriously interrupted results in a strengthening of the sense of being real, and with this goes a growing capacity on the part of the infant to tolerate two sets of phenomena: These are:
>
> 1. Breaks in continuity of True Self living;
> 2. Reactive or False Self experiences, related to the environment on a basis of compliance.
>
> *(1960, p.149)*

One example of this second phenomenon, he suggests, is an infant taught to say 'ta' when handed something. In this case they are being taught 'to acknowledge the existence of an environment that is becoming intellectually accepted. Gratitude may or may not follow' (p.149). This is perhaps also like the child made to say 'sorry' for the infraction of some rule – a compliant response is made; I apologise because refusing to do so is too difficult (incurs too great a personal cost). In effect, the child is taught the value of an expedient lie to ease social living. Remorse may or may not follow.

This quality of enabling resilience to be built would seem important. As we move through life, escalating impingements inevitably become part of living as we are increasingly called upon to attend to matters beyond our immediate needs and desires: socially, academically, economically, we must work to live. So, managing to continue through life without completely collapsing into compliance, or accepting some need for compliant behaviour without losing access to what *we* think, is an important capacity. If an educational aim is to develop adults able to engage critically in our democratic social structures and institutions, then the ability to think through our responses to social difficulties in those institutions and in the world is important – and, conversely, unthinking compliance (following the herd) can become deeply problematic. Concern about compliance takes us to the False Self Structure.

False Self Structure

In a description of False Self organisations, Winnicott sets out different functions and levels of intensity that can pertain (1960, pp.142–43). At its least intense, 'in health', he sees the False Self Structure as a necessary defence put in place to protect the True Self from intrusion. It is, he says, 'represented by the whole organisation of the polite and mannered social attitude, not "wearing the heart on the sleeve", as might be said'. Of course, anyone trying to live entirely through the True Self would be cut off from contact with external reality, a state that might be thought of as psychotic, a state of mental ill health. Thinking back to the definitions of experience in previous chapters, this would mean an exclusive focus inwards, no 'to-and-fro', not life in the space between inner and outer, no creative living. This 'healthy' use of the False Self as a defence that guards against the exposure of the True Self and helps to maintain the necessary separation between the inner and outer, between me and not-me, is unconscious – it is not something we can control. At this level, the False Self protects the gains made from all those very early processes of self-knowledge and separation. It protects the gains won from the first big risks: the giving up of primary omnipotence to separate self from other.

This minimally defending False Self is built in part on early identifications: a desire to 'be like' other people and so to fit in with our early social spheres. As hugely dependent individuals – as children, and again later in life in different ways – we survive (literally and metaphorically) at the whim of others; keeping them sweet is an important survival strategy! So, as well as defending the True Self, the False Self can also be active in searching for the conditions that will enable the True Self to live and find expression in the real world. Still operating in the realms of 'health' the False Self knows itself and learns to read its surroundings. Where there is 'two-way' communication, it can negotiate a place for the True Self to communicate while still helping to maintain a level of secrecy and privacy. For Winnicott, in health, the False Self neither entirely hides nor over-exposes the True Self; it mediates without overwhelming.

However, if the environment is experienced as consistently dangerous, if over time there has apparently been no way to negotiate a safe theatre for the True Self then, Winnicott suggests, the False Self can entirely take over; it can 'set up as real' such that others mistake this False Self as the real person while the True Self becomes entirely hidden. This extreme level of compliance to the world outside is highly problematic.

The emergence of an overwhelming False Self corresponds to a complete or catastrophic failure of the facilitating environment. But, as we are reminded every time we consider the 'good enough' (m)other, some failure is a necessary and inevitable feature of any environment; it is the appropriate level of challenge that leads to learning. The important thing is whether or not the failures come in a way and at a time that can be tolerated and managed without risking a sense of (or causing) annihilation. Annihilation here refers to the exposure, destruction or exploitation of the true self, a stopping or failure of the ability to 'go on being'. We can make sense of this if we think back to the example in Chapter 4 of the young girl using a stolen school book to secretly collect quotations and excerpts from novels that expressed things she felt to be true and moving. Her discovery that her mother had found and read the contents of the book was experienced as catastrophic. Her mother had looked into a private, hidden place of personal exploration, had looked into her soul. If such an exposure of the True Self would be so catastrophic, then setting up a guard to protect it would be equally important; this is part of the role of a False Self Structure.

Adam Phillips identifies three functions of the False Self:

1. It attends, within severe limitations, to the mother
2. It hides and protects the True Self by complying with environmental demands; and
3. It is also a 'caretaker', like a nurse looking after a child, taking over the caring function of the environment that has failed. It is a primitive form of self-sufficiency in the absence of nurture.

(2007, pp.133–34)

That is to say, when the child is unable to find himself in his mother's face – when she is unresponsive, distracted or absent – he is forced to forgo his own feelings and has instead to take on his mother's: 'This perception that pre-empts apperception is an early form of compliance; unable to get the mirror to notice and approve, the child is compelled to see only what the mother feels' (Phillips, 2007, p.130). In a small way (at stage 1, above) there is self-preservation here. Learning not to anger or over-tax the person one is dependent on, and learning to pick one's moment, is a key social survival strategy. This is true in the classroom or workplace as much as it is in the nursery. Asking for help, a favour or a pay rise is more likely to result in a favourable response if you can time the request right. At a more perilous level (2 and 3 above), we might imagine a child who has been asked to 'write an exciting story' and spends the lesson constructing a complex tale of peril and rescue set in a mystical landscape described in great detail. Delighted with his story, he takes it to his teacher who, rather than focussing on the content of the narrative (the 'exciting story'), instead corrects the spelling and punctuation. The child does not see his own excitement and satisfaction mirrored in the teacher's face, and her words convey not praise for a task well done, a brief fulfilled, but petty criticisms about spelling and punctuation perhaps with warnings that, if he produces such a story in the upcoming tests, he will not get the grade he might otherwise have been capable of. What should such a child trust: the initial request for an exciting story, or the subsequent demand for an accurately written story? The teacher expresses her disappointment and her feeling that he has let her – and himself – down. This turning out to take care of the 'environment' because the environment is not taking care of him requires him to comply with demands 'out there' so he can be seen – at the very least – as a 'good boy' who is then worthy of love and attention. In this way, the infant and the learner begin to take care of themselves by managing the environment for themselves.

Reading Winnicott, one gets a sense that the True and False Selves are multi-dimensional: there are degrees of False Self *and* degrees of split or separation between the True and False Selves, all of which will affect the ways in which any one individual responds to their own desires as well as to demands from the outside. At its most extreme, when trust in the environment (mother, teacher, school) has been entirely lost, a False Self can come to dominate the whole of the way an individual relates to the world. And, Winnicott suggests, where this individual is intellectually able, the intellect may become entirely split off from knowing about the individual's personal life. In such persons, while social and academic success may be evident to onlookers, for the individual concerned with a feeling of emptiness, of not belonging, of futility, it may come to dominate their sense of self. Completing tasks for someone else's satisfaction is rarely personally satisfying; and indeed, what might be personally satisfying can be lost entirely. When I think of this, I am reminded of the reaction of some people to academic success: pleasure tempered by surprise. I have been told by students on programmes from Undergraduate to Doctoral levels, on successful completion of their degrees, of a feeling that might be expressed as 'I feel as if I have been let into the wrong playground and I am going to be found out and told off!' They have surprised themselves as some forgotten quality of the self has erupted into the outside world. They have become so used to focussing on the demands of the university and the task, on the deadlines and assessment criteria, that when they succeed and are praised they are surprised.

Among the plethora of books aimed at helping people prepare for or adjust to retirement *It's never too late to begin again* (Cameron, 2016) was written in response to new retirees attending creative writing classes who struggled to connect to their creativity beyond a desire to rediscover it. The book structures activities to help people remember their old interests and desires, affects that may have been drowned out by the noise and hectic activity of life and living. After years of attending to the demands of their careers and families and suddenly with time to fill, many can struggle to reconnect to that inner voice – to their True Self Structures – and to begin to play and live creatively again. Compliance has (hopefully only temporarily) deafened them.

Split off intellect: performing the good student

This leaves us with the idea of an extreme separation between the True and False Selves to consider: the idea of a split-off intellect. Given education's valorisation of intellect, this high degree of False Self Structure can come to be misrecognised and celebrated. We might want to question whether this is really such a good thing.

> ... where there is a high degree of split between the True Self and the False Self which hides the True Self, there is found a poor capacity for using symbols, and a poverty of cultural living. Instead of cultural pursuits one observes in such persons extreme restlessness, an inability to concentrate, and a need to collect impingements from external reality so that the living-time of the individual can be filled by reactions to these impingements.
>
> *(Winnicott, 1960, p.150)*

Winnicott describes the beginning of this state of affairs by considering the 'bright' infant and her mother colluding together in the management of the baby's needs. So, he suggests, an alert child can come to recognise 'from noises off' that a feed is being prepared and so learn not to cry – that is, not to pay attention to her own hunger – and instead, to focus out at what can be anticipated. This use of the intellect to manage internal life through a turning out to the world is an early act of compliance and instantiates a beginning of loss of contact with internal reality. Faced with an intelligent baby able to not scream with hunger, it would be an unusual mother who did not collude with this!

The resulting 'poor capacity for using symbols' suggests difficulty drawing on the potentially rich meanings of words and phrases, limiting the speaker to a literal life and the very concrete meanings of words, phrases and interactions. Under these circumstances, everything becomes 'real' and concrete, the metaphorical, the poetic, the associative are unreadable – no play is possible. The issue of the failure of symbolic thinking, of the concrete and literal use of language, will be explored in more detail in Chapter 9.

An inability to concentrate and the restless filling of life with impingements suggests an extreme outwards focus and an associated inability (or perhaps more accurately, refusal) to take the rest associated with a movement inwards, with relaxation and reflection. Such an inability may stem from fear: perhaps when I turn inwards I will find I have no response, perhaps I am empty, a hollowed-out shell? The anxious seeking for 'what the teacher means' to the extent that this prevents thinking or seeking one's own responses to a task is familiar, not least from observations in some classrooms. Classrooms are places that can satisfy a need (for teachers and students alike) to have stuff to do all the time to distract self from (lack of) self. The example that follows, taken from a year 5 literacy lesson, charts a moment when, for one boy, the opportunity to attend to his own, second language learner interests, was overwhelmed by the need to pay attention to his teacher's needs as the environment failed him. It is a moment of learning compliance. As the researcher, I was sitting with and supporting Shanhrul, as the teaching assistant had had to leave the room:

> A copy of the story is given out, and they are to use coloured pencils and a key to highlight good examples of vocabulary (red), punctuation (yellow) and so on. After 10 minutes of this, they go back to the white board and look for more examples. [The teacher] then goes through and asks for examples of [each element]. Children make suggestions, which are generally accepted. Interestingly 'crypt' is suggested as a good word, but she disallows it as it is 'just the place'. I get the feeling that often the 'interesting word' is 'a word I don't know' – Shanhrul frequently asks what words mean.
>
> After a while during this activity, Shanhrul stopped asking me what words meant and started to focus on whether they were 'interesting'. He was looking at the 'target record' sheet in the front of his book, this listed 'Level 4 connectives – *although, besides, even though, before*' and he was searching for these in the text. They weren't there. This caused him some confusion. I explain that these are just examples and that what is important

> is that the words are interesting. I suspect this demand from the teacher is what prompted the change in what he was looking for.
>
> Shanhrul also started to ask if particular words were connectives. He often asks about words that are unfamiliar and near the centre of a sentence. I realise that I don't really understand this 'connective' thing; it seems to me that punctuation can connect clauses without some special word but perhaps I am missing the point? It makes me wonder to what extent Shanhrul is (as they used to say) 'barking at text'? He is clearly very good at assimilating rules and following them, but I do sometimes wonder what sense he is making of them – especially in Literacy.
>
> *(Field notes)*

In this moment, and elsewhere in the 18 months of the project, Shanhrul, who had come to the school the year before (aged 8–9 years) from Bangladesh and with very little schooling or English, stopped attending to his own interests and felt needs and focussed instead on what the teacher wanted. In literacy lessons and throughout the curriculum he moved from a playful interest in words to a mechanical adherence to the task. We can almost visualise the growth of a false sense as it reacts to the playful qualities of his curiosity being at best ignored and occasionally rebuked. The teacher's demand for 'interesting words' assumes a shared aesthetic; like requests for suggestions of a good read, contributions can be wide of one's personal mark. Reflecting on Shanhrul's experience of lessons and demands like those that characterised this lesson I wonder how he was supposed to judge whether or not words were 'interesting' – such judgements come with experience and rely on understanding of the word itself – what it signifies and its context. How is any 10-year-old, indeed how is any *any*-year-old, to develop such an understanding except through attention to the way their own tastes are received in a world that is beyond their control? And what does it mean for a teacher to curtail such access? The next chapters pick up and pursue these questions further. Chapter 7 particularly provides a more detailed exploration of compliance while Chapter 8 attends to refusals of compliance – an insistence on the voice of the True Self and the difficulties such behaviour visits on education.

References

Cameron, J. 2016. *Its never too late to begin again: discovering creativity and meaning at mid-life and beyond*. New York: TarcherPedigree, Penguin Random House.

Phillips, A. 2007. *Winnicott*. London: Penguin.

Winnicott, D.W. 1960. Ego distortion in terms of True and False Self. In *The maturational processes and the facilitating environment: studies in the theory of emotional development*, edited by D.W. Winnicott (1965, 2007 edition, pp.140–152). London: Karnac.

7

ALL THE GOOD GIRLS AND BOYS

Compliance and its vicissitudes

> The child's freedom, the child's self-fashioning project, depends upon her being able to treat orders and instructions as though they were hints and suggestions; as open invitations rather than prescriptions. Rules are not merely abided by, they are also sounded out; they require that unfounded competence called guesswork.
>
> —*(Phillips, 2007, p.90)*

Adam Phillips is pointing to the importance of space and room to move, to a certain latitude in responding to the world, which is central to our becomings. It is important to be able to say no, to refuse, to repudiate. If compliance is the False Self's way of fitting in, then the nature of what it is trying to fit in with becomes hugely important. Interestingly, this suggestion shifts responsibility for 'behaviour' away from the individual and implicates the environment. For Winnicott, if the environment that needs to be fitted in with is relatively benign – if it recognises the person trying to fit in, if it is trustworthy, if it is caring and makes sufficient adaptations so that the fitting in needed is not too much or too difficult – then the False Self remains proportionate and the True Self can still be attended to. However, if the environment is experienced as harsh or hostile – as judgemental, uncaring, inattentive or over-attentive – then the False Self will strengthen and tense, becoming more rigid, increasingly hiding the True Self and perhaps even taking over entirely. So, while extremes of compliance may become problematic, there are also levels that are necessary: as Winnicott reminds us, we need to learn to say 'ta' (at least occasionally) in order to fit in. It is a matter of working to develop (relatively) sure-footed balance.

Before thinking about the difficulties that can come to be associated with compliance, however, it is worth spending some time thinking about compliance for social acceptance – which, of course, may still be problematic! Some of the earliest forms of compliance are perhaps unsurprisingly the most hidden, the most apparently 'natural'; they are part of the veneer that is layered over our infantile omnipotences and the rawness of our immediate affects. The two that particularly interest me because of their implications for education are compliance to what counts as 'good knowledge', that is, compliance to demands that we curb our curiosities; and compliance to time and to the control of appetite. These two compliances are enmeshed and not entirely separable; I do so here only to enable discussion.

Curiosity

Lest we forget, it was curiosity that killed the cat! This admonition suggests that there is something dangerous about curiosity although where the danger lies is less clear: Is it in the answer we may receive? Is it in the demand, desire or expectation of an answer, or is it in the question itself and the audacity of the ask?

Listening to scientists or artists who have made it to the top of their professions we can be struck by the extent of their curiosities and perhaps particularly the degree to which these curiosities were given permission – encouraged even – by parents or teachers. Dave Goulson, the professor of biological sciences who first alerted the UK government to the effects of a class of pesticides on bees and the potential for ecological catastrophe that their falling numbers might herald, was interviewed on BBC Radio 4's *Life Scientific* (12 November 2014). In a brief introduction, he described his childhood; he was clearly a child with a burning curiosity about the world, and he was allowed to pursue his own questions in his own way. He went from collecting and nurturing live animals (at the age of 4 it was caterpillars and worms) to keeping a range of pets including snakes; from picking up and dissecting dead animals and road-kill to learn 'what was inside' to (not very successful) self-taught taxidermy. Through all of this, he had no particular memory of any parental interference apart from his stinkier projects being banished to the garage. Similarly, on both *The Life Scientific* (BBC Radio 4, 22 November 2016) and *Desert Island Discs* (BBC Radio 4, 23 July 2000), the Nobel Prize-winning mathematician Roger Penrose has talked about how, at school, a teacher recognised that his slow rate of work in mathematics was not a sign of any lack of ability, but was rather due to his personal need to find answers from first principles. As a consequence, he was given as much time as he needed to take tests at junior school (aged ≤ 11) and is frank in saying that, if that had not happened, he would probably have given up. These two happy examples, which we hear about because of what these individuals went on to achieve, raise new questions about curiosity, not least about what happens to it in the rest of us?

How then should we think about what we might mean by 'curiosity'? Crucially, the young searchings of the scientist and the mathematician above were not identical, yet both were passionately curious. So where does curiosity come from, what does it represent, how does it shift its focus and what does it mean to encourage this quality?

Within psychoanalysis, the question of curiosity is linked to infantile sexuality (Freud, 1905). This is a phrase that troubles some people – infants, they might claim, are asexual or perhaps pre-sexual. But this is an unhelpful transposition of the meaning of adult sexuality – with its focus on genitals – onto children and infants. Infantile sexuality refers to a desire to understand and find pleasure (in their own terms) in the body and its sensations. The oral, anal and genital pleasures associated with taking things in through the mouth by sucking, biting, chewing; with emptying their bladder and bowels and finally with their genitals.

The theoretical journey of infantile sexuality from Freud and through Klein has been explored by, among others, Deborah Britzman (2003, 2006). The trace of love and curiosity through the infant's – through our – learning and our lives is multi-faceted. Britzman (2006, p.166) spells out three of the complexities implicated in making sense of infantile sexuality. First of all, 'it begins with views that love is not the absence of aggression', that is, a recognition that the absence or opposite of love is not hate, but rather a lack, perhaps indifference. Hate is far from indifferent, it is passionate, and it needs love to be mobilised. Secondly, she points out 'that our parental love and our love for our parents involves sexual feelings'. This suggestion, that parental feelings include sexual feelings, can be lost if we maintain a singularly adult focus on children's experiences (a reference to the Oedipus Complex). Finally, she reminds us that 'infantile sexuality is the basis for all that follows'; that is that curiosity and questing form us and knowledge. In calling children 'little sex researchers', Freud (1905) drew attention to the fact that they are passionately curious about their own pleasures, and their own and other bodies. Children are drawn to wonder about people and how they relate to themselves and each other, to wonder anxiously where the child himself came from and, in an interesting link back to Dave Goulson's experiences, to wonder what happens within their own, and inside their mothers' bodies.

Verhaeghe suggests there are 'three questions that form the child's curiosity: "What is the difference between me and the other sex, where do children come from, and what is the relation between my mother and father?"' (cited in Britzman, 2006, pp.174–175). This curiosity about what makes us the same and/or different, about what happens out of sight inside bodies, where I was before I existed and how the world went on without me and in the relationships that created me, that existed before me in which I am therefore both implicated and invisible, are fundamental questions of existence that shape the questing of adults as well as of children. While we may, through science, have reached some rational answers, the larger existential questions remain. I understand about conception and I know 'where babies come from', but I still want to know what my existence could mean before 'I' was conceived. This is a question of a different order, the rational answer – that there was no 'I' until I was conceived – just raises new questions about when, post conception, 'I' becomes a meaningful word or what it means to exist as an idea or a desire: as a twinkle in a parent's eye. These questions evade rationality, they continue to be about the inside world and to be the stuff of the paradoxes that trip up and muddle our lives.

Back with the hated paradoxes, Melanie Klein's route through certainty to uncertainty and deeper understanding of children's 'voice' and questions, has important messages for educators. In the early stages of her career, Klein believed that if only adults would give children direct and truthful answers to their questions about time, origins, sexuality and relationships, then later adult neuroses could be averted. This was psychoanalysis as prophylactic: words and talk as a preventative, a pre-cure. However, her own work later disproved this theory and instead highlighted her own desire, a desire also familiar to many teachers: to 'save' children from difficult and often bruising aspects of growing up. This is the problem of transference and of our repeated forgetting that the other person is not us – we are not they (Boldt, 2006).

The hard lesson that Klein learned and that we as adults continue to become enmeshed in and struggle with, is that the adult's desire to answer – and end – the child's questions satisfies only the adult (if that!). Literal interpretations of the child's question miss the question's (the child's) unconscious purposes; an answer to 'Where do we come from?' that informs about relationships and conception, doesn't quite hit the mark and more questions follow. As intimated earlier, Klein found that, even when her son knew how babies were born, he still 'wanted to know where he was before he was born'. So we are left, wobbling in the in-between space of experience, with both a passion for ignorance (a desire to turn in towards our dreams) and a desire for answers that can end the questions – that make life certain and unambiguous. This fantasy of a knowledge that can have all the answers leaves knowledge idealised and vulnerable to failure.

So, somewhere there is a balance to be struck between the child's own questions and the questions we think they should want to ask or that we are prepared to answer. As teachers, we often mark a difference between good knowledge (that is worth knowing) and bad knowledge (which is mad, bad or dangerous to know), and we list the good knowledge and call it the curriculum dismissing 'bad' knowledge as irrelevant. But, as Britzman reminds us:

> knowledge is not just an investigative procedure. The process of coming to know creates the self and knowledge. ... we use knowledge as a defence, as an attempt to settle the longing and the emptiness. At the same time, resistance to knowing this emptiness will be the counterforce. [...] in the crevices of the Oedipus Complex, [is] not so much the story of exclusion but the yearning for knowledge to complete the mystery of existence.
>
> *(Britzman, 2006, pp.173–180)*

We struggle to tolerate paradoxes and yearn for certainty. However much we try to codify the good knowledge thereby eliminating the 'bad knowledge', the knowledge we try to render outside and abject will keep creeping back in. We can pre-emptively answer all the children's questions we can imagine, but still our answers will miss their target. Sex education does not teach children about sex, or sexuality, they teach each other about that – although we may be able to engage in their conversations: importantly, theirs are not *our* conversations (Britzman, 2012). At stake in relation to the compliance of social acceptance is our willingness to keep an open mind, that we maintain a desire and an ability to look and explore. Paradoxically, both key to education and put at risk by education is the belief that one's questions are worth asking and that one's curiosity is safe and worth pursuing.

The dangers of curiosity and miscommunication between adults and children in school was highlighted for me by research that a group of children undertook supported by the Economic and Social Research Council (ESRC) project's researchers (discussed also in Chapter 9). This particular group of 10-year-olds felt they would like to know their teachers better – after all, their teachers knew a lot about them. However, a high level of suspicion greeted their desire to interview the teachers and support staff. Staff felt it was our way of snooping on them when in fact it was entirely the children's own curiosity. The level of openness with which the adults responded to the child interviewers varied from fairly whole-hearted and playful to non-existent and hostile. Once the children had the transcripts to analyse they responded with disappointment, anger and disbelief to examples of insincerity and evasion: how could these adults who they were trying to deal with honestly and with integrity betray them in these ways? What was the use of being compliant, of being good and considerate when this gets you nowhere? Or not nowhere, but nowhere you were trying to get to.

One of the children's interviews stood out as particularly troubling. Rezwana had chosen to interview one of her teachers: Ms Naidu. Theirs was a difficult relationship so we questioned her choice, but Rezwana was determined. During the interview Ms Naidu's responses were little more than monosyllabic, leaving me wondering why she had agreed to be interviewed at all. Towards the end of the interview Ms Naidu seems to have become impatient, and she started to read Rezwana's prompt sheet, taking over her planned questions:

REZWANA: What is the most important thing you have ever learned?
MISS NAIDU: Maths. It's true. Now which one?
R: What is the least, huh? Oh yeah. What is the most important thing you have ever learned? Boring. (whispers)
MISS N: That's not very nice is it?
R: I tried it on some other teachers and they had more interesting things to say.
MISS N: I can't understand what you're saying.
R: Nothing. Read the question.

Even several years later, this remains a difficult piece of data to read and engage with. The teacher's impatience, her lack of thought or awareness of the trouble Rezwana had undergone to plan and prepare for the interview – perhaps Rezwana's thwarted hopes for some reparative work – is hard to accept. The curt and cursory nature of this teacher's answers and her barely veiled contempt still upset me, as does the memory of Rezwana's resigned disappointment: 'Silly me for hoping otherwise'. This sad moment might make us wonder about the nature of unsafe curiosities and dangerous questions. Where can curiosity not go? This is hard to answer, but responses characterised by contempt – by expressions of hatred – might act as warnings, as trip-wires to warn us that we are treading on dangerous ground. Questions that seek to explore or to know the limits of love, the edges of knowledge: does my teacher know everything? Does my mother love me as much as she loves my brother? Can I really be treated the same as my peers? And what would any of that mean?

Time and appetite

> Compliance and appetite are always uneasy bedfellows and appetite is another word for imagination.
>
> *(Phillips, 1998, p.4)*

The second of the 'everyday' compliances for social living that I want to consider is not unrelated to the first. Phillips associates appetite with imagination. I want to explore this and also to ask about greed and aggression, which are also in the picture here: We greedily devour, heartily attack, whatever we desire to satisfy our appetites – polite nibbling won't really cut it! To go back to Winnicott's writing about an infant's coming into being (discovering itself and the world) and the first moments of the good enough mother's maternal preoccupation – in the beginning there is sensation and the breast: hunger, a feed and satiation. Winnicott identifies time as the first impingement. The 'good enough' mother initially holds this at bay by feeding her baby when it demands feeding. During this early stage and immediately afterwards, as infant and mother begin to establish their relationship and routines they can live with, an infant becomes aware of their demand and the aggression inherent in it. The urgency of their demand and need for a feed result in an attack on the breast, a devouring delight. As a capacity for concern emerges with a tacit recognition that self and other are separate, limits are put on greed and desire so that the loved object (which is also simultaneously the hated object) can be protected. With an infant's growing strength, the way they excitedly bite a nipple becomes more painful and their mother starts to exclaim pain and to request gentleness. To guard against the hated absent breast (the nipple withdrawn perhaps as a result of pain), expressions of appetite, urgency and joy are moderated. Reflecting on an infant's aggression ('muscle eroticism'), on their joy in biting, hitting, tearing and generally causing reactions in their immediate environment, and a mother's sense of emotional as well as physical hurt in the face of the assault of a feeding frenzy, Winnicott explores what it might mean:

> If it is true, then, that the infant has a vast capacity for destruction it is also true that he has a vast capacity for protecting what he loves from his own destructiveness, and the main destruction must always exist in his fantasy.

> And the important thing to note about this instinctual aggressiveness is that although it soon becomes something that can be mobilised in the service of hate, it is originally part of appetite, or of some other form of instinctual love. It is something that increases during excitement, and exercise of it is highly pleasurable.
>
> Perhaps the word *greed* conveys more easily than any other the idea of original fusion of love and aggression, though the love here is confined to mouth-love.
>
> [...] there is a theoretical greed or primary appetite-love, which can be cruel, hurting, dangerous, but which is so by chance [the acts – biting, tearing – are painful but not intentionally so]. The infant's aim is gratification, peace of mind and body. Gratification brings peace, but the infant perceives that to become gratified he endangers what he loves. Normally he compromises, and allows himself enough gratification while not allowing himself to be too dangerous. But to some extent he frustrates himself; so he must hate some part of himself, unless he can find someone outside himself to frustrate him and bear being hated.
>
> *(Winnicott, 1984, p.76)*

In linking hunger and imagination, Phillips is developing Winnicott's point that the initial hallucination is a way of coping with absence: that the breast can be conjured as a place-holder until the real breast arrives (as if by magic or out of desire). Beyond the primary omnipotence of our earliest infancy, our 'I wonder what would happen if …?' or 'I wonder what it would be like to …?' conjure answers for us to play with and that can feed our affective lives, our true selves. Again, we need to tolerate a back and forth between the literal and the metaphorical: the feeds that fill our stomachs and the feeds that fill our minds and our souls. We can link curiosity to appetite here and so the two forms of compliance are entangled. And, as Winnicott warns, appetite that conjures a feed needs to take care not to 'bite off more than it can chew'; it needs to take care not to hurt or diminish the source of goodness and not to overload the biter (we need to take care of our questions).

Beyond breast feeding, and as impingements are allowed in, lie the processes of weaning. In both literal and metaphorical weanings, the move off the breast and on to solid food, or from complete dependence towards self-reliance, puts the delivery of what we want on a timetable. Weaning involves moving away from feeding 'on demand'. As time is allowed in as an impingement in relationships, we are nurtured towards a control of our appetites (our desires): bedtime and awake time, school time and home time, work time and play time, breakfast, lunch and dinner time. 'You can watch TV when you've done your homework', 'You can have a glass of wine when you've planned your lessons'. Notice, as an aside, that reward follows work, the thought that you might work harder or better *after* a break seems impossible in these bargains, so completely have we internalised the imperative to earn what we might need. Over time, the requirement that we comply with when and where our needs might be met – not unconnected to sexuality – conveys messages about our worthiness to receive the love and food that nurtures us. How long must I wait? How many people are ahead of me? How many people are more worthy than I?

In the following rather long extract from a group interview with 9- to 10-year-old girls, the researcher (Alice) starts by reflecting back the previous comments:

ALICE: So, when [your teacher] ignores you you feel less like learning and then you get the question wrong and you feel guilty

SABRINA: Yeah

A: I'm not quite clear about why you feel guilty

[...]

SALLY: Well I feel like that, it's because [my teacher] like, I put my hand up and she never chooses me, especially like in maths, she loves the other year 5 class and then like um she blames me if I've got it wrong, it's like 'Sally you don't understand' but it's her, she doesn't understand and then when I'm ignored I don't like it, I feel left out and nobody ignores me! But then she says I only ignore you, it's because you're so clever, but then that's not true [... because] she doesn't like me, no Alice it's true, I don't think she likes me that much

[...]

A: And what happens to you when you're trying to get on with learning things and you feel that your teacher doesn't like you? Does that make a difference

SALLY: Yes, it's a bit difficult to like concentrate and then she's like 'you're not concentrating properly', but then when you tell her that 'you're leaving me out' then she doesn't know how you feel because it's not happening to her!

A: Because she's not being left out

SALLY: Yeah cos she's being, like everyone's surrounding her going Miss! Miss!

SABRINA: If I was [my teacher] yeah and [my teacher] was me yeah, I'd just squash her like a fly.

This exchange highlights some of the difficulties of being in and experiencing the classroom. This group of bright and 'clever' girls was among the good and compliant members of the class; they worked hard and were chosen to do responsible jobs; they did well in tests and assessments and they were popular amongst their peers. And yet they report experiences of feeling fraudulent, of fearing themselves to be unlovable. Feelings of guilt, unworthiness, envy and anger dominate this and other conversations with different researchers over the five terms of the project. The vengeful turn – if I was my teacher, and she was me, I'd just squash her like a fly – speaks of a contempt that appears to run through the relationship. The fury, envy and indignation in Sally's comment: '"Sally you don't understand" but it's her, she doesn't understand and then when I'm ignored I don't like it, I feel left out and nobody ignores me!' The costs of compliance and the silencing of curiosity are painful to witness. Associated with issues of appetite and greed, and mired in dependency, are the questions: What can I ask? Are my needs/questions allowable? If I am hungry can you, will you, feed me? Am I manageable – or am I too much? Is my hunger too devouring?? Will you feel the need to defend yourself against my ravenings? And what will happen to me if you do?

Examples abound from the classroom: of children not asking their questions because they are afraid they are stupid questions, or that the teacher will ignore their raised hands. The example of Shanhrul in the previous chapter and the death of his curiosity were painful to witness and left me, as a researcher, wondering about (struggling with) the ethics and balance of activity in participant observer research roles.

The use (and abuse) of compliance in schooling

Infants get their first taste of social living at home and in the family. From the first acceptance of me and not-me, to the recognition of self and (m)other, and the recognition of people beyond the dyad – father, siblings, teacher – a child progresses to school and wider social circles. As Winnicott explains:

> The school, which stands for the home, but which is not an alternative to the child's home, can provide opportunity or a deep personal relationship with someone other than the child's parents. It provides this opportunity in the persons of the staff and the other children, and a generally tolerant but steady framework in which experiences can be lived through. … [T]he school has to be able to take over the function of the mother who gave the infant confidence at the beginning.
>
> *(1964, p.192)*

And so school begins to use the social learning and compliances that a child has initially acquired at home. Here, Winnicott is signalling similarities and differences between the new and complex institution of the school and the simpler and more familiar institution of the family. For teachers, managing large groups is difficult. Of course, social compliances can smooth the transitions ('ta') so schools are able to build on what has (hopefully) been started at home developing new behaviours to regulate the need to take turns with a teacher's attention, with toys, with passing through doorways. What was started at home is picked up and extended: The old limits to curiosity and appetite/greed are there to be used, but these limits need extending and redefining in this new context.

The extent to which we learn and internalise compliance was brought home to me recently when I found myself unable to write. Overwhelmed by the need to attend to a plethora of external calls on my time and attention, I was reduced to endlessly writing lists in an attempt to gain purchase and some control over the looming chaos. And writing the lists did indeed help; the chaos receded just enough for me to recognise my joy in lists and to retreat from letting this take over. I managed to get back to my thinking and writing, but it was not easy.

Compulsive busyness is often an attractive option for teachers; we often have a strong work ethic, a call that rivets our (compliant) attention outside ourselves.

What place is there for creativity in schools?

In the previous chapter, I touched on Winnicott's (1971) assertion that 'in any cultural field it is not possible to be original except on the basis of tradition' (p.134); that new ideas come from what is already known and not from the ether. I want to think about this suggestion in relation to the demands placed upon learning by the curriculum: At what point can children, or perhaps more properly young people, become creative?

There is a school of thought that you need to know the canon *before* it is possible to be creative; conventions and basic skills are the tools of creativity, and before you have full mastery of these you cannot use them and therefore cannot be creative. This argument insists that schooling needs to 'give culture' to children who must demonstrate their knowledge and understanding of 'the basics' and the canon before they learn to express themselves and are perhaps able to be innovative and creative in their turn. This is an issue that Britzman touches on in a consideration of Kant, who is credited with having expressed these ideas during the early days of the Enlightenment. She points out that 'Kant's unthought problem is an aggressive faith in education as a representative of knowledge capable of transcending what he saw as "the second nature" of adult immaturity' (2006, p.171). Kant's desire, she is suggesting, is for an education that can protect us from our susceptibility to our own desires: for certain knowledge, for 'real' creativity and originality, to be special and recognised as unique. This returns us to Melanie Klein's problem of knowledge that fails to protect children against the need to grow up and make their own knowledge the hard way – out of experience, with effort and in relationships that are full of compromise. The paradox of uncertain knowledge amongst people anxious about dependency (all of us) is that the more you try to guard against dependency, the more visceral and present vulnerabilities become.

Despite this, most people seem to be happy that very young children are creative in their sloppy use of paint and crazy junk modelling – the carefree, artless (?) creativity of the nursery proudly displayed on fridge doors. Running counter to Kant is the suggestion that the conventions we need to live by (the canon) might be learned *through* creativity, that the two might be developed together. There is broad acceptance that correcting children's creative use of language is socially necessary: 'I runded' respoken as 'I ran' and spellings such as 'sosijis' and 'dire rear' (two of my favourite spellings of sausages and diarrhoea) are patiently corrected. However, we might pause to notice that we correct these communications even though we understand them perfectly well; we do not hesitate to provide the 'correct' form in each case. Gunther Kress (2000) has pointed out that such 'mistakes' are simultaneously both *correct* and *wrong*, nicely capturing the moral overtones that such pedagogic work carries. And, of course, our sacred pronunciations, spellings and punctuations are only conventions (organised/organized, colour/color) that could, 'imho',[1] as easily have been, or could easily become, something else. Yet despite policy certainties (with which we may or may not agree) places of difference creep in to trouble us: dialect and, most obvious in relation to second language learners but an issue for everyone, a balance between inhibiting through (over)correction and/or allowing expression. Compliance to the canon remains highly contested in all areas of knowledge: can creativity in maths ever be contemplated?

The issue of how much to 'put in', the degree to which basic skills and conventions need to be provided as a prerequisite to creativity is perhaps more important than UK governments' constant revisionings of the curriculum or the Californian maths wars (Schoenfeld, 2004) suggest. There is more at stake here than whether Jane Austen or Harper Lee should be on reading lists and whether principled maths knowledge or algorithms are more valuable. More importantly, my deciding what will be interesting to you and overriding your desire to learn something else appears to me to be an extreme arrogance. That I can dismiss your curious questioning with educational certainties is taken for granted in classrooms around the world. As an adult I can decree, because I think I know how and where I made my knowledge, when and how you can make yours. These facts are troubling.

It is not that teachers should never lead learning or make suggestions; my question is one of degree and intent: Is the curriculum all that can be learned? Must it be learned in this way and not that? In this order rather than another? To suggest that it must is to participate in the communication that Benjamin (2004) characterised as one-way, it is to enforce a persecuting doer-done to pedagogic relation. From the point of view being explored in this book, such behaviours represent a complete and potentially catastrophic failure of the classroom as a facilitating environment. Depending on the level of False Self-defence already in place, children will find it more or less threatening and be more or less able to cope with the lack of space and time to pursue their own questions, the curtailing of their own curiosities. And as Winnicott reminds us, the refusal of questions and curiosities signals an untrustworthy environment in which the emergence of a desire for experience – small pieces of the True Self – would be dangerous. Similarly, the dangling of a prize for the right knowledge, and uneven access to it (perhaps based on gender or race or class or all of these) can produce a tantalising environment that exposes students to a kind of pedagogical sadism (Bibby, 2011). In such relationships there is a serious risk to an individual's 'going on being' and an associated threat of annihilation.

Something else needs to happen if two-way communication and a creative 'potential space' are to be managed. Winnicott is clear on this matter:

> If teachers are living healthily they are engaged in a mutual sacrifice of spontaneity and independence, and that is almost as important a part of education as the teaching and learning in the set subjects. At any rate,

> education is poor stuff, even when the subjects are well taught, if this object lesson – 'give and take' is absent, or is overridden by dominance of one personality over another.
>
> *(1964, p.203)*

'A mutual sacrifice in spontaneity and independence', a give and take, a willingness to surrender power, a desire for learning through conversation not fiat. While most teachers would like to think this is what they provide, I suggest that even in the best of times this is difficult. And we are not living in the best of times. Providing these experiences in classrooms is becoming increasingly difficult – a problem I have discussed at length elsewhere (Bibby, 2011, 2015).

To think about Winnicott's suggestion in greater detail, I want to go back to a comment he made about a patient:

> A patient said to me: 'Good management … such as I have experienced during this hour is a feed' …. He could not have said this the other way round, for if I had fed him he would have complied and this would have played into his False Self defences, or else he would have rejected my advances, maintaining his integrity by choosing frustration.
>
> *(1960, p.142)*

Winnicott is here marking a difference between looking for food and being told to 'open wide while I put this in your mouth', between active, curious looking and passive compliance. To allow oneself to be pre-emptively 'fed' is not the same as deciding to make something to eat and looking in the fridge to see what there is, riffling through cookery books and writing a shopping list. As Phillips has pointed out 'Thinking about a meal won't make me full; but neither will eating a meal I have no appetite for. Only my hunger turns the food into a meal' (Phillips, 1998, p.4): Knowledge and teaching are only satisfying if I am 'hungry' for them. Yet the alternative is slower; the difference is between 'here is a meal I prepared earlier' and hunting through hunger and desire, the cupboards, books and shops to plan and prepare a meal. But apparent speed and efficiency are seductive qualities; they are the dangers of an 'open wide' school of teaching.

> The child fits in with the teacher's need to teach and by implication, with the culture's demand that these are the things one learns, and this is the way one learns them. At this stage competence is a kind of imitation, the context defines the project.
>
> *(Phillips, 2007, p.55)*

This fitting in, a submission (not surrender) to the school's demand, marks a new level of compliance, and new aspects of the False Self Structure may well be instantiated. At home, and again at school, a child

> gets seduced into compliance, and a compliant False Self reacts to the environmental demands and the infant seems to accept them. … the child may grow to be just like mother, nurse, aunt, brother, or whoever dominates the scene. […] compliance is then the main feature with imitation as a speciality.
>
> *(Winnicott, 1960, p.146)*

This seduction into compliance, so relied upon, used, and manipulated by schools, is deeply problematic. A seduction is not the same as an invitation: seduction plays on love; it flirts with desire; it controls responses; an act of seduction is a power play, potentially an abuse. How flattering must it be if, unaware of the seduction that has been perpetrated, one sees oneself being imitated: I must be loved! How delightful to teach the child who appears to like what you like, and who is able to anticipate the administrative needs of the classroom. So, classrooms play on the False Self using and developing the 'everyday' social compliances instantiated at home to manage the behaviour of individuals in groups. But already we have indications that these small compliances incur costs: costs to our creativity and costs to our experiencing of ourselves as worthy of receiving love/being taught. If we reimagine the 'good girls and boys' as victims of their parents' and teachers' seductions into compliance, our praise and valorisation of them might feel less comfortable. And, as with many acts of seduction, what price submission and compliance?

Going back to the idea of health as a state of being in which I am aware of myself as a thinking and feeling individual able to know myself well enough so that I can respond creatively to life, we might now also think of this in terms of the healthy individual not being dominated by a False Self, of retaining a connection and a capacity to communicate with their True Selves. Seductions into (or demands for) compliance signal an unreliable environment, an environment that fails to facilitate, a place of too many impingements and too little visibility, of persecutory one-way communications. Such an unreliable environment is a hostile place to fit in with; it will result in escalating levels of compliance – increasingly dominant False Selves and hidden True Selves. In Winnicotian terms, this is emphatically not a place of health.

In classrooms and school cultures characterised by rigidity, we need to think carefully about what academic success might mean. The passing of tests, the meeting of teacher and exam-setter expectations, particularly where there are narrow criteria for success, require high levels of compliance. In such cases, Winnicott warns,

> 'success may so easily mean no more than that a child has found the easiest way to deal with a particular teacher, or a particular subject, or with education as a whole, is by subservience, a holding open of the mouth with the eyes shut, or a swallowing without critical inspection'.
>
> *(Winnicott, 1964, p.203)*

Again, data from the ESRC project on learner identities highlights some of the difficulties. In the classroom a series of red and yellow slips (pieces of paper that names would be written on) were used to record moments requiring praise or censure. This system of rewards and punishment was a topic of massive importance to the children and was a frequent topic of conversation with researchers. The boys (correctly) felt they were disadvantaged by the system. As the field notes record:

> The boys recognise that the easiest way to get rewards is by being seen to be helpful. However, they are never given opportunities to be helpful, and there are a few girls [...] who are very good at manipulating the teacher's attention to ensure that they get picked to do the chores and therefore get the rewards. Many of the boys in the class are very exercised by this and harbour a sense of injustice. [Their teacher] appears to have no awareness of this. If this pattern continues it will be unfortunate, but perhaps unsurprising, if the boys stop trying and perhaps even turn to spoiling tactics. [The boys] also feel unseen when they are working – as if [their teacher] can only see girls behaving well and can only see boys when they are misbehaving. They feel this is extremely unfair – if the boys work quietly they become invisible in some way.
>
> *(Field notes)*

The workings of gender stereotypes reinforced who and how it is possible for any one individual to be in the classroom. They were acutely aware of their own, and other peoples' positions. That compliance here is shown to extend beyond the overt rules and curriculum of the school to broader social expectations of race, ethnicity and gender just underlines its pervasive pull. And the costs of compliance are potentially huge not least because compliance is always experienced (by children and adults) as demeaning. Yet compliance is not the only possible response to a failure of the classroom as a facilitating environment. Even 'in health', Winnicott suggests, 'compromise ceases to become allowable when the issues become crucial. When this happens the True Self is able to override the compliant self' (1960, p.150). Here he is suggesting that, just as the False Self can take over and swamp or drown out the True Self, so too, the True Self can come out fighting. This second response, a non-compliance associated with defiance, Winnicott identifies as 'a recurring problem of adolescence' (1960, p.152) and is the subject of the next chapter.

Note

1 Text speak and the rise of twitterisms like this one (In My Honest Opinion) are causing all sorts of difficulties for grammar and spelling purists.

References

Benjamin, J. 2004. Beyond doer and done-to: an intersubjective view of thirdness. *Psychoanalytic Quarterly*, 73, 5–46.

Bibby, T. 2011. *Education – an 'impossible profession'? Psychoanalytic explorations of learning and classrooms*. London: Routledge.

Bibby, T. 2015. Thinking and learning? On (not) dreaming in the classroom. *Psychoanalysis, Culture and Society*, 20(1), 49–66.

Boldt, G.M. 2006. Parenting and the narcissistic demands of whiteness. In *Love's return: psychoanalytic essays on childhood, teaching and learning*, edited by G.M. Boldt and P. M. Salvio (pp.143–160). London: Routledge.

Britzman, D.P. 2003. *After-education: Anna Freud, Melanie Klein, and psychoanalytic histories of learning*. Albany: State University of New York Press.

Britzman, D.P. 2006. Sigmund Freud, Melanie Klein, and little Oedipus: on the pleasures and disappointments of sexual enlightenment. In *Love's return: psychoanalytic essays on childhood, teaching, and learning*, edited by G.M. Boldt and P.M. Salvio (pp.165–184). London: Routledge.

Britzman, D.P. 2012. The adolescent teacher: a psychoanalytic note on regression in the professions. *Journal of Infant, Child and Adolescent Psychotherapy*, 11, 272–283.

Desert Island Discs. 2000. Interview with Roger Penrose. [Radio programme] BBC, BBC R4, 23 July 2000.

Freud, S. 1905. On sexuality: three essays on the theory of sexuality and other works. In *The standard edition of the complete psychological works of Sigmund Freud*, edited by J. Strachey (Vol. VII, pp.125–248). London: Vintage.

Kress, G. 2000. *Early spelling: between convention and creativity*. London: Routledge.

Life Scientific. 2014a. Interview with Dave Goulson. [Radio programme] BBC, BBC R4, 12 November 2014.

Life Scientific. 2014b. Interview with Roger Penrose. [Radio programme] BBC, BBC R4, 22 November 2016.

Phillips, A. 1998. *The beast in the nursery*. London: Faber and Faber.

Phillips, A. 2007. *Winnicott*. London: Penguin.

Schoenfeld, A.H. 2004. The math wars. *Educational Policy*, 18(1), 253–286.

Winnicott, D.W. 1960. Ego distortion in terms of True and False Self. In *The maturational processes and the facilitating environment: studies in the theory of emotional development*, edited by D.W. Winnicott (1965, 2007 edition, pp.140–152). London: Karnac.

Winnicott, D.W. 1964. *The child, the family and the outside world* (1991 edition). London: Penguin.

Winnicott, D.W. 1971. *Playing and reality* (2008, Routledge Classics edition). London: Tavistock Publications.

Winnicott, D.W. 1984. Aggression. In *Deprivation and delinquency*, edited by C. Winnicott, R. Shepherd and M. Davis (1990 edition, pp.73–85). London: Routledge.

8

DEFIANCE

Insult or sign of hope?

While compliance may be a quiet problem that passes under the radar in many schools, defiance is an altogether touchier topic. What does it mean to suggest that acts of defiance or antisocial behaviour might be an unconscious, creative response from one's affective core, one's True Self? How are schools to make sense of children who steal, lie or otherwise defy their teachers? Is it ever possible to understand children who display aggression to others or who are destructive of their own, their peers' or school's property? Or is seeking such understanding a form of condoning the actions concerned? Should such behaviours be thought about at all? Should we use zero-tolerance policies to shut them out of our schools and out of our minds? When rocking back on a chair comes to be defined as disruptive (OfSTED, 2014), how can we even think about more extreme behaviours? Are there other ways of thinking about non-compliance that can help us think constructively about 'disruptive' behaviours wherever and whenever they occur? Might we be able to find any sympathy with Winnicott for his belief that antisocial behaviour is best understood as a child's S.O.S. to the adult world?

Winnicott provides us with innovative ways to think about the normal travails of adolescence as well as what he called 'the antisocial tendency'. His experiences during and after the Second World War forced him to rethink issues of deprivation and failures in the facilitating environment. To explore his ideas more fully, we need to remind ourselves that, as a London-based paediatrician working throughout the 1940s, he came into contact with many children who had been evacuated out of London and into foster homes. His written legacy includes talks about the difficulties of the evacuation programme for *everyone* involved: his talks addressed the mothers who had to send their children away and the foster carers who took those children in (or on whom they were billeted), as well as social workers, teachers and magistrates. There can be no doubt that many of the children who were evacuated found life very difficult, although others thrived. But however the fostering went, the daily experience of the loss of their homes must have been very hard for the children (and their families) to bear. Parents also suffered the effects of trauma, including nightly bombing raids and untimely bereavements, making it even more difficult for them to be reliably (emotionally) present and to provide a good enough facilitating environment. Winnicott also commented on the post-war legacy and the way it played out in the increasingly liberal 1950s and 1960s. As a result, his writing on issues of childhood disturbance spans his own maturing sense of his professions (paediatrics and psychoanalysis) drawing on, and developing beyond, the work of both Freud and Klein.

One unfortunate legacy of the time at which he was writing is the language: He talks of 'antisocial tendencies', of 'delinquency' and 'maladaptation' and the institutions of 'approved' or 'reform schools', borstals etc. The range of behaviours described – from 'nuisance' through to 'delinquent' – are all forms of what Winnicott called an 'antisocial tendency'. Such behaviours might nowadays be covered by the rather imprecise and general notions of 'non-compliance' or 'defiance' with the criminalisation of damage, assault and theft occupying the 'delinquent' extreme. Perhaps we need to reclaim the idea of 'antisocial' behaviours when we think about those that interrupt, or that are disruptive of social forms of living? However, despite the fact that more modern sensibilities have changed both our use of language and our institutional practices, the issues he highlights remain helpful in thinking through the difficulties of children's defiant behaviours.

To think about 'the antisocial tendency', Winnicott starts by considering what 'normal' might look like, quickly puncturing any idealisation or fantasy of perfection that might be connoted with the term:

> What is the normal child like? Does he just eat and grow and smile sweetly? No, that is not what he is like. A normal child, if he has confidence in father and mother, pulls out all the stops. In the course of time he tries out his power to disrupt, to destroy, to frighten, to wear down, to waste, to wangle, and to appropriate. Everything that takes people to the courts (or to the asylums, for that matter) has its normal equivalent in infancy and early childhood, in the relation of the child to his own home.
>
> *(1946, p.99)*

'Normal children' then are difficult and challenging. Or perhaps, being difficult and challenging is just a normal part of childhood. And so we begin to get some sense of the difficult job that parents may have in tolerating the aggression inherent in children's loving impulses as they try out their *power to disrupt, to destroy, to frighten, to wear down, to waste, to wangle and to appropriate.* He continues:

> If the home can stand up to all the child can do to disrupt it, he settles down to play; but business first, the tests must be made, and especially so

> if there is some doubt as to the stability of parental set-up and the home (by which I mean so much more than house). At first the child needs to be conscious of a framework if he is to feel free, and if he is to be able to play, to draw his own pictures, to be an irresponsible child.
>
> *(1946, p.99)*

All children (i.e. all of us) respond to the boundaries that provide a framework within which we think and act. Under anxious conditions, for example, the need to write an essay or perform a task, we seek criteria and deadlines. Assessment criteria, for example, are demanded and tested: 'Can I ...?', 'What will happen if ...?', 'What does ... mean?', 'Will it be okay if I ...?' For teachers it does not matter how precise we are with our criteria, they will always be unclear to the students. Indeed, sometimes it seems that the more precise and exact the criteria are, the more anxious the students become. Perhaps this is because there are now more ways to get things wrong? Assessment criteria therefore perform two tasks: Not only do they set out expectations, but also they put limits around (or define) the edges of creativity that are contextually appropriate. It is a rare student who pushes at the limits of creativity, perhaps saying more about the demands for unthinking compliance in academic work than any lack of imagination among students.

Winnicott stressed that it is important that these testing moves are survived. However lamentable their aggressivity may appear to adult eyes, he suggests that aggression is an inherent and vital part of learning to live and love: It is central to the child's developing sense of confidence in self and trust in the environment.

> ... the early stages of emotional development are full of potential conflict and disruption. The relation to external reality is not yet firmly rooted; the personality is not yet well integrated; primitive love has a destructive aim, and the small child has not yet learned to tolerate and cope with instincts. He can come to manage these things and more if his surroundings are stable and personal. At the start he absolutely needs to live in a circle of love and strength (with consequent tolerance) if he is not to feel too fearful of his own thoughts and of his imaginings to make progress in his emotional development.
>
> *(1946, p.99)*

Aggression lies at the heart of coming into being. Previous chapters have explored the importance of aggression for finding and creating the not-me. It is through aggression that objects are (in fantasy) destroyed and, if they survive their destruction, can be rediscovered as existing beyond omnipotent control. Destroying the (subjective) object releases it from omnipotent control allowing it to be an objective entity with a separate existence. In this way the object becomes real and so can be relied upon and used to grow and learn. The earliest objects include the object mother, especially those parts of the mother first recognised: breast, eyes, mouth, arms but not yet known as an integrated whole.

What happens, then, if the environment fails before the child is ready for it to do so, if the impingements come in too fast or are too much to cope with? What if it fails at a moment when the child is in a state of relative dependence? Or what occurs if the extent to which it fails is beyond what the child can manage? One answer was offered later in William Golding's (1954) novel *The lord of the flies*. Winnicott himself put it like this:

> The popular idea is that, finding himself 'free' [the child] proceeds to enjoy himself. This is far from the truth. Finding the framework of his life broken, he no longer feels free. He becomes anxious, and if he has hope he proceeds to look for a framework elsewhere than at home. ... He seeks an external stability without which he may go mad. ... Often a child gets from relations [aunts, uncles, grandparents] and school what he missed in his own actual home.
>
> The antisocial child is merely looking a little farther afield, looking to society [peers, gangs, sporting groups, the law etc.] instead of to his own family or school to provide the stability he needs if he is to pass through the early and quite essential stages of emotional growth.
>
> *(1946, pp.99–100)*

So, Winnicott establishes a continuum of difficult, aggressive and challenging behaviours from the 'normal' through the 'antisocial' and to 'delinquency'. As the level of self-control diminishes and the challenge to others escalates, it can be difficult to hold in mind that all these behaviours signal a significant failure in the facilitating environment and are not a sign of any inherent 'badness' or 'evil' in the child. Winnicott is keen to remind us that between the normal difficulties of childhood and the more extreme reactions of 'antisocial' behaviour there are many who can still come to fit in with society if conditions experienced as loving and containing can be provided so that while 'failures will eventually come to the courts, ... successes become citizens' (p.101).

In here then is the challenge to schools: If children will, as a part of their development, seek to *disrupt, destroy, frighten, wear down, waste, wangle, and appropriate*, how can teachers understand these behaviours in a way that enables them to continue their primary task (the overlay of knowledge on the developing child) (Bibby, 2011) while neither stopping a child's development nor behaving as if antisocial behaviour were social? That is, there is a difficult balance to be found between the outright rejection of the 'naughty' child and condoning the 'naughty' behaviours. This is a balance teachers typically sense needs to be found even if the school rules suggest otherwise. If a school's systems are sufficiently flexible, difficult moments can often be managed by sensitive and nimble practitioners; if not, then strict rules (table points deducted, playtimes taken away, children sent out) can inadvertently escalate unwanted behaviours.

Aggression as a part of life

Overt displays of aggression can be frightening to witness and to perpetrate. A (real or apparent) loss of control suggests a stepping beyond rationality and a disinhibition about causing hurt or harm. To live in the world and to enable society to function as smoothly as possible, we prohibit acts of aggression placing limits on the extents and implications of physical and verbal violence. For children in schools, this prohibition is still being learned, so at times it will feel unfair or unreasonable, but it is a social rule we expect everyone to come to terms with eventually. Society provides acceptable outlets for aggression in sport and other competitive pursuits, and it is expected that we will all be able to make appropriate use of these.

A central difficulty with this prohibition of aggression is that it can make our own anger frightening to us, stop us from recognising the aggression inherent in destructiveness and other acts of defiance and stop us thinking about the more positive aspects of aggression. As Winnicott pointed out:

> It is comparatively easy for us to get at the destructiveness that is in ourselves when this is linked with anger at frustration or hate at something we disapprove of or when it is a reaction to fear. The difficult thing for each individual is to take full responsibility for the destructiveness that is personal, and that inherently belongs to the relationship to an object that is felt to be good; in other words, that is related to loving.
>
> *(1960, p.117)*

To understand the link between aggression and loving, Winnicott began with the baby's aggression. Primary aggression, or 'muscle eroticism', (a baby's enjoyment of thrashing about and feeling a reaction to its movement) leads babies to bite their mother's breast in an attempt to take inside what is felt to be good about her. These bites have no moral force; they are responses to a felt desire to incorporate the goodness and have it as part of oneself. As we develop a sense that our biting hurts the one we love, we may start to inhibit our oral aggression. But biting, along with other forms of aggression, may take on moral overtones and become increasingly socially problematic. It causes trouble in nursery schools, and we might recall the international condemnation brought down on Luis Suarez when he bit a fellow footballer during a match (*The Guardian*, 2014). Yet despite the social prohibition, biting and nibbling remain private, erotic pleasures for many. Also familiar is the desire to (playfully and lovingly) bite tiny babies whose toes and bottoms seem to call to us. More openly, we may gnash our teeth with frustration, bite nails, chew pencils, behead and dismember jelly babies, and make 'biting' remarks: all signs of (unconscious) aggression.

So, a blanket ban on aggression makes it difficult to think about the multiple dimensions of destructiveness. This may be part of the reason that the defiance of others can be so hard to take: The blanket ban and the moral overtones make our desires seem more frightening to us, and if we cannot think about our own 'unacceptable' sides, we are even less likely to be able to think about other people's. It is hard not to feel personally violated when we are burgled or a child steals in a school we work in. Defiance offered to one teacher can come to be read as defiance to a whole institution. Being a victim of theft can leave us feeling persecuted, so it is perhaps no surprise that, as Winnicott points out, it can feel easier to leave someone else to deal with acts of defiance than deal with them ourselves.

For us to be able to think about our own aggression we have first to spot it then think about its effects as a way of perhaps making sense of where it came from and its aims. For Winnicott, it is important to note that learning the effects of our defiant behaviours requires first that we *are* defiant; without the act there is nothing to recognise and process. To illustrate this I will use, as an example of defiant behaviour, something an otherwise well-mannered professional might slip into. I do that to offer a deliberate provocation: it is not only the young and unruly who behave inappropriately and with aggression!

So, imagine a teacher, a professional colleague whose work is generally thoughtful. She has her day ruled by the clock and, while she makes it to the start of lessons, she is often late to staff meetings. This unconscious refusal to be on time, an act of defiance, is an aggressive act. It attacks the school's procedures, which the teacher experiences in a visceral way with a suffocating sense of constriction, of being hemmed in. The act of defiance is a lashing out, an attempt to break free of constricting expectations that limit actions elsewhere (perhaps a quiet five minutes to collect herself or to tidy the classroom). In fact, in defying the school's timetable she actually creates difficulties for her colleagues who have to wait for her to arrive. The knock-on effect is that the rest of the staff must either curtail their discussions or allow the meeting to run late making everyone else late for upcoming commitments. If she is never late to a meeting – if she is reflexively compliant to all the demands on her time – she never has to think through what the meeting times mean and what they represent for her. However, having been defiant and seen the impact of her 'lashing out' she may come to fully understand the purpose of the start time: Not only does it enable the complex institution to function smoothly, but her receipt of collegial love and acceptance require that she collaborate fully as a member of her teaching team. She may now also be able to think about *why* she hates the meeting time so much: how controlled she feels by a faceless bureaucracy, how much she hates the impersonality of much of her work and how she resents her students' apparently endless demands that *she* makes sure *they* learn. All this, while no one seems to care for or about her, no wonder she feels hemmed in and suffocated! If she could think this through, she might be able to ask for the meeting time to be changed, and this request may or may not be successful but it could be thought about. Unrecognised, an act of defiance will generate a split between the on time and the late, the conscientious and the lazy, the good and the bad, a defence against the difficulty of facing up to the demands of institutional life.

Being a part of something

As a result of his clinical work, Winnicott came to see the importance of what he called 'contributing in'. His suggestion is that we need to be able to make a contribution to social life and thereby be allowed to be known as constructive before we can be expected to see and think about our own destructive behaviours. If our imaginary teacher had not felt part of a team or had not had a recognisable team to identify with, and some positive history working within it, then the learning described above may have been more difficult. 'Contributing in' can take many forms, but Winnicott suggests, it is the way it is looked at that matters:

> ... you can look at the positive way a person mends, and you can cleverly say 'Aha, that means unconscious destruction.' But the world is not helped on much if you do this. Alternatively you may see in someone's mending that he or she is building up a self strength which makes possible a toleration of the destructiveness that belongs to that person's nature. Say you somehow block the mending, then to some extent that person becomes unable to take responsibility for his or her destructive urges, and clinically the result is either depression or else a search for relief by the discovery of destructiveness elsewhere, that is to say by the mechanism of projection.
>
> *(1960, p.122)*

This mending, whether of broken clothes, sentences, bodies or ideas, is a form of 'contributing in', which allows the 'mender' to feel good enough about themselves that less positive aspects of their self can be considered. As well as literally repairing something, the mending is also a reparative act in that it enables the mender to act on unconscious guilt and to make things better. Stopping someone from 'contributing in' (through their hobbies, relationships, or work) deprives them of an opportunity to think and, Winnicott is suggesting, leads to splitting: The unthought destructive behaviours are then 'projected' elsewhere so that the destructiveness met in life can be seen as someone else's doing and becomes persecuting. By not thinking about our own compulsion to destroy, we enable ourselves to believe that only others are destructive; our contempt enables us to hate them and bolster our own sense of moral superiority. The example that comes to mind is of animal lovers who judge animal abandoners very harshly: How could they? They should never be allowed to have another pet! They should be fined. While in no way wishing to condone acts of animal abandonment, a refusal to acknowledge our own dark moments faced with the expense, frustration and hate they can engender (alongside the delight, joy and love) is unhelpful. How much easier is it to shout angrily about abandoning owners (who are perhaps already heartbroken and feeling a deep sense of shame) than to admit our own shameful or hateful feelings, the moments when, driven to distraction, we, feeling like shit, walk away from their shit?

It is worth pausing here and going back to Winnicott's remark (above) about the 'clever' comment. It is not that the interpretation – 'Aha, that means unconscious destruction' – is 'wrong' but that it does not help the world much. The comment focuses attention on the cleverness of the commentator, but when turned around, it could instead help us think about the development of the one doing the mending. This matters hugely for schools: How can we enable children to 'contribute in' to the life of the classroom and maintain a sense of their own goodness so that they can come to know their own aggression without necessarily acting on it? Similarly, how can we enable teachers to 'contribute in' to the life of the institution? Is it possible for teachers and institutions to know about their own aggressivity so that they do not retaliate when they see, or imagine they witness, an attack on them? Can schools and teachers, for example, think about the aggression inherent in lateness, torn work, forgotten homework, stolen calculators or swearing without their own aggressive retaliations: stolen playtimes, exclusions, shouting and zero-tolerance policies?

The facilitating environment revisited

To think in more detail about Winnicott's antisocial tendencies it is useful to revisit the idea of the facilitating environment and to think again about what can happen when it fails. The failures that need thinking about now go beyond the small, managed environmental failures a mother makes as she de-adapts to her infant enabling it to learn about the world beyond itself. While making small failures the mother must still not 'let the baby down'; she must continue to be there in a reliable, trustworthy way. Being a moment delayed in providing a feed or picking up a crying child, perhaps talking to them as the delay is endured, is not the same as ignoring their plight.

For Winnicott, it is the reliable presence of a trustworthy, good enough facilitating (m)other that enables the child to experience its ruthless impulses and to come to recognise the effects of these. With time and the continuing presence of a good enough environment, the child can come to develop a sense of guilt, a desire to make reparation and a capacity for concern. These are all developmental achievements and as such can be missed, only partially achieved, lost or distorted by circumstances: Nothing is certain and forever. This work is a lifelong project for all of us.

Guilt and reparation

The aspects of aggression discussed above matter because they contribute to an aspect of a sense of guilt. Destructive and aggressive impulses towards the one we love (mother, teacher, friend, ally) will hurt them if we act upon them, and knowledge of this – that is, of our desire to hurt the ones we love – if it is met with love (acceptance, tolerance, non-retaliation) generates guilt at an unconscious level. A willingness to recognise a state of ambivalence, of being able to tolerate the paradoxical realisation that both good and bad exist together in others as well as in ourselves, is central to the development of guilt. Winnicott himself explains that, when things go well:

> ... the opportunity for giving and for making reparation that the environment-mother offers by her reliable presence, enables the baby to become more and more bold in the experiencing of [unconscious impulses]; in other words, frees the baby's instinctual life. In this way, guilt is not felt, but lies dormant, or potential, and appears (as sadness or depressed mood) only if opportunity for reparation fails to turn up.
>
> *(1963a, p.89)*

In schools and other educational institutions, the environment and teacher can similarly provide opportunities for reparation: if a student's insult to their teacher in a lesson is not carried forward in the form of a grudge or resentment they may find an opportunity to 'make it up' to her – perhaps by putting in a bit more effort. Each lesson, and each episode in a lesson, provides students with new opportunities to 'contribute in' and to be experienced by them as constructive. Winnicott suggests that students are not forced to experience their guilt unless their teacher starts to retaliate, perhaps by withdrawing opportunities for them to attempt to repair the damage they may have done (perhaps by sending them away to another room). It is experiences of 'contributing in' and of feeling valued for oneself within a group that enable a sense of concern to develop.

The capacity for concern

This cycling between guilt and reparation describes a process of learning; a process of coming to recognise when our impulses cause hurt and that responding to these impulses can impact the classroom and institution. A process of repair may overcome the damage of a moment of environmental failure: All is not necessarily lost. In schools (and other institutions), learning about ourselves inevitably goes hand in hand with learning about mathematics or geography (or institutional processes). It is the adult separation of personal and academic learning that can create difficulties in this regard. Such a stark separation (or dichotomising) is a split, a defence against the difficult and inconvenient interconnectedness of personal and academic learning, of the affective and the cognitive, of the hidden and planned curriculum. An insistence on compliance to the demands of the institution and institutional knowledge forecloses possibilities for developing concern and can result in the creation (or reinforcement) of a False Self that cuts itself off from personal responses. It is a personal and institutional inconvenience that developing a capacity for concern has to be done repeatedly in different contexts (across place and time) throughout life. This is not only a task for childhood. Indeed, according to Winnicott, 'most of the processes that start up in early infancy are never fully established, and continue to be strengthened by the growth that continues in later childhood, and indeed in adult life, even in old age' (Winnicott, 1963a, p.87).

One who has developed a capacity for concern 'cares' or 'minds' about others and 'feels and accepts responsibility' for their actions (Winnicott, 1963a, p.73). Winnicott suggests that the capacity for concern develops when the environment-mother (the mother who is reliably there for me) and the object-mother (the fragments of mother that meet particular needs), initially mentally held in a split state to keep them safe, can come together in the infant's mind:

> The favourable circumstances necessary at this stage are these: that the mother should continue to be alive and available in the sense of not being preoccupied with something else. The object-mother has to be found to survive the instinct-driven episodes, which have now acquired the full force of fantasies of oral sadism and other results of fusion. Also, the environment-mother has a special function, which is to continue to be herself, to be empathic towards her infant, to be there to receive the spontaneous gesture, and to be pleased.
>
> *(1963a, p.89)*

It is in relation particularly to the object mother (the unintegrated fragments associated with need: breast, mouth, eyes etc.) that attack and destruction play out. In infancy, the (biting) eating of the mother to take possession of her; in childhood, the biting of a biscuit while it is imagined that the mother is bitten. In both instances, the desire is to take in and possess (to introject) what is felt to be good about the object-mother. In parallel, a baby's relation to the environment-mother may engender much worry and guilt: 'If I eat her, she will no longer be available for me to eat'; 'If I eat her I will hurt her, she may retaliate'. Such concerns can cause an infant to become inhibited or to turn away. Winnicott points to this as 'a positive element of the infant's experience of weaning and one reason why some infants wean themselves' (1963a, p.89).

Translating this to schools and other educational contexts, the required availability of a teacher (free from preoccupation) suggests that they need not be so consumed with other children that one student becomes invisible, that their attention is in *this room* and on *this class* during lesson time, not on marking or planning or dealing with unconnected administrative tasks. A reliable teacher is able to survive biting remarks and other forms of aggression/defiance (forgotten books, torn or lost homework, challenges to authority, refusals of knowledge and a lack of gratitude) without retaliation, a theme explored in greater detail in Chapter 9.

Deprivation: the loss of something that was …

Winnicott draws a clear distinction between deprivation and privation. Deprivation involves loss. Privation is a state in which nothing has been lost because it was not there in the first place. This is an altogether different matter;

privation is catastrophic for the individual concerned and leads, Winnicott suggests, to serious mental illness. Significantly, Winnicott suggests that a slide towards antisocial behaviour signals hope. He stresses here that there is a *morality* in childhood, born in the ruthless use of objects, that we tend to lose sight of as adults: an *integrity* that relates to staying true to one's self and in the face of which 'the *mores* of local society are mere distractions. Adolescent children' he says, 'are more concerned with not betraying themselves than with whether they smoke or not, or whether they do or do not sleep around. … the false solution [someone else's solution] is OUT' (1966, p.96 emphasis in original). Adolescents retain some contact with their internal/affective life until it is eventually swamped by demands for compliance to social and institutional life.

As the pattern above suggests, for children who display an 'antisocial' tendency – or who are defiant – there has been a deprivation, a loss of something that had been experienced as good at a time when they were relatively dependent on that factor in their environment. Deprivation may result either from a temporary loss or from a loss that has endured for long enough that the experience of its absence outlives the child's ability to keep the original good experience alive in its mind. This experience of deprivation will vary from individual to individual. What one person might experience as a minor matter, someone else might feel acutely, and what is felt acutely at one time or in one context may be better tolerated at another time or in another place.

To go back to the development of a capacity for concern and Winnicott's reference to the two aspects of the good enough mother/facilitating environment: the object-mother and the environment-mother. These two aspects of good enough parenting jointly facilitate not only a child's excited/active, ruthlessly outward focussed life and reflective, inward focussed life, but also its creative moves between them. A failure of the facilitating environment will involve a loss of access to one or both of the two aspects of the mother and therefore an inability to move between them: an inability to think or play.

Winnicott suggests that if the environment-mother is lost, the child will seek 'that amount of environmental stability which will stand the strain resulting from destructive behaviours' – he will fight the metaphorical arms until they notice him, respond to him again and hold him as he requires. If on the other hand the object-mother is lost, then the child will seem to be searching for something in different places, for as long as they remain hopeful they may 'steal' things in the hope of replacing that which was lost. So, Winnicott identifies two main forms of antisocial tendency: The first, which is characterised by destruction, and the second, by object-seeking. Whichever is manifest it is, Winnicott suggests, of primary importance that the 'bad behaviour' be seen for what it is: an S.O.S., a cry for help:

> The antisocial tendency represents the hopefulness in a deprived child who is otherwise hopeless, hapless and harmless; a manifestation of the antisocial tendency in a child means that there has developed in the child

> some hopefulness, hope that a way might be found across a gap. This gap is a break in the continuity of environmental provision, experienced at a stage of relative dependence … The wickedness goes if the gap is bridged.
> *(1963b, pp.103–104)*

This image of a facilitating environment becoming fractured (a 'break in the continuity of environmental provision') and creating a gap is helpful to me. It is as if the failure creates a crack, a fissure in the continuity of being, and the antisocial act – the moment of defiance – is an attempt to reach back over that gap to the moment *before* the deprivation happened and to repair the fracture or perhaps to magically find that the fracture never happened. The 'naughty' behaviour is a request to press a psychic rewind button. For Winnicott, the child is unconsciously using being a nuisance or displaying more challenging behaviour to ask the adult to go back with them to *just before* the moment of failure and to try again. It is important to note here that the cause of defiance is an environmental failure, a failure of adult care. It is *adult* failure that has hurt the child whose antisocial act now tries to prompt adult reparation. Of course, thinking about schools, it is likely that the source of the environmental failure and the 'victim' of the defiance are not the same person. But what good can it do to further hurt (punish) the child for an environmental failure that has already caused pain? By what right do we, as teachers, visit the 'sins of the father' on the child? And how prepared are we to accept that the environmental failure might also be our failure? Again, we need to remember that these children are not just children: They are *anyone* in a position of relative dependency in relation to someone else. This would include postgraduate students and the university, and employees and their institutions/teachers and their schools.

The ordinary child: just a 'ruddy nuisance'

Before considering the more challenging aspects of defiance, it is perhaps useful, like Winnicott, to think about the more minor antisocial nuisances that most children confront adults with as a general part of living. In discussing the infant's being a nuisance, Winnicott makes reference to the baby who urinates on its mother's lap while feeding and the way, at a later stage, on waking (a moment of vulnerability and regression) children often wet the bed. The small ways in which the many minor nuisances of childhood pass, often unnoticed and unremarked, reflect both the everyday nature of these instances of 'reaching back' and the frequency of small environmental failures.

A friend of mine has a strong childhood memory (perhaps helped by this story having become something of a family fable) of a trip out with his father when he was a toddler. Upon returning home, his mother asked whether they had had a nice time, and my friend reportedly responded 'I was a ruddy nuisance'. The image still makes me chuckle, and I can hear his exasperated father telling him this. Given the time at which this happened (the mid-1960s) it would have been relatively unusual for a father to take his very small son out, so perhaps this was something of a memorable occasion in itself. It can be imagined that the small boy took the opportunity (unconsciously) to *disrupt, destroy, frighten, wear down, waste, wangle and appropriate* his father's time, energy and money. Perhaps he dawdled or repeatedly dropped his glove, demanded an ice cream, needed his nose wiped, wanted a toilet when they were furthest from toilets, kept asking 'why?' and 'what is …?'. Perhaps his shoelaces kept coming undone, he was too hot or his ears were cold, his jumper scratched or his socks fell down; history does not relate. But these are the endless irritations of being with a small child who walks too slowly, struggles to manage his being in unusual or unfamiliar circumstances and is not interested in what we had planned for them to be interested in. In school, the nuisance is the child who never has a pen or whose pencil always needs sharpening, who endlessly misplaces their book or 'loses' their coat because it has been hung in the wrong place, who always forgets to go to the toilet at playtime, who calls out without putting their hand up. All the small acts of carelessness, thoughtlessness and forgetfulness … the nuisances and minor irritations of the classroom are legion!

As difficulties escalate and develop beyond the immediate family, we begin to see children who find it difficult to respond to the small cures offered by their environments. In this way, defiance in school can snowball becoming increasingly difficult to manage. Once the school and defiant child become caught up in an escalating tit-for-tat one-way shouting match of action and reaction, the chances for understanding and repair diminish. If the moment is missed, or if the S.O.S. is misunderstood or ignored and the moment of hopefulness is lost, then the gap widens a little more as a new insult has been added to the injury. Unfortunately, now as then:

> Time after time one sees the moment of hope wasted, or withered, because of mismanagement or intolerance. This is another way of saying that the treatment of the antisocial tendency is not psychoanalysis but management, a going to meet and match the moment of hope.
>
> *(1956, p.106)*

In the hopeful moment the child has recognised something that seems trustworthy – perhaps some attitude of their new teacher suggests that *this time* actions will match words. In this moment they feel an urge that Winnicott called 'object seeking', a desire to poke and prod the environment to test and check their perception: Is this person really as reliable as they want me to believe? And so small acts of nuisance begin to creep in to test the relationship. So, a new class or class teacher may see the resurgence of difficult behaviours that the last class teacher thought she had 'sorted out'. However annoying this might be, it is worth considering whether this might be a positive move, another moment of hope. What if the first teacher had not read the acts of defiance as an S.O.S., but had instead reinforced compliance? If she had overridden a child's efforts to sound out her apparent reliability in such a way that they retreated behind their False Self and compliant behaviours? A child's loss of hope and simultaneous caving in to compliance may have driven the hurt back under the protection of a False Self. A new teacher may then provide a new opportunity to experience, notice and learn and so the defiance resurfaces to provoke new opportunities, a hopeful act. If we accept this reading, then it is possible that the child has not suddenly 'forgotten how to behave' with their new teacher but is asking (again) for an opportunity to go back to a place before the original loss occurred. The fact that their need to ask again has not (yet) resulted in despair may be a minor miracle rather than another annoyance!

Destruction

There are many literal and metaphorical forms of antisocial destructiveness: from bed wetting and messiness to the destruction of a working atmosphere in a classroom and the outright breaking of equipment, to scribbling in books and the vandalism of tagging on walls and windows, to the tearing or ripping of displays, and the cutting of self-harm. All such behaviours can best be understood as a claim to an environmental provision that was lost: a claim to have access to a personal response, to a reliable presence. Most particularly, Winnicott suggests, destructiveness is an unconscious search for the mother's body and her arms, the first environment that contained its movement, its hunger, its despair and its delight.

> ... the child is seeking that amount of environmental stability that will stand the strain resulting from impulsive behaviour. This is a search for an environmental provision that has been lost, a human attitude which, because it can be relied on, gives freedom to the individual to move and act and to get excited.
>
> It is particularly because of [this] trend that the child provokes total environmental reactions, as if seeking an ever-widening frame, a circle which had as its first example the mother's arms or the mother's body. One can discern a series – the mother's body, the mother's arms, the parental relationship, the home, the family including cousins and near relations, the school, the locality with its police stations, the country with its laws.
>
> *(1956, p.107)*

So, the destructive testing of the environment, which is often experienced as an affront to the institution, is a seeking after stability and boundaries. While this may become a demand for rules and strictness, the blanket imposition of general rules in advance will lack the personal qualities required of such communications and potentially lead to an escalation of defiance or a growing inability to contain the self without strict rules. Yet in violence we can see 'an attempt to reactivate firm holding ... without such a firm holding a child is unable to discover impulse, and only impulse that is found and assimilated is available for self-control and socialization' (1964, p.135).

Destruction can be thought of then as the desire to relocate boundaries. The explosion of aggression marked by the destructive act unconsciously re-evokes the moment at which the fracture in the framework occurred. It is a reaching back to the moment just before the framework within which life felt safe was breached. The desire (need) for firm boundaries can be one reason some children appear to do so well in very authoritarian contexts, and the recent militarisation of school life is one policy response to perceptions of increasingly unruly, violent youth (Chadderton, 2014). The provision of inflexible, zero-tolerance, highly authoritarian learning environments pre-emptively assumes that the institution can know that the children coming in will be difficult/defiant, and that they will respond well to their rules and punishments. As a form of communication, however, it fails to listen and respond to anything individual children might want to say – it is effectively a 'one-way' street. Even where the environment might be the kind of thing that would be wanted, it has not yet been 'asked for', so it is impersonal and may not prove to be acceptable.

Stealing and lying: object seeking

Like destructiveness, theft in schools can be experienced by the institution as a ruthless assault on its being: an attack on its values and a denial or repudiation of its worth and goodness as an institution. Theft (like destruction) provokes the desire for revenge. To manage the extremes of what we might want to enact by way of revenge we have laws and institutional punishments. But, what is the theft aimed at, and how best might we understand it?

> When a child steals sugar he is looking for the good mother, his own, from whom he has a right to take what sweetness is there. In fact, this sweetness is his, for he invented her and her sweetness out of his own capacity to love, out of his own primary creativity, whatever that is. He is also looking for his father, one might say, who will protect mother from his attacks on her, attacks made in the exercise of primitive love. When a child steals outside his own home he is still looking for his mother, but he is seeking with more sense of frustration, and increasingly needing to find at the same time the paternal authority that can and will put a limit to the actual effect of his impulsive behaviour, and to the acting out of the ideas that come to him when he is in a state of excitement.
>
> *(Winnicott, 1946, p.100)*

Importantly, the mother being looked for here is the object-mother (not a whole, real person), a fantasy created out of need in the earliest days of life. Later, when the child 'reaches back' to this time of care before environmental failure he looks to steal comfort. Importantly for Winnicott, comfort is an infant's right under the conditions of primary maternal preoccupation, it is provided without thought by the 'good enough' mother. No wonder chocolate is so comforting, melting sweetly and effortlessly in our mouths, providing an unconscious link to times of sweet dependency met. Yet Winnicott is clear here that the thief also experiences unconscious concern: concern that thefts from their mother will damage her. So, a father (in the form of the rules and laws that protect the mother), is also simultaneously wanted. There is a desire to devour the sweetness but also a desire for someone to witness the need and the theft, and to protect that which is stolen from and to help regulate unruly appetites.

It is common for thefts to occur in schools, and the response is often to ban the bringing in of items of value. This is one reason mobile phones have been forbidden in many schools and the bringing in of toys and books may also be discouraged. Yet perhaps these prohibitions just push the stealing elsewhere (to pencil cases, bags, dinner money, and the school's or teacher's property or off-site). And, do they perhaps also miss the point?

> ... the mother in her adaptation to the small child's needs enables the child creatively to find objects. She initiates the creative use of the world, when this fails, the child has lost contact with objects, has lost the capacity creatively to find anything. At the moment of hope the child reaches out and steals an object. This is a compulsive act and the child does not know why he or she does it. Often the child feels mad because of having a compulsion to do something without knowing why. Naturally the fountain pen stolen from Woolworths is not satisfactory: it is not the object that was being sought, and in any case *the child is looking for the capacity to find*, not for an object.
>
> *(Winnicott, 1967 cited in Abram, 2007, p.63)*

Amongst older students, thefts are more typically those of ideas, and so plagiarism can become a problem in the university. In school, the issue is generally more one of copying or cheating, stealing answers. The links here are to the loss of a capacity to create an idea or to have one's own thoughts. Of course, the stolen ideas are not satisfactory; someone else's ideas are not what I might want to say, but if I have lost my connection to my own creative impulse I no longer know what I want to say; the theft is a way of highlighting my loss. It is the capacity to think that is being re-sought, so punishing a student for being unable to think and asking for help seems perverse. Of course, copying and plagiarism, like all thefts, are not good ways to ask, but in a regressed state, there may be no other way. Even knowledge of what has happened may be lost.

On pulling one's punches

I have struggled with writing this chapter and, somewhat late in the day, I have realised that the social prohibition against aggression – or even the appearance of aggression – extends to writers and indeed to myself. There are things I seem not to be saying here, and the examples I have used have been relatively 'quiet'. This seems strange and worth thinking about rather than just quietly rectifying.

Being confronted with defiance, non-compliance or nuisance can be not just 'a bit annoying' but entirely consuming, enraging and thought destroying. I want therefore to return to a data extract I analysed extensively elsewhere (Bibby, 2015), not to repeat that analysis but to make a different point. The data was collected as part of an auto-ethnographic study by Laura Teague, and I remain grateful to her for her permission to reuse it:

> ***Daisy and Mr Baxter***
> I collect the class [of 6- to 7-year-olds] from assembly and notice Daisy is stood up along with Jay. I take the rest of the children back to the class and see them out to play. I then return to the hall. Jay is apologising to Mr Baxter and he is then sent out to play. Daisy refuses to apologise. She is staring at the floor and sucking her fingers. Mr Baxter walks over to her, tells her to stop behaving like a baby, and pulls her fingers out of her mouth. He tilts her head up to make her look at him. He then shouts at her, telling her what a rude, horrible child she is. He asks her repeatedly to apologise and she refuses (by not saying anything and looking away). He tells her he can't be bothered with her and that she needs to see him at lunchtime. He marches out of the hall. Daisy continues to stand still, staring into space.
>
> *(Field notes Autumn 2011, Teague, 2015)*

We have no way of knowing what it was that precipitated Mr Baxter's rage, but his fury is entirely apparent. Jay has managed to apologise and has escaped leaving Daisy to face his wrath and perhaps more unable than unwilling to respond. The aggression in this apoplectic, visceral reaction to apparent non-compliance is startling. I would go so far as to say it is frightening. I am fairly confident that it frightened Daisy, and it may indeed also have frightened Mr Baxter to find himself so out of his own control. It would be easy and perhaps comforting to dismiss Mr Baxter as a 'bad' teacher; as I am a 'good' one, I know I myself would never behave in such a crass manner. Except I have. I know this can come out of me with the right wrong trigger. There is absolutely no doubt that Mr Baxter's outburst is inappropriate. His aggression is overwhelming for the small child who really cannot be expected to make sense of this. But how best can we think about the adult's aggression? What is *he* reaching back for? Who would he want to stand with him to enable him to come back from this no-thought to thought? What fracture has breached his ability to process his affective responses?

I was struck when I remembered this data by the extent to which, in this chapter and perhaps elsewhere, I too have 'pulled my punches'. I was struck too by the metaphor I had used: to pull punches, to soften blows, to lessen the force of one's argument. And twice 'struck' – hit – by my (in)actions. Writing, like much academic work, is full of places to hide unseemly affects (so much easier if they only belong with youngsters!) not least the use of the passive voice: Has 'the chapter' pulled its punches or have I? Where is *my* aggression? Perhaps in my raging desire to shake the teaching profession to its complacent foundations and to demand that we all take greater responsibility for what happens in schools! To press faces to windows and force a witnessing. How can this be allowed to happen? And there is anger directed towards myself: shame and depression because I don't have – can't have – answers. Because, as part of the teaching profession I am and have been complicit in acts of failing to see, recognise and respond to clumsy requests for help. Mr Baxter's facilitating environment was the school he worked in, and there are messages in Winnicott's work for managers who might also (fail to be) good enough, who fail to see (or see and fail to act with) others in a state of need and dependency. We cannot all be adult all of the time, and the times when this infuriates me the most are the times when I am perhaps least able to do anything constructive. I return to these difficulties in the final chapter.

For now, though, Winnicott paints a difficult picture of antisocial behaviour:

> the antisocial set-up is on the whole a complex defence against delusions of persecution, hallucinations, and a going to pieces without hope of recovery. I am speaking of something which is worse than unhappiness, and on the whole one would feel pleased when an antisocial child, or adult for that matter, reaches the stages of unhappiness. At this point there is hope and there is also a possibility of providing help. The hardened antisocial has to defend himself even from hope because by experience he knows that the pain of losing hope again is unbearable.
>
> *(1961, p.176)*

What is it like for teachers to be faced with antisocial behaviour? Can we be surprised that levels of depression and attrition are high in the profession (NUT, 2017)? How are they supposed to survive relatively benign attacks? And what about more serious, perhaps literal physical attacks? How can teachers respond thoughtfully when their first reaction may be to retaliate? And how about teachers who want to think but who work in institutions where the only mandated response is punitive? What are the options available to them?

The final two chapters of this book consider what it means for a teacher to survive the aggression of nuisance, destruction, theft and lying and what it means for institutions to take on board these messages and to provide good enough working environments for pedagogic relationships and learning to flourish in. How might we survive those who try constantly to disrupt, to destroy, to frighten, to wear down, to waste, to wangle and to appropriate? How can we learn to recognise and respond to our own efforts to disrupt, to destroy, to frighten, to wear down, to waste, to wangle and to appropriate? What will it take to manage to maintain enough control to not retaliate and to think? And how can institutions enable the active not doing, the balancing acts required for non-retaliatory, non-punitive teaching in an aggressive and unforgiving policy environment?

References

Abram, J. 2007. *The language of Winnicott: a dictionary of Winnicott's use of words* (2nd edition). London: Karnac.

Bibby, T. 2011. *Education – an 'impossible profession'? Psychoanalytic explorations of learning and classrooms*. London: Routledge.

Bibby, T. 2015. Thinking and learning? On (not) dreaming in the classroom. *Psychoanalysis, Culture and Society*, 20(1), 49–66.

Chadderton, C. 2014. The militarisation of English schools: troops to teaching and the implications for Initial Teacher Education and race equality. *Race Ethnicity and Education*, 17(3), 407–428.

Golding, W. 1954. *The lord of the flies*. London: Faber and Faber.

NUT (National Union of Teachers). 2017. Teacher recruitment and retention. Published online www.teachers.org.uk/edufacts/teacher-recruitment-and-retention (accessed 1/3/17).

OfSTED. 2014. Low-level disruption in classrooms: below the radar. www.gov.uk/government/publications/below-the-radar-low-level-disruption-in-the-countrys-classrooms (accessed 11/3/17).

Teague, L. 2015. *Pedagogy, subjectivity and counter politics in the primary school: an ethnography of a teacher's practices*. Unpublished PhD Thesis. Institute of Education, London.

The Guardian. 2014. www.theguardian.com/football/2014/jun/24/luis-suarez-bite-uruguay-ban-world-cup (accessed 4/3/17).

Winnicott, D.W. 1946. Some psychological aspects of juvenile delinquency. In *Deprivation and delinquency*, edited by C. Winnicott, R. Shepherd and M. Davis (2012 edition, pp.97–102). London: Routledge.

Winnicott, D.W. 1956. The antisocial tendency. In *Deprivation and delinquency*, edited by C. Winnicott, R. Shepherd and M. Davis (2012 edition, pp.103–112). London: Routledge.

Winnicott, D. 1960. Aggression, guilt and reparation. In *Depravation and delinquency*, edited by C. Winnicott, R. Shepherd and M. Davis (2012 edition, pp.116–123). London: Routledge.

Winnicott, D.W. 1961. Psychoanalysis and science: friends or relations? In *Home is where we start from*, edited by C. Winnicott, R. Shepherd and M. Davis (1986 edition, pp.21–38). London: Penguin Books.

Winnicott, D.W. 1963a. The development of the capacity for concern. In *Deprivation and delinquency*, edited by C. Winnicott, R. Shepherd and M. Davis (2012 edition, pp.86–90). London: Routledge.

Winnicott, D.W. 1963b. Morals and education. In *The maturational processes and the facilitating environment: studies in the theory of emotional development*, edited by D.W. Winnicott (1965, 2007 edition, pp.93–105). London: Karnac.

Winnicott, D.W. 1964. Youth will not sleep. In *Deprivation and delinquency*, edited by C. Winnicott, R. Shepherd and M. Davis (2012 edition, pp.134–135). London: Routledge.

Winnicott, D.W. 1966. The absence of a sense of guilt. In *Deprivation and delinquency*, edited by C. Winnicott, R. Shepherd and M. Davis (2012 edition, pp.91–96). London: Routledge.

PART III

Working it through

Chapters 9 and 10 focus on what it means to be a teacher in the face of compliance, nuisance and defiance. How can teachers work productively with aggression? This section also turns the tables on the 'adults' to ask whether only students or children are compliant, or aggressive and defiant? What role can and do institutions play in the establishment or destruction of reliability and trust?

9

HATE AND BEING A GOOD ENOUGH TEACHER

The chapters so far have privileged the position of the one learning or developing, referencing the role of the (m)other or facilitating environment without troubling to give that experience much consideration. This chapter begins to redress the imbalance. While there are undoubted challenges to providing good-enough learning environments, we need to resist the temptation to see this as a task of bestowing goods upon children that only adults can perform. As Thomas Ogden (2009, p.100) reminds us, 'every stage of development involves facing emotional experiences for which one feels unprepared'. As the example of Mr Baxter (Chapter 8) reminds us, we need to remember that, at different times, we can all be vulnerable, we can all be the one learning, developing and needing support through the process.

The facilitating end of a facilitating environment

For Winnicott, central to coming into creative being is a child's (our) capacity to make use of objects. As part of facilitating someone else's becoming, an important function of the (m)other is to present objects (herself, toys, ideas etc.) to a child/learner in such a way that they feel they have created or found them for themselves. Once a (m)other has allowed an infant to develop the illusion that they have omnipotently created the world, she needs to wean them off their utter dependency by gradually disillusioning them: they do not control their world. Importantly, she must also survive the aggression and destruction that run alongside processes of disillusion, a child's frustrated fury at their loss of magical control. In Chapter 5, the continuing importance of a feeling of 'discovery' was discussed in relation to play and creativity. The value to students of the feeling that they have 'discovered' ideas for themselves is instinctively recognised by many teachers who will allow such moments of 'discovery' even if the novelty of a creative discovery is 'only' personal. In this a child uses the (m)other to enable them to grow and learn. This use is a tacitly licenced 'taking advantage of', a use Winnicott suggests the infant has the 'right' to expect. This chapter takes the adult's perspective to consider what it means to be used in this way, why this matters and the difficulties of surviving use.

For myself, as an educator, Winnicott's paper on the use of an object (1971) provides a powerful metaphor for what it means to learn. He identifies the hard bit of the process as the movement *from* object-relating *to* object-use suggesting that this movement 'is the most difficult thing, perhaps in human development' (p.120). Here we might draw a parallel with the hardest part of learning: making a move from thinking you know about something – a kind of knowing that we can be deeply attached to – through realising perhaps you don't, and being prepared and able to make the effort needed to adjust your worldview and develop and take account of new knowledge. We must first admit ignorance or insufficient understanding, letting go of our image of ourselves as knowers, and then put in the effort to learn. As teachers, we deal all the time with students who seem to prefer to write themselves off as forever unable, for example, to understand maths, speak a foreign language, write coherently or manage relationships rather than expose themselves to the risk of failure that accompanies learning. And as teachers, we may also find it hard to accept our own ignorance; knowledge can be such a familiar defence. It can be hard to allow the possibility that a student's demeanour in the classroom or their past performance in our subject might not tell us everything we would like it to. How can we really be sure that apparent failure has to do with the student and their work and not us and our teaching? In an ironic twist, there is also the double refusal of knowledge in the position of the teacher who (for example) teaches mathematics but claims not to understand it or who teaches art but claims not to be able to draw.

Winnicott spent a lot of time considering the implications of object use for psychoanalysts but suggested that it was something teachers should be able to take for granted. It seems that if we accept this it can leave us, as teachers, stuck with our own omnipotent fantasies and unable to think about the children (or colleagues) for whom object use becomes difficult or impossible, to stand with learners or colleagues for whom a reliance on defensive strategies seems to be the only possibility. I am sure Winnicott is right and we do tend to take object use for granted, but unlike him, I think it is helpful to question the assumption. The task here is not to think 'how can teachers behave as analysts?' (that way disaster lies!); it is to use his writing as an object with which to rethink learning and the pedagogic relationship, to see if the theory can withstand the violence of recontextualisation.

In his consideration of object use, Winnicott (1971) identifies a sequence that leads up to this capacity: '(1) Subject *relates* to object. (2) Object is in process of being found instead of placed by the subject in the world. (3) Subject *destroys* object. (4) Object survives destruction. (5) Subject can *use* object' (p.126 emphasis in original). Winnicott considers the fact that psychoanalysts are often quite happy to talk about object-relating, that first part of the process enumerated above, suggesting perhaps that this enables them to discount their own part in the story of an analysis. In an uncompromising move, he points out that 'in examining usage there is no escape; the analyst must take into account the nature of the object, not as a projection, but as a thing in itself' (p.118). That is, the analyst needs to consider his own part in the client's analysis. This means the analyst must not imagine that what the client is going through or telling him has nothing to do with him; the analyst is not a catalyst or a 'fly on the wall' but a part of the process. In exactly the same way, the teacher is an integral part of the students' learning. The way teachers respond to children and the way they present ideas are key to the ways these ideas come to be known and the ways students can come to see themselves as knowers (or not) (Bibby, 2009). Winnicott demands that we accept the full implications of the relationality of experience: of analysis and of teaching. This means rejecting the analyst's and the teacher's desire to be able to take a 'god's eye-view', that is the desire to be able to stand apart as an expert or a 'grown-up' and to observe and interact with clients/students *as if* the effects of that interaction could be known in advance and affect only them leaving us untouched as knowers. To put it more directly: There is a demand for an acceptance of mutual complicity in, and mutual responsibility for, learning, teaching, and becoming knowers.

Finding and making an object to use

To recap the argument encapsulated in the sequence of events listed above and discussed in previous chapters: Initially, there exists a subjective relationship to the object that is omnipotently or magically 'owned' and controlled; the object is found because it is needed. A baby 'conjures' a breast out of hunger. In this moment, subject (baby) and object (breast) are merged (there is no 'not-me') and indistinguishable to the subject although this state of affairs is unstable and subject to change. But how can we think about this subjective object beyond trying to imagine life for an infant? One suggestion is that subjective objects are those that populate our unconscious and our fantasies. Of course, the unconscious is unknowable, but our fantasies are made partially visible in the transitional space of play and culture, and so we might usefully look to films and novels.

The subjective object: the teacher of dreams

Even before starting school, stories from parents and older siblings provide images about what a child might expect from a teacher, school and classroom. Indeed, throughout our lives, we are met with images of schools and teachers that real schools and teachers might want to embrace but may also feel constrained by. Idealised schools and teachers in films such as 'Goodbye, Mr Chips' (Wood, 1939), 'To Sir, With Love' (Clavell, 1967), 'Stand and Deliver' (Menendez and Musca, 1988), or 'The Freedom Writers' (LaGravenese, 2007) portray the promise of pedagogic or teacher love triumphing over adversity. In such films a caring, often maverick, teacher puts in a Herculean effort and wins over disaffected students freeing them from fates that are presumed to be 'dead-end' or hopeless. The powerful fantasy of teacher as saviour (Moore, 2004) is one embraced by many early stage teachers; the omnipotence and narcissism inherent in the fantasy (by my efforts *I alone* can save these children) is either celebrated, or it passes unremarked. In this way, films such as these keep alive the fantasy that teachers alone transform lives at once displacing and devaluing other influences (peers, parents, families, other members of the school community) and insisting that real teachers and real schools in real communities identify with these impossible, magical desires.

Idealisations of the saviour or hero teacher can also be read as aggressive and destructive attacks on real teachers and real schools. It is not unusual, even for university lecturers, to find students who seem to believe that they live in their offices so that turning off email or delaying a response to a query is seen as a personal slight. Such students deny the reality that lecturers also have multiple demands on their time; they too have complex professional lives and a right to a private life including holidays. Students (of any age) can display real surprise at meeting a teacher in 'real life' doing mundane chores like picking up groceries in a supermarket: "What, you buy food?", "And wine?" There is an aggressive envy in the assumption that teachers or lecturers can afford to buy whatever they want, can write without effort, read without difficulty. On the whole, at an unconscious level at least, students often expect real teachers, like the teachers in books and films, to be omniscient and endlessly caring, patient and creative: everyone a Miss Honey, no Miss Trunchbulls (Dahl, 1988). It is a rare film that deals with the disappointments and misjudgements that are part of the reality of classroom life (although see, for example, 'The Class' (Cantet, 2008)). The degrees of disappointment (anger, frustration and outrage) evidenced when teachers let students down by dint of their human fallibility can take us aback. The recent case of a student suing his university over his failure to get a first class degree is only a very extreme example of a more general trend towards students placing the whole responsibility for their learning on their apparently inadequate teachers (Taylor and Sandeman, 2016). Even students who are also teachers can fall prey to idealisations of their own work. The issue of institutions and institutional defences is taken up in more detail in the final chapter.

Children's curiosity about teachers is generally hidden, but in the Economic and Social Research Council (ESRC) learner-identities research project one group of child-researchers chose to interview their teachers (also briefly discussed in Chapter 7). The experience of facilitating this work was interesting. In discussing interview topics, questions and ethical considerations – especially the need for confidentiality – the children (aged 10 years) showed a high degree of sensitivity and thoughtfulness. The interview schedule (which was shared with the teachers in advance) showed their curiosity about their teachers' professional and personal lives: What did they do all day? Why had they chosen to be teachers? What did they like to do in their spare time? Had their personalities changed when they became teachers (the children wondered if they had become more bossy)? And, did they like teaching some subjects more than others (just as the children enjoyed learning some subjects more than others)?

They spent a long time deciding which teachers they wanted to interview and who would be the best person to conduct particular interviews. The ways in which different teachers responded to the interviews varied hugely, with some clearly being relatively open and honest and responding as rounded individuals and others providing highly managed and restricted teacher-only answers. At first, the children seemed unaware of the variations, but once they started to analyse the transcripts they became upset and angry: Could it really be that teachers only like teaching maths and literacy? Did they really only eat and plan lessons in their spare time? And why did the two teachers who were married to each other not mention the fact? The more they considered many of the answers the more disappointed the child-researchers became. As a qualitative researcher I am well used to the idea of managed responses and respondents providing answers they think are wanted. We discussed this, and the child-researchers acknowledged that they too do such work when they are answering questions about their lives, but this did nothing to diminish the sense of betrayal they seemed to feel. Having been offered a greater presence and an existence beyond idealisation and fantasy, many of the teachers refused. This restriction that some of the teachers used seems problematic to me; it is not that I would want children to know everything about their teachers (even if such were possible) but existing as rounded individuals with complex feelings and a mutual investment in the classroom and learning environment has the potential to offer a wider range of objects for children to work with, a richer range of ways of coming to know.

If students are to move beyond idealisations and unrealistic fantasies about teachers and, by extension, themselves as learners, they will need to be able to 'destroy' their teachers – place them out in the real world and insist that they demonstrate their (our) common humanity – *and* their teachers will need to survive those attacks. In the example of the children's research, some teachers refused the offer – their interviews had a retaliatory quality; they were brusque, evasive and disingenuous. They refused to be more than the two-dimensional storybook teachers they were comfortable being. Yet it is only when teachers take on a real existence and are allowed their associated human frailties – including fallibility, intolerance and the ebbs and flows of interest and energy – that students can engage fully (and passionately) with knowledge, learning and classroom experiences.

Aggression and destruction in the making of the object

Whether it takes the form of ruthlessness, and necessary destruction, anger, frustration, or 'muscle eroticism', aggression hurts or damages the object and generates a reaction, perhaps a noise (ouch!) or a flinching. In this way, a subject/baby may begin to experiment with generating reactions and noticing what these are.

It is through such moments of action and reaction that a not-me quality begins to emerge, and objects are allowed an objective existence in the world.

In fantasy, the subject destroys the object. This idea of destruction seems rather violent or extreme but Winnicott is clear:

> The word 'destruction' is needed, not only because of the baby's impulse to destroy, but because of the object's liability not to survive, which also means to suffer a change in quality, in attitude.
>
> *(1971, p.124)*

It is through destruction that the object subjectively perceived (omnipotently created) is put beyond self and becomes available for use. The teachers who were able to allow the children to see them as people survived the questions – all questions that demand an answer are a form of attack. As we move beyond babyhood and infancy, the way in which we make the separation changes to some extent, but destruction remains a central part of the process of locating the object in the world and acknowledging the object's separate existence, life, interests and needs. The teacher who told them that he liked to watch football and probably spent rather too much time and money travelling to matches to support his team took on a new aura; he was a teacher and more. He was no longer exclusively there to serve their needs; they had new topics for conversation in the playground when he was on duty, and the new vibrancy in their relationship had the potential to carry across to lessons. It is only through allowing the world out there its separate existence that the movement back and forth between subjective knowing and seeing reality can be made and creative living be enjoyed.

What has to survive? And what does survival look like?

For Winnicott, survival means remaining reliable (not suffering a change in quality or attitude) and not retaliating. In failing to survive an object might cease to exist; it might either literally disappear or change beyond recognition because its quality or attitude is transformed. Or it might respond with aggression of its own, an act of retaliation, causing the one testing reliability to retreat in fear or escalate their own testing and destructive behaviours. Further, Winnicott indicates that it is the whole context within which the destruction takes place that has to survive:

> If it is in an analysis that these matters are taking place then the analyst, the analytic technique, and the setting all come in as surviving or not surviving the patient's destructive attacks.
>
> *(1971, p.122)*

At issue then is both who and what is being destroyed, and who and what needs to survive: The teacher, her pedagogy, and the subject being studied all need to survive their destruction as do the classroom and school. While finding examples of destruction and failure to survive is relatively straightforward, examples of survival may be harder to locate (although see perhaps Bibby, 2015).

Nuisance and other antisocial actions poke and prod at the facilitating environment – the (m)other, the subject matter, the classroom, the school – and (unconsciously) seek to provoke the holding environment into providing the good enough care that is felt to have been (even temporarily) lost. As discussed in Chapter 8, nuisance tests the sincerity, limits and constancy of reliability. Here, and in the toleration of defiance, lie the most overt challenges to teachers and schools; (the challenges of compliance are more hidden). Disrupting, destroying, frightening, wearing down, wasting, wangling and appropriating are all acts of aggression aimed at destruction. They have the potential to destroy (to varying degrees) relationships, which is why they are for Winnicott all signals of an antisocial tendency.

Any level of verbal or physical aggression demonstrates a desire to destroy. Acts of destruction focussed towards education are not necessarily out-of-control physical attacks on teachers (although they might be). Concrete thinking that only recognises overt and extreme violence as 'antisocial' is a convenient way of not considering the aggression inherent in more coded forms of attack and the ways in which teachers as well as children can be aggressive in the classroom. As well as anger that lashes out with fists or feet, biting, cutting and witheringly sarcastic remarks, pointed or incisive comments made in frustration or from hubris, dejected fatalism and idealisation are all forms of aggression. Mundane varieties of destruction were described by Winnicott in a talk he gave in the 1950s to psychology and social work students. Adam Phillips describes the two stages Winnicott suggested students go through when learning psychology:

> The first stage of learning can be called, in Freud's language, identification; the student becomes like somebody who knows these things. In Winnicott's language it would be called compliance: the child fits in with the teacher's need to teach, and, by implication, with the culture's demand that these are the things one learns, and in this way one learns them. … At this stage competence is a kind of imitation; the context defines the project.
>
> In the second stage something akin to what Freud calls dream-work, and Winnicott differently calls object-usage, goes on. Each student, consciously and unconsciously, makes something of their own out if it all; finds the bits they can use, the bits that make personal sense. The teaching is radically recontextualised according to personal need. … [T]he student attacks the subject with questions and criticisms, and finds what is left after the assault; whatever survives this critique – this hatred – is felt to be of real substance (resilient, incorruptible, worth banking on). In this way the student makes (or fails to make) the subject true for her.
>
> *(Phillips, 1998, pp.55–56)*

To put this back into the language used throughout this book: In the first, compliant, stage of learning and of knowing the subject remains inert. Knowledge may be swallowed to please the teacher or out of some other sense of duty, but it seems useless and irrelevant as no connection has yet been made between the subject matter and the learner's life and interests. In the second example, however, the creative movement between subjective and objective knowing enables psychology to 'come alive' for the student. The affects and the facts can co-exist and be moved between; neither the facts nor the experience of learning then dominates, and the student can use each to think of and understand the other. The aggression in the student's attacks and the subject's subsequent survival mean that she is able to use psychology as a way to understand her world and the issues that interest her. This second, alive, creative and satisfying way of knowing stands in contrast to the first.

One problem with Winnicott's two-stage example is that it casts as inevitable an initial stage of compliance: 'the child fits in with the teacher's need to teach, and, by implication, with the culture's demand that these are the things one learns, and in this way one learns them. [...] At this stage competence is a kind of imitation'. The slip in language between child and student, and talk of stages, can signal a danger that we succumb to an unconscious adult desire for linear growth and for an eventual maturity beyond the need to learn. I do not believe that Winnicott is attributing age to these two ways of knowing; development is often stuttering and recursive, its achievement can never be certain or taken for granted. That fantasies of adult capacity with their associated assumption of juvenile incapacity can so quickly seep through linguistic cracks provides an example of the power of the unconscious and a timely reminder about the complexity of the issues. Novice learners (at whatever level of education or stage of life) typically move between compliant acceptance of new ideas and destructive/creative use as they encounter greater levels of complexity within a topic and increased fluency with new ideas. Confronted with new ideas we can bite off more than we can chew, leave things to stew on the back burner, chew them over so we can take them in, digest them and make something new from them – either shit or muscle as seems possible or appropriate to us. Learning at any age will progress through and oscillate between these two stances if new knowledge is to be made.

This leaves open to consideration the dynamic of a teacher learning from experience in the classroom, a teacher whose subject is the learners in her class; mutual learning in a more reciprocal relation. In this case, where can a teacher's aggression be focussed? Can it be safe for vulnerable learners? These are important questions, perhaps especially for critical pedagogues. How can one balance being a person and being a teacher (a question the teachers interviewed by children were faced with), how can they present their subject in ways that both honour that subject and reveal its social power? These questions challenge us to think about ways to make objective and subjective knowing simultaneously available across the learning environment, to provide the possibility of the classroom or a lesson being a transitional object that can be played with creatively. Of course, questions are a form of attack, an outlet for aggression (have you noticed and wondered about my use of questions throughout this book?, she asked). But we need to remember, in the case of both learners and their teachers, that life continues beyond the hours of lessons. Thinking, dreaming and processing happen in the intense moment of a classroom exchange, but they continue in other places too. And of course teachers are a nuisance to their students and they *disrupt, destroy, frighten, wear down, waste, wangle, and appropriate* just as children do. Teachers do not think twice about disrupting conversations and play; destroying games; frightening with deadlines, tests and examinations; wearing down with repetition; wasting time demanding silence during dull administrative tasks; wangling compliance and appropriating ideas and examples of work. Is it really possible to think that teachers/adults are above (or beyond) the behaviours Winnicott highlights in children?

The survival of the object

Teachers are explicitly charged with the intellectual development of young people, and, by extension, are implicitly charged with overseeing their emotional development. Or at least, they are required to share time and space with those developing emotionally as well as intellectually. Teachers therefore need to be aware of their students' need to find and use them as people and as bearers of knowledge (including, but not only, curriculum knowledge). I suggest that one important implication of the reading of development through dependency offered by Winnicott and in this book is that we have an ethical responsibility to think about this use and to consider our responses.

It is only if the object does not retaliate, if it survives the destruction, that it can it be used. Importantly, this survival signifies both that 'the object is available for me to use' and 'I am now in a position and have the capacity to use the object'. I have felt able to destroy the object (to take a risk to learn), and it has been placed in the world beyond my omnipotent control; the object now has an independent existence and has become real (it is no longer only my fantasy), and it has become reliable (my fantasy is an unsafe place; things might not be reliable there). There might be relief at this movement: I no longer have to rely on myself; I can begin to trust outside myself and turn my gaze beyond its first focus. The example Winnicott uses to illustrate this stage is clinical:

> ... two babies are feeding at the breast; one is feeding on the self in the form of projections, and the other is feeding on (using) milk from a woman's breast [and is therefore able to 'get fat' and grow].
>
> *(1971, p.119)*

To re-contextualise this example: the baby feeding on milk has its equivalent in the child able to use the teacher and the classroom. Such a child is able to take in and use ideas, knowledge and a model of what a learner, or one who knows, might look like to 'get fat'. They can develop as one who knows and can respond to opportunities to learn. Children and students unable to develop themselves as knowers and learners can't make use of the teacher and classroom. They are left 'feeding on projections', perhaps their own sense of futility read in the teacher's presumed disinterest or a passive swallowing of what they are told without any engagement. A teacher's real or apparent failure to survive throws students back on themselves leaving them isolated and 'feeding on the self in the form of projections', a form of compliance and a False Self defence to a failed environment.

If nuisance and other antisocial acts are cries for help, S.O.S.s that ask for reparative work, how is a teacher to respond? If this is a request for maternal holding are we to regress with the children to a state of maternal preoccupation? What might the holding involved in teaching look like? Winnicott is very clear about a progression from the womb to arms, lap and beyond. In psychoanalysis, the couch provides the 'lap' and warmth, but how can a school or a teacher make appropriate sense of this? What does it mean to offer a regressed and angry 13-year-old a metaphorical 'pair of arms' or a 'lap'? I suggest that institutions provide safety through their relationships and the procedures, rules and boundaries that shape these. Many such boundaries are cultural, for example deference to age or status. But culture and tradition are still being learned, and therefore they too are going to be attacked and need to survive if they are to be accepted; this is the nature, particularly of adolescence. Ultimately, it is the quality of the relationships and the pedagogic care that matter in school; rules need to be experienced as personal. As with the care of the infant, the impersonal is anathema: generalised rules, whether these be school or cultural rules, have nothing to do with *me* and are therefore irrelevant, or worse, are an attack on my being. Survival means continuing to exist; it means existing for oneself and being alive so that you can be found again in the world and used; it means going-on-being. But what might this look like? Beyond the obvious physicality of the teacher, as Winnicott reminds us, the institution and the subjects being taught also need to survive attack and use.

Thinking through an attack on mathematics: 'Oh no, don't make me do Pythagoras!'

To think about attacks on the object teacher as holder of knowledge we might consider this familiar student (and adult) complaint. The attack in the rejecting demand 'why do I need to learn about Pythagoras?' suggests at least one observation, and two questions need to be considered. The observation is that the attack here is on the subject not the teacher; this particular attack is not personal, although it may feel it. To react *as if* it were personal is likely to confuse a complaining child and to be experienced as an attack *on them*. While answering attacks on our (curriculum) subjects may seem tedious and unnecessary, they are still attacks that need surviving. So a teacher needs to be able to stand with a learner and to observe and consider objects that she may be passionately attached to and tired of having to defend: aspects of her own subject. Meeting the 'Why do we have to do this?' with a demand for unthinking compliance is not survival; it is counter-attack (retaliation). An unwillingness to hear the question and to respond with a stock answer provide two examples of the kind of one-way communication Benjamin (2004) talks about; the exchange will be experienced by both the teacher and learner as persecutory; very wearing!

Of the potential questions raised for the teacher in this situation one might be: Why *do* students need to learn this apparently arcane piece of mathematics? One answer to this might be a nod towards its place on the curriculum and therefore its likely appearance on an examination paper. Such an answer suggests that Pythagoras' theorem matters because of the wider cultural importance (access to the next levels of education and employment) of achieving at least a passing grade in mathematics examinations (Stobart, Bibby and Goldstein, 2005; Brown, Brown and Bibby, 2008). Such a response relates to the first 'stage' of learning identified above; it demands compliance rather than that a connection to the topic be sought. Or it might be that, later, the rules and work done here will lead to learning about other aspects of mathematics; that is, it might have significance for the subject that is not yet visible. Again, this a request for compliance on the promise of gratification deferred.

With completely disinterested and hostile students, a further pedagogic question might be: What do they risk by not knowing this (about Pythagoras or whatever) at this point? Is this a battle worth fighting? Does it really need to be fought right now? As a teacher I may enjoy this area of maths, but can I let it go without students suffering unduly? When I think of the bigger picture of their maths learning, can this corner of the curriculum be relinquished? Questions such as the last ones are often unthinkable in schools. Pressure and surveillance from outside can be very great, but at this point the curriculum issue may be acting as an impingement and enabling the student to destroy the whole subject. It is possible that, if this area of maths fails to survive, necrosis will set in and the entire subject will be lost. Such choices and possibilities require careful and professional consideration; a 'You do it because if you don't, I get into trouble' answer is utterly inappropriate. It may be possible to find a workable solution that is not collusion but is a temporary, tactical withdrawal.

A slightly different question to ponder might be: Am I teaching this in such a way that it can be found to be relevant? Or, am I providing opportunities for the students to make personal relevance from this topic? This does not necessarily mean relevant to some unknown future. Much of the curriculum lacks the relatively easy direct relevance of reading, writing and basic calculation, but that does not mean the 'basics' are all that schools need to teach. Relevance can also be internal to the subject, and this can come to have meaning if other pleasures can be found. In this example, we might look beyond the typical practice exercises of the textbook to investigate what happens to the sum of the squares in the sides of non-right-angled triangles, or to explore the sum of the areas of other shapes on the sides of right-angled triangles. By providing more varied ways to engage with a topic we might help students learn to look within subjects for relevance and thereby provide opportunities for the subject to survive hatred and attack. Richer opportunities for engagement provide more opportunities for a student to experience and find value in the movement between reflection and experience that indicates a creative and therefore satisfying life within (in this case) mathematics.

Making these creative teaching moves potentially involves a risk for teachers in their relations with their institution. There is a possibility that an institution might read them as an attack on their procedures (their schemes of work and programmes of study), and consequently an institution's capacity to act as a facilitating environment might be called into question: Will the institution facilitate a teacher's professionalism or retaliate?

Being the object that does not survive

It is worth playing with the idea of the object-that-fails-to-survive to think about what it might look like and mean for a student. As discussed in previous chapters, small failures are inevitable, even required: We are fallible; to err is human.

Beyond the small, necessary failures, Winnicott sees problems begin to emerge if the object fails to survive; that is, if its response is retaliatory because of its non-acceptance or rejection of a challenge. The example Winnicott gave is the mother who responds with moral outrage to the baby that bites her nipple ('*You shouldn't hurt me!*' Or perhaps '*You shouldn't excite me*'). He goes on to emphasise that 'this language involving "the breast" [and "mother"] is jargon. The whole area of development and management is involved, in which adaptation is related to dependence' (1971, p.124). That is, all moments, places and phases of development – including, for our purposes, the places of education – are accompanied by relationships infused with dependency. Environments where dependency is in play need to be reliable and trustworthy if they are to be good enough. Qualities like reliability and trust have to be felt if they are to be believed and used. Jan Abram draws on her experience as a psychoanalyst to describe what happens when an adult has had repeated experiences of an environment (or environments) that have failed to survive their destructive attacks:

> Many patients in analysis are more familiar with a non-surviving object that persecutes and causes an incommensurate sense of guilt. They feel obliged to protect the analyst from their conviction that relationships are dangerous and simultaneously they are sure they will damage the analyst with their need. If this need is seen they feel the analyst will surely disappear; certainly not survive.
>
> *(2004, p.37)*

This sounds like a despairing situation, and indeed it might be: To be unable to trust help offered and to repeatedly sabotage even one's own efforts to move beyond stuckness is a terrible place to be. In a different context it might also be what is happening when a student or child ignores the 'come and see me' comment at the bottom of the homework covered in crosses or corrections: does my teacher really mean their offer of help? What is the point of my going to see her when I know that she can explain it a million times and I still won't understand? Last time I tried to get help I failed. I won't chance it again; I'll ignore the comment and she probably won't notice. And unfortunately, very often, she does not notice.

Winnicott (1971) is clear that attacks and use might be hard to take especially when they are expressed in ways that elicit reactions from us that trouble us. While we may not always be aware of our responses they can haunt and shame us (or they might if we had them pointed out to us): I didn't mean to get angry; I don't know why I responded like that; I just lost it when .... In his own context, Winnicott includes here, the analysts' use of an interpretation as a defence. We might extend a kind of defence to any adult use of knowledge, of experience, of relative maturity as a defence against adolescence or immaturity.

As teachers, we too need to think about the times when we use knowledge as a defence; times when we override a student's desire to know and their aggression in our haste to provide answers or suggest that 'you would have done better if you'd worked harder', or paid attention, or done your homework. Such examples of the rush to fix ignorance are often provoked by anxieties: those of students, teachers and institutions. For example, a common teacher response to approaching assessments, pressured by outside expectations, is to drill a whole class in aspects of the curriculum and exam technique regardless of individuals' desires or needs and the potential costs to present and future learning. The existence of the curriculum, of the linear ligature of chronological time (so different to subjective or unconscious time) and of metrics that measure and extrapolate teacher worthiness from student performance ensure the environment that teachers operate in paradoxically defends against the uncertainties of knowledge and knowing while failing to respond to other professional needs and desires.

An internal object that survives

During the process of aggressive attack and destruction, an object may accept or react negatively to the (real or imagined) pain of the (literal or metaphorical) flailing around and either accept (continue) or reject (retaliate) their destroyed and discarded status. It is through repeated experiences of objects surviving their ruthless destruction that a surviving object may be internalised. That is, as well as having reliable objects 'out there', we may also come to have some of them 'inside'. Having access to our own 'object that survives' does not signal an end to the need for external objects we can count on, but it can provide us with some access to our own desire and mind, some resilience:

> ... ruthlessness in maturity means that the individual is able to take responsibility for her own feelings and is able to distinguish between the Me and the Not-me world. The consequence is that the subject is able to say 'no' when she feels pressure from the other to say 'yes'. This is the mark of integrity and the capacity to know one's Self.
>
> *(Abram, 2004, p.37)*

An internal 'object that survives' may therefore provide us with some recognition of our own desires and agency (always limited by the ultimate unknowability of the unconscious) and provide us with resources to engage creatively in the transitional spaces of culture. The process of coming to know the self in a reliable way (of developing an 'internal object that survives') is, Abram (2004) suggests, a task that is ongoing throughout childhood. It may reach some fruition at the end of adolescence, but this achievement is by no means certain and never final. There appear to be two periods when activity with this aim has peaks. The 'first two years of life and adolescence will', she suggests, 'be the most intense time for the subject to test the environment's capacity to survive' (p.38), a fact that has implications for those teaching adolescents and others (see also Britzman, 2012).

Being a teacher

It is uncomfortable to think of (aspects of) oneself as someone else's object. It is also difficult to accept that one's automatic reactions to challenge might be thought of as 'a failure to survive' when it feels as if they are the only way to survive in the classroom! It seems to be a strange reversal of everything we tell ourselves to accept that our admonitions or even our turning away might be received so negatively and have such potentially hurtful and damaging consequences for students and their learning. As a way of making this more directly applicable, I will again follow Winnicott as he turns to hate and discusses the desire for revenge.

To be reliable as a teacher I must be allowed (and allow myself) to exist in the world. I need to be experienced as trustworthy and provide space in my mind for two-way communication to develop, for the student to feel that they exist and matter to me. I need to provide my students with opportunities to engage with the ideas they are ready to engage with by presenting them in a way they can recognise and move on from. I need to value their contributions even if I then have to help them develop these further. I need to respond to their communications, and I need to hold at bay the impingements that could crowd the space they need to grow into and become in. All these things that I need to do and be as a teacher will be repeatedly pushed and tested to the limits (and beyond) before they are trusted. As a teacher I need to survive all these tests because on this survival hangs a child's/student's ability to trust in and make use of the learning being offered. This is a big ask, especially in the current climate when teachers are expected to know the solutions before they have understood the problem and to pre-emptively smooth the path to knowledge and academic success. Both the climate of the schools and the question of who will look after the teacher are explored further in the final chapter. In the meantime, why would anyone subject themselves to such a demanding and potentially demeaning profession?

> ... after each phase [of destructiveness and transference] there comes reward in terms of love, reinforced by the fact of the backcloth of unconscious destruction.
>
> *(Winnicott, 1971, p.124)*

Winnicott's suggestion is that the very difficulty of the task makes the reward, the love, sweeter. But the love can feel like a long time coming and seem like thin gruel. How are members of a caring profession to endlessly love their charges? Winnicott would suggest that they cannot.

Love and hate in the classroom

In real life there is never only love; 'simple', 'uncomplicated' love is the stuff of idealisation and fairy tales. In the face of the endless irritations and nuisance generated by 'low level disruptions', let alone the full-blown acts of defiance, is it possible to think of and use the hate evoked? Winnicott wrote about this in relation to the analyst's experience of hate engendered by his work with clients. He issued a stern warning:

> However much he [the analyst] loves his patients he cannot avoid hating them and fearing them, and the better he knows this the less will hate and fear be the motives determining what he does to his patients.
>
> *(1947, p.195)*

The suggestion is that it is only by being aware of the hate and fear stirred up by the grind of routine and small rejections, low level disruption, outright defiance and threats of violence or loss of control that teachers can learn to recognise and manage their hate and their desire to wreak revenge. The issue of hate is difficult to think about; it is a word infused with such negative associations that it is almost taboo in 'caring' professions; how can a caring professional hate anyone? And more especially how can they hate a child? To think about what objective and justified hate might look like, Winnicott turns to the ways in which a mother hates her baby (1947, p.201) providing a long list of examples. To select and play with a few that have strong resonances for teachers:

> The baby is not her own (mental) conception.
>
> *The student in the classroom is not the student the teacher thought she would be teaching. His learning does not follow the lines of her planning: What was the point in all that planning and thinking? She feels she needn't have bothered!*
>
> The baby is an interference with her private life, a challenge to preoccupation.
>
> *Schools would run a lot more smoothly if it weren't for the students. They make a mess and endless demands so that, when teachers are in school they can't think. This is why they need their holidays: so they can have space to think in!*
>
> The baby must first dominate; he must be protected from coincidences; life must unfold at the baby's rate, and all this needs his mother's continuous detailed study. For instance, she must not be anxious when she holds him.
>
> *In school, when teaching, the children have to come first, and they must be protected from impingements. Teachers need to pace learning at a rate that students can manage and, if this feels too slow (because this is 'supposed' to be taught/covered in two lessons') then that is the teacher's anxiety. If a student needs four lessons, then four lessons is what the teacher must find a way to provide.*
>
> He excites her but frustrates – she must not eat him or trade in sex with him.
>
> *Working with children can be exciting, but it is also frustrating. A teacher must not overwhelm (devour) a student and take over their work (the student's story must remain their story however much it excites her) or bribe them with love (if you do this I will. . . .)*

Of course feelings of hate and fear might be aroused in many ways. Students can arouse negative feelings if they tread too close to something personal in us reminding us of some quality in ourselves that we unconsciously defend against. Of more importance is what Winnicott terms 'objective hate', hate that is aroused 'in reaction to the actual personality or behaviour of the patient, based on objective observation' (1971, p.195). Unlike psychoanalysts who would (at least consciously) expect to have to think about their hate, teachers are much more likely – like most people – to avoid or deny it. Added to the general distaste aroused by thinking about emotions as loaded as 'hate' is the additional burden created by the context of children one is supposed to love unconditionally. One way in which teachers can manage negative feelings is by displacing their hate onto the institution. So, for example, hate engendered by students' endless chatting and the need to constantly provide clear boundaries is displaced onto the institution whose boundaries the teacher starts to transgress replaying the students' behaviours in the staffroom – perhaps through lateness or talking out of turn or inappropriately during meetings – and leaving management to re-establish boundaries.

The desire for revenge

Faced with behaviours that hurt us it is entirely natural to flinch or hit back:

> Crime produces public revenge feelings. Public revenge would be a dangerous thing were it not for the law and those who implement it. First and foremost in court work, the magistrate gives expression to public revenge feelings, and only by so doing can the foundation be laid for a humane treatment of the offender.
>
> I find that there can be a very strong resentment over this idea.
>
> *(Winnicott, 1946, p.98)*

The desire for revenge and the scale it is enacted upon are to be expected in situations where there is a breakdown in sociality, in the face of antisocial behaviours. Winnicott (1947) suggests a variety of ways in which a mother shows her baby that she hates it: by singing lullabies with violent undertones (Rock-a-by baby …) and by putting them to bed despite their protests. Similarly, he suggests that the end of the analytic hour is the analyst's expression of hate. Rules and boundaries, like the law, can provide safe spaces, outlets and expressions of hate: The insistence on unavailability during break times, the requirement that children go outside to play, the end of the day, the timetable. In the management of hate and the desire for revenge, the enemy, Winnicott suggests, is sentimentality:

> … threat comes from the adoption of a sentimental attitude towards crime. If advances seem to come but are based on sentimentality they are useless; reaction must surely set in, and the advances had better never been made. In sentimentality there is repressed or unconscious hate, and repression is unhealthy. Sooner or later the hate turns up.
>
> *(1946, p.98)*

This suggests that a lenient 'oh they don't mean it' attitude from schools and teachers is unhelpful; hate needs to be acknowledged and responded to in a personal way. For Winnicott antisocial acts are absolutely meant. To dismiss them as not meant, or to ignore them, is likely only to store up an escalation of the behaviour and require (or get) a bigger reaction later. A child or student pushing boundaries will continue to push them until they find the limits they are looking for. To keep extending deadlines for the serially disorganised student (rather than the temporarily distracted adult student whose child is in hospital or who is moving house) colludes with their hatred of systems and the need to learn to manage; this will not be forced until a crisis is reached.

In comments made in response to a committee on punishment in prisons and borstals (since 1982 replaced in England and Wales by secure children's homes and young offender institutions), Winnicott (1961) explores the desire for revenge and the ways in which society protects itself from such desires:

> ... the offender has committed an offence [and] the community has to react somehow or other to the sum total of offences committed against it in a given length of time. It is one thing for a psychoanalyst investigating the causes of thieving, and another thing to be the person from whom a bicycle is stolen at a critical moment. ... The psychoanalyst is also a member of society and joins in as a member of society in having to manage reactions which are natural to the person hurt by the antisocial act. ... we cannot only think in terms of treating individual criminals, forgetting that society has been wounded and also needs treatment. ... those of us who are working for the extension of the principle of treatment rather than punishment must not blind ourselves to the great danger of producing a reaction by ignoring society's need to be avenged, not for any one particular crime, but for criminality in general.
>
> *(pp.174–175)*

In terms of satisfying itself, Winnicott identifies two routes an institution might take in managing extreme antisocial behaviour amongst young people; these seem still to resonate and Winnicott's concerns also remain pertinent. He begins by acknowledging a public appetite for 'military discipline'. Such an appetite remains and, since the *Troops to Teachers* initiative was launched in England in June 2013, has again regularly been mooted as an attractive proposition. Interestingly, Winnicott's original comments about military-style discipline relate to young boys in borstal homes; that is, to boys who had already been officially declared criminal. The slippage (or escalation) of the revenge to ordinary school contexts seems particularly dangerous. Winnicott says:

> ... there are probably only two alternatives: one is military discipline after the Nazi pattern and this keeps everything nice and quiet because the boys are so fully occupied that they have no time to think or grow; and the other is a rather horrifying extreme of allowing the boys to reach down to the hopelessness which is the bottom of their illness, but which may be the beginning of their growth.
>
> Military discipline however makes every case hopeless because no young man can develop individual responsibility and personality in that atmosphere.
>
> *(1961, pp.177–178)*

So, the use of military-style discipline used as a punishment appears to remove hope from the picture. Winnicott's original suggestion was that antisocial acts and delinquency were signs of hope (Winnicott, 1939); the nuisance and defiance were a reaching back and a request to repair a point of fracture in their experience of being. Such a regime fills the day with demands for compliance. Current schools demanding these kinds of discipline also fill the psychic space with compliance: deference to others, to uniforms, to the minutiae of finely parsed rules and regulations (Mills and Pini, 2015). Winnicott suggests that the alternative, allowing the boys to reach down into their hopelessness, may look more disturbing but allows the possibility of hope to be re-found.

A problem with institutional punishments (like the blanket demand for military-style discipline) is that they are impersonal. This impersonality means it is hard – impossible? – for an individual to feel it is a response to *their* S.O.S. and *their* antisocial act. If the reaction punishment is not felt to be an appropriate response then it cannot be used to learn from and is likely to result in cycles of escalating behaviours and recidivism as the unconscious demand for help is repeated ever more urgently.

> [T]here are two aspects of the problem. Society demands that the individual be punished. The individual being ill is not in a state to derive benefit from punishment, and is indeed most likely to have to develop pathological trends, masochistic and other, for dealing with the punishment as it comes.
>
> In a favourable case punishment may succeed, that is to say, a boy who has come to doubt the existence of a father, his own father having been absent for some years because of war, may recover the sense of having a father through the strong line taken by his father when he behaves in an antisocial way. This is a rare type of case, however, and is unlikely to be met with in a borstal. Punishment is only valuable when it brings alive a strong and loved reliable father figure for an individual who has lost exactly that. All other punishment can be said to be a blind expression of the unconscious revenge of society.
>
> *(Winnicott, 1961, p.179)*

This raises the issue of the institution even more urgently. If it is the institution that provides the framework (the law) within which revenge can be tempered and safely expressed, what is the institution's relationship with the teacher? What if, for teachers, the school fails to survive the impossibility of their professional tasks? This last possibility extends Winnicott's metaphors and takes us to the arguments of the next and final chapter.

We might wonder whether teachers are capable of being a nuisance to their students and their institutions. Does nuisance (and other antisocial tendencies) end at adolescence? Do we 'grow out of' such tendencies? And if we do, is the 'growth' a function of age? Or of something else? For example, if nuisance is an S.O.S., and a 'reaching back' to a moment before an experience of loss or failure in the facilitating environment, does a teacher whose own background is of a relatively middle class schooling and a privileged university experience a degree of 'deprivation' when they go to teach in working class schools? Do they suffer some loss? Might they then 'reach back' through the commission of 'antisocial' acts within the school? What else might such antisocial teacher acts look like?

In the final chapter, therefore, the role of the 'institution' is considered in more detail.

References

Abram, J. 2004. *The survival of the object: does Winnicott's work constitute a paradigm shift in psychoanalysis?* Unpublished PhD Thesis, Middlesex University.

Benjamin, J. 2004. Beyond doer and done-to: an intersubjective view of thirdness. *Psychoanalytic Quarterly*, 73, 5–46.

Bibby, T. 2009. How do children understand themselves as learners? Towards a learner-centered understanding of pedagogy. *Pedagogy, Culture and Society*, 17(1), 41–56.

Bibby, T. 2015. Thinking and learning? On (not) dreaming in the classroom. *Psychoanalysis, Culture and Society*, 20(1), 49–66.

Britzman, D.P. 2012. The adolescent teacher: a psychoanalytic note on regression in the professions. *Journal of Infant, Child and Adolescent Psychotherapy*, 11, 272–283.

Brown, M., P. Brown, and T. Bibby. 2008. "I would rather die": reasons given by 16-year-olds for not continuing their study of mathematics. *Research in Mathematics Education*, 10(1), 3–18.

Cantent, L. 2008. *The class (Entre les murs)*. Haute et Court.

Clavell, J. 1967. *To Sir, with love*. Columbia Pictures.

Dahl, R. 1988. *Matilda*. London: Puffin.

La Gravenese, R. 2007. *Freedom writers*. Paramount Pictures.

Menendez, R., and T. Musca. 1988. *Stand and deliver*. Warner Brothers.

Mills, M., and B. Pini. 2015. Punishing kids: the rise of the 'boot camp'. *International Journal of Inclusive Education*, 19(3), 270–284.

Moore, A. 2004. *The good teacher: dominant discourses in teaching and teacher education*. London: RoutledgeFalmer.

Ogden, T.H. 2009. *Rediscovering psychoanalysis: thinking and dreaming, learning and forgetting*. London: Routledge.

Phillips, A. 1998. *The beast in the nursery*. London: Faber and Faber.

Stobart, G., T. Bibby, and H. Goldstein. 2005. *Moving to two-tier GCSE mathematics examinations: an independent evaluation of the 2005 GCSE pilot and trial. Final report*. University of London, Institute of Education.

Taylor, M., and G. Sandeman. 2016. 'Graduate Sues Oxford University for £1m over his failure to get a first'. *The Guardian*, Sunday, 4 December. www.theguardian.com/education/2016/dec/04/graduate-sues-oxford-university-1m-failure-first-faiz-siddiqui (accessed 5/12/16).

Winnicott, D.W. 1939. Aggression and its roots. In *Deprivation and delinquency*, edited by C. Winnicott, R. Shepherd and M. Davis (2012 edition, pp.73–85). London: Routledge.

Winnicott, D.W. 1946. Some psychological aspects of juvenile delinquency. In *Deprivation and delinquency*, edited by C. Winnicott, R. Shepherd and M. Davis (2012 edition, pp.97–102). London: Routledge.

Winnicott, D.W. 1947. Hate in the countertransference. In *Through paediatrics to psycho-analysis*, edited by M.M.R. Khan (Vol. 1975, pp.194–203). London: Hogarth Presss and The Institute of Psycho-analysis.

Winnicott, D. 1961. Comments on the report of the committee on punishment in prisons and borstals. In *Depravation and delinquency*, edited by C. Winnicott, R. Shepherd and M. Davis (2012 edition, pp.174–179). London: Routledge.

Winnicott, D. 1971. The use of an object and relating through identifications. In *Playing and reality* (2008 edition, pp.115–127). London: Routledge.

Wood, S. 1939. *Goodbye, Mr Chips*. Metro-Goldwyn-Meyer.

10

INSTITUTIONS

Both mad and maddening

This book has moved back and forth between life in schools and the work of Winnicott to consider, and reconsider the everyday lives of those who live, work and play in institutions that have a focus on learning: schools, universities and families. The chapters have sought to explore what can go right and wrong with learning and with the pedagogic relationship. They have explored Winnicott's developmental theories and more general psychoanalytic acknowledgements that development is far from a straightforward linear process. In schools and universities, this means that teaching involves both teacher and student in teaching and learning from each other. Throughout this book the notion of learning has been expanded to cover far more than the curriculum to acknowledge that growing into 'wellness' (what Winnicott called 'health') through learning about the self and other, is as much a part of what happens in school as learning about reading, writing and arithmetic. The ways in which life can impinge upon development and create the kinds of compliance and defiance that stop us from living creatively have also been explored. The roles of hard-to-think-about affects, such as hate and aggression as well as love and depression, have been considered. And the endlessly impossible role of the teacher has begun to be exposed in a somewhat more complex way than government policy, or public fantasy, generally allows.

In this final chapter, I want to turn the ideas that have been central to this book back on teachers as employees and colleagues and on institutions including schools and universities. In this way, I will expand Winnicott's notion of the good enough facilitating environment beyond the new mother and family. This is perhaps a somewhat maverick move. Winnicott's theories relate to individuals; institutions are different. While he was obviously aware of (and spoke about) families, his main focus was on pairs: mother and infant, analyst and client, with institutions present as frames but not generally his specific focus. However, thinking about learning without acknowledging and exploring the tensions between the group and the individual seems far from adequate. I want to draw attention once more to the timeless nature of the unconscious, to the uncertain nature of knowledge and to the sheer difficulty of living life. It is endlessly hard to tolerate our nested and unstable moment-to-moment experiences of being the dependent learner floundering in new ideas, the annoying adolescent testing our place in the world and the adult trying to provide a safe, reliable and facilitating environment for those who, at any moment, may be less experienced or more regressed than we are. There is a lot here to juggle, and so it should come as no surprise that we defend against the difficulties. The challenge of this chapter, and of the book, is also Winnicott's challenge. Can we survive the struggle and learn to recognise the times when we do and do not manage to live creatively, when we do and do not facilitate others to live creatively? And can we accept our place(s) in the quiet and tumultuous chaos that is a life lived in relationship with others in schools and classrooms?

The paradoxical institution

Institutions are somewhat paradoxical structures. On one level, they are cultural creations – concepts or ideas – and as such they provide social defences against anxieties (Menzies Lyth, 1960); institutions are a thing in the minds of individuals and groups. Going back to Freud's (1930) consideration of group and individual anxieties we can think of people coming together to form schools to defend against their (social) anxieties generated by unstable and uncertain knowledge, by society's fear of stalled or reversed progress, and by the threat of apparently recidivist, 'evil' or 'out-of-control' youth. Coming at it from another direction, institutions are groups made up of individuals, and in groups we can lose our sense that we are unique; we can become submerged in group anxieties (Bion, 1961). And, out in the 'real' world beyond our fantasies, institutions also exist as physical buildings: bricks and mortar, concrete and glass, objects to house activities (and latterly objects to be turned into houses).

Despite its physical presence in the world, and the people who perhaps actually *are* the institution, the dominant 'reality' of the school (nursery or university) as institution is that it is an idea. It has a strong and singular symbolic presence in our minds and culture, but we can also reify that idea. By doing so, we turn the idea (or ideas) into a thing, we make it concrete as a way to help us think and act with it. In this way, we create *the institution* as singular and monolithic.

In this chapter, I want to try to avoid referring to 'the institution' and the smother of its comforting, normalising singularity and determinism and talk instead of 'an institution' or 'institutions' (Murris, 2017) – but this is a difficult thing to do. Attributing intent to a reification is problematic: An idea has no independent agency. To say that an institution is 'corrupt' or 'doesn't care' or 'refuses to change' can feel natural, but it is the people in the institution who hold the agency. It is people from among those who constitute an institution whose behaviours may be corrupt or uncaring or – whatever. Unfortunately, they may feel or act *as if* this is not the case by pointing to policies and their compliant actions or injustices to justify their 'natural' responses. Others within the same institution may seek to block independent thoughts or actions, to subdue them to group processes – it can, for example, be hard to gainsay the apparently 'uncaring' acts of others and to stand against a 'zero-tolerance' policy. So, while it is tempting to try to think about an institution as providing a facilitating environment (or not), this is not a project that can have a helpful outcome. So, an institution cannot provide a reliable, facilitating environment although together, the people who constitute it at a particular location may do so. Our individual and collective actions, the policies we put in place, the thought and energy we give to their implementation and so on, all of these can make a difference. If we play with the idea (the metaphor) of a reified institution, we are in danger of absolving ourselves – as members of that institution – of responsibility for our part in the way our institution works. This paradox, this doubling back, this mutual implication, is the subject of this chapter: The hated idea that we may be the very institution that frustrates us and that we hate, while perhaps also being the institution that supports us and that we love.

The institution as groups of individuals

If an institution is good, healthy, productive and creative it is good, healthy, productive and creative because of the people in it not because of any quality we might want it to possess independently. But institutions certainly have effects. These effects seem to emerge out of the ways in which institutions have been developed to manage the anxieties of their constituent individuals and 'parts' and that the paradox that doubling back generates.

As Freud (1921, 1930) noted, being in a group is difficult. We are susceptible to other people. Bion (1961) developed these ideas and others have taken them on and re-contextualised them to new contexts. Anziu (1984) puts it well:

> When human beings are together to work, to play, to defend themselves, to steal, to kill, to believe, to change the world, to be taught or cared for, feelings, desires, fears and anxieties excite or paralyse them. They may experience a common emotion which may give them an impression of unity: conflicting emotions may tear the group apart; several members may withdraw and defend themselves against group emotions that they feel to be threatening, whereas others, frantically, joyfully, let themselves go; or most members may withdraw when faced with invasive emotion, in which case the group is dull, apathetic and wordy.
>
> *(In Britzman, 2003, p.113)*

Even an apparently unified group, the teaching staff, the history department, the support staff, the whole staff, will be made up of smaller groups coalescing around their – conscious and unconscious – responses to particular events. Despite political desires for stability and consistency, policy is enacted by the people who work in an institution. We may all think we implement policy in the same way, but we do not. Whether mandated/statutory or not, policies will always be interpreted in context (Ball, 1993). Policies in action offer a reflection of the beliefs and values of the people who write them and those who enact them. While the stated purpose of education may be to teach or perhaps instil knowledge in minds, beliefs extend this perspective. For example, one person may believe that education is about fitting individuals to participate productively in society. It is equally possible to believe that schools are places of exploration and self-actualisation or that they exist to ensure civility, to reinforce the status quo or to manage progress towards a more socially just society, or they may simply be exam factories preparing individuals for a next and 'better' stage in life (see for example Williams, 1961). Or they may be all of these and more! Even this brief reflective exercise highlights that, when 'institutions' turn in upon themselves to reflect or dream their affects, it is far from certain what they will pay attention to. Individual teachers in an institution will enact the same policy differently, understanding statements like 'is literate' or 'can measure' differently, with all the little differences in teaching style that go with these differences in perspective.

The idea that an institution is a unitary and unified thing in the world defends against the complexity of 'institution' as an abstract idea constituted in individual minds and group processes. For education, the unified and unitary school also defends against the fact that learning itself, like all development, is uncertain and circuitous, that steps can be taken backwards as well as forwards, or that one can march on the spot and go nowhere. This is unstable and shifting ground. The wobbly institution in the mind is a compelling place from which to try to reconsider the notion and possibility of a collectively constituted facilitating education environment.

The divided institution

One of the things that we might notice from the first sections of this chapter is that there seem to be (at least) two ways of looking at everything – the unitary idea is divided: institutions are both real *and* imagined; institutions are both individual/singular *and* group/multiple; institutional effects exist for individuals *and* for groups and society. The staff of an education institution is also typically divided between, for example, those who are 'academic' and those whose focus is administration, or those who teach and those who support and, more familiarly, between those who teach and those who learn.

It is not that there is no overlap between these pairs of roles but, to use the language of the university, academic staff members teach, do research, and some administration associated with teaching and research while the administrative staff administers the institution itself: the admissions, the finances, the building/plant, the qualifications etc. The academic/administrative divide (all of these dichotomies) represents a split in the fabric of the institution and must therefore defend against some unbearable piece of knowledge. Increasingly, this divide may be due to the growing realisation that universities are no longer valued just for being universities; schools are no longer valued just for the education they provide. However, the drive for commercial independence and exam success may cover over an older terror: the impossibility of education itself and the uncertainty of knowledge (How can I be sure that you have learned what I think I have taught you? How can I be sure that our efforts will be well received by those who judge us?). If we accept the idea of this older terror then the teacher/learner, teaching/support and academic/administration splits begin to seem more understandable; each insulates the singular institution from the messy and potentially disappointing chaos of its constituent parts.

But my language is slipping with this talk of splits. Let us return to Winnicott and his suggestion that the early facilitating environment needs to provide *both* handling *and* holding. For Winnicott, the early 'good enough' mother is able to attend to the subjective experiences of her infant: she is able to mirror their experiences and is sufficiently attuned to their cries and wrigglings to provide what is needed or wanted and withstand their hate and aggression. In this way, she is able to provide what is required while keeping impingements at bay, allowing these in gradually as the infant develops capacities to deal with them. That is, initially the good enough (m)other mediates both outside world and inner child for the infant. Later, she mediates the world and leads her infant to new developmental challenges through both active actions and active no-actions; she is able to tolerate the frustrations associated with watching faltering learning without either taking over or walking away. Her reliable presence provides a holding that prevents annihilation; her thoughtful handling presents the world in ways that can be experienced as tolerable. For Winnicott, in health, holding and handling are concurrent.

With this dual role in mind, it is possible to imagine that the administrative staff tends to the objective body of the institution, they guard and feed it, and in so doing provide a portion of the care. The academic/teaching staff tends to the affective life of the institution, paying attention to its thoughts, its imaginative and internal life. Of course, that is too crude (as splits are) but, as anyone working in education knows: The split between administrative and teaching staff is very real and their tasks are different. But for Winnicott (and indeed for me) it is the lively to and fro between the inside and the outside – between subjective experiences and objective reality, between care of the mind and care for the body, between holding and handling – that allows space for the creative apperception that can make life feel vivid and bearable.

It is the discovery of this safe 'third space' in communication (Benjamin, 2004), of a mind between the psyche (the unconscious) and the soma (the world) (Winnicott, 1960) that makes creative living possible. For institutions to be experienced as nurturing environments *both* teachers *and* students, academics *and* administrators, teachers *and* support staff, staff *and* parents need to negotiate the dual and tandem nature of their roles – they need to tolerate the doubling back and paradoxical qualities of their roles for themselves, their colleagues and their students. The silos and categorical certainties we retreat to in times of over-work, anxiety, fear, stress and over-management compound the very problems they are put in place to defend against. This is the madness of an institution and of the institution's members.

The primary task of the institution

Elsewhere, I have suggested that the primary task of the school is twofold: the creation, control and transmission of knowledge and its overlay on the developing child (Bibby, 2011). But in *Education – an 'impossible profession'?* I did not consider that 'the institution' (as a home for, or mother to, education) might have a different or additional primary task: perhaps its own survival as an institution. Stokes (1994) has discussed the ways in which the overt tasks of the health service and the prison service might be multiple and not coincident across the minds of people working within them, let alone the minds of people outside the service. Discussing the health service, he points out:

> While an organisation may have one publicly stated idea of its primary purpose or mission, there are often also hidden conceptions at work. Put simply, there is the level of 'what we say we do' but there is also the level of 'what we really believe we are doing' and also 'what is actually going on'; the members of an organisation may be quite unconscious of this third level. [...] [A]t this third level the health service is unconsciously seen as a 'keep-death-at-bay' service; while the stated task is the treatment of illness, there is also an unconscious task of providing each member of society with the fantasy that death can be prevented.
>
> *(p.121)*

So, one unconscious impossible task of the school is to provide each member of society with the fantasy that ignorance (and other 'social ills' such as teen-pregnancy, lack of qualification, economic failure) can be prevented. Another possibility in the current climate is that the dominant primary task of the institution becomes its own survival. When policy and social contexts stress 'austerity', value for money and an anti-intellectual ethos alongside public fears about job insecurity, rising debt and increasing credential inflation, then educational institutions face a toxic situation. Those who identify with the administrative requirement to ensure the survival of the institution may feel pressured to focus on the financial side of the balance: the imperative to make money/a profit, to attract students (especially low-cost students, high paying/grant-attracting students or both) and research grants and to cut costs. Those whose focus is on creative living are likely to feel shouted down in direct proportion to the real or imagined costs of failure or fears of annihilation. When we attend exclusively either to pressures from outside or to desires from the inside, the movement between the inside and out is stifled, the possibility for creative living is lost and institutions – and the people housed in them – become imperilled.

The divided institution and loss of thought

If learning institutions are indeed constructed around a split, or if they embody a split, then it is not surprising that they are so hard to think in or with. Splits – dichotomies that simplify our lives – represent unconscious efforts *not* to think. In the language of Winnicott, a failure in the environment leads to an inability to live creatively. The loss of a capacity to tolerate moves between listening to one's inner voice and listening to calls from outside, from the other, are catastrophic for creative living. Compliant and defiant responses to real or perceived threats cut one off from relations to both self and other; they isolate. If either handling or holding fail, then the institution fatally wounds itself. This loss of movement may result in a False Self structure coming to dominate and be characterised by an attitude of compliance. Or it may lead to an over-valuing of the inner voice, the affective experience, and result in a refusal to tolerate the demands placed upon one for social compliance resulting in defiance – another loss of thought.

So, what might a creative institution look like? And, what does a (reified) education institution make difficult – for itself and for others – and how does this happen?

Living creatively in an institution (institution as potential space)?

To return to a quote I used earlier and to add to it some additional ideas:

> In order to study play and then the cultural life of the individual one must study the potential space between any one baby [student or teacher] and the human (and therefore fallible) mother-figure [teacher or institution] who is essentially adaptive because of love.
>
> *(Winnicott, 1971, p.135)*

The transitional space of apperception, of play and of cultural life relies on the back-and-forth of communication; communication with self and with others. Such a space is kept safe from impingements that 'steal' the piece of self that has been exposed for exploration. Creative living relies on the possibility of recognising and chasing down one's own questions and fantasies, of holding impingements at bay while someone else chases down their questions and fantasies. It is also dependent on the possibility of 'relaxation' – of being able to take a breath and stay with an idea, a thought, a moment of reverie without being propelled forwards by someone else's agenda all the time. It relies on the possibility of repudiation: of recognising what is mine or me and what is not me, of rejecting an idea or a thought that offends or intrudes. It means being able to bear to look at something unexpected and perhaps surprising or unwelcome. It means allowing others their space even as you take up your own. This requires tolerance, self-awareness, thought and effort. While policies and cultures can (and do) help to hold spaces open, in the end it is the people in the institutions who bear (or fail to bear) the uncertainties that desires and experiments generate.

So is the notion of an institution as a potential space (a transitional phenomenon) a fantasy? Is this an impossible ask? Groups of people can and do hold spaces open. Does the size of an institution matter or just the experience of its hostility and inflexibility? Someone is usually able to make the most of whatever is available. Just because an opportunity, an institution's actions or policies, does not seem to accord with my idea of the purposes of our institution, does that make it 'wrong'?

Being able to be creative and to live creatively, in the broadest sense, requires the presence of support, a reliable and trustworthy handhold that can help one steady oneself through a moment of productive teetering. When we are 'well' we do not need to cling to a handhold all the time, just to know – to trust – that it is going to be there when we need it to be. We need to be able 'to be alone' while we tolerate the uncertainties that our own thoughts generate and play with the ideas to see where they might go: we need to be able to think. We need to feel able to 'contribute in' to act within the relationships that contain us and within which we contain others. We may need qualities such as bravery, honesty and integrity if we are to demonstrate (and find) reliability and trustworthiness in both our colleagues and ourselves.

I am repeatedly struck by the fate of planning as a professional pedagogic activity and as a potentially creative activity or a potential space for teachers. Of course it depends rather on what planning is felt to be. For some, planning is the creation (or even the adoption of someone else's creation) of a forensic programme by which knowledge might reliably and efficiently be inserted into minds that are supposedly lacking that knowledge. For others, planning is the process of thinking about a piece of knowledge or a skill that they want to pass on or to offer as a tool for thinking – a challenge. For a teacher of this second sort, planning is a way of thinking through something that may already be intimately familiar. It is a way of exploring the less familiar complexities and ramifications of a well-known space so that the idea can be put into the potential space of the classroom for students to play with in a way that will be accessible to them. Such a teacher would want to make the idea attractive so that it might be seen as appealing. Doing this requires that one has some measure of the tastes of one's students and their preferences. It means being sufficiently acquainted with the ideas of the lesson that they can be presented in a variety of ways and challenge, but not overwhelm, the intended audience. It requires having some awareness of any built-in difficulties that the topic might bring (in addition to the more general impingements of the classroom and school). It means having some ideas about the ways in which groups and individuals might respond so that opportunities for them to 'contribute in' to the class and their own coming to know can be built in.

These two forms of planning – the forensic and the more processual – facilitate two very different kinds of teaching. The first offers a fantasy of the clean, efficient, reliable and clinical insertion of knowledge into minds. The second provides a description of the landscape in which a dance may take place. The first is designed, through the careful selection of activities and assessments, to hold at bay the uncertainties of knowledge, learning, teaching and assessment. The second is structured to make space for the uncertainties of knowledge, learning and teaching and to allow minds to explore possibilities together, to circle around and play.

Many years ago I was watching a maths lesson in a class of children aged 7 to 8 years. The teacher was introducing division and, as often happens, was using food as a 'real-life' context. She proposed that a mother had '5 fish fingers to share between her two children for tea' and asked 'How many fish fingers would each child have?' The children – all of them – were confident that they knew the answer to this: It was easy, it was 'one'. But they quickly discovered they were all 'wrong'. In an area of poverty, five fish fingers are enough for two siblings to have 2½ dinners or for two diners and for there to be one left over. But because the required answer was '2½', not 1 fish finger at 2½ meals, or 1 fish finger at 2 meals with one left over, the teacher was lost. She became annoyed by the children's refusal to entertain the possibility of eating more than one fish finger at a sitting; this would, they protested, be greedy. They would not be moved and, because she had not thought through the numbers or the scenario she had nowhere else to go with it. Impasse. No speculating about (playing with) what might happen in a rich person's house or turning the question around (how many meals ...?), or of abandoning the scenario entirely to think about the numbers.

We can only speculate about the children's experience of this lesson, of having their lived experience deemed 'wrong', of their ideas and contribution being rejected. How can maths become relevant if it does not touch your life? How can maths touch your life if it behaves differently in classrooms and out in the world? Similarly, we can only speculate about the teacher's experience of this lesson, of having her 'reality', her generosity rejected, perhaps her denied fears of hunger or insufficiency visited upon her. Perhaps her carefully planned lesson had been approved by a surveilling eye (her own or someone else's)? Perhaps she had been pleased by its forensic intent, so clearly right on paper; how might she understand its unravelling? And for a teacher whose planning is for creative thought, play and process – how can this fit on the planning sheet provided? There are difficulties all around. What does (what can) a teacher, a school or an assessment do with right wrong answers?

Forensic planning sits well in intensively surveilled institutions; it aligns with their needs. It can be easily read, the intentions are clear and stated, the assessment is built in. From an institutional point of view it is exactly what is needed. It enables the knowledge deemed important to be portioned out rationally across the days, weeks and terms of the school year (2½ ideas per week, 2½ levels per year). It is seemingly efficient; it can be reused year after year and by different teachers.

How useful it is for teaching is another matter, but that is only tangentially an institution's concern. In such a context, when children fail it is the fault of the teacher unable to perform the surgery, not the planning that allocated the time and resources for the learning to be done in and with. The space of the classroom as institutional space is constricted by its own and outside impingements; it is a series of demands for compliance. The potential space of a classroom shaped by mobile pedagogic relations is somewhat different. The question is whether the institution – as matrix of learners and knowers – can tolerate the uncertainties and think with, and for, itself. Is it even allowed to be like this?

Taking planning as an activity is one way to investigate and underscore the difficult paradoxes of turning back. As teachers, can we risk holding open the possibility of learning from the learners, of being taught by our students? What will it mean if our desire for recognition, if our need to have our generosity accepted, if our fantasy of a shared reality is exposed to us? What happens if – or when – we realise that not everyone in the class thinks of us as 'good teachers'? If (or when) we realise a lesson has missed its mark because it is too hard, or 'boring', or hard to connect with? When (or if) our reality and that of our students are not congruent? And if this is all painful when it is exposed to us in relation to our students, what about when it is exposed to others beyond the classroom door? How can we bear the trauma of difference? And, for an institution, can teachers be trusted to plan? Can the uncertainty of knowledge be allowed? Can a year of not knowing be held safely before assessments perhaps tell us something (what?) about the learning that has taken place? Could narrative planning that spills out higgledy-piggledy over a page or pages be trusted to hold ideas as safely as the boxes on a planning grid? To return to the quotation at the start of this section and Winnicott's comment, to the punch that tickles at the end of that sentence: It is love that makes play and learning possible. It is love, the love of the teacher, her colleagues and their institution that enables them to adapt to the needs of learners. So big questions are: Does that love exist? And if it does, what does it look like? Can it be allowed? Or is it too risky, too painful, too dangerous?

Failures of love, failures in the facilitating environment – small or large, deliberate or accidental – are the stuff of relationships. They may be learned from if they are experienced as tolerable or defended against if they are too much to bear. In the next section, I look again at issues of compliance and defiance, turning them back to explore the difficulties of maintaining thought and creativity in institutional spaces.

Institutional compliance: avoiding annihilation

Winnicott saw compliance as a defence against the terrors of annihilation, a necessary way of managing to continue to survive by fitting in with the environment (fitting planning onto a *pro forma*). The survivals he pointed to ranged from social survival (saying 'ta' and perhaps learning gratitude later) to literal survival depending on the level of hostility in the environment: We might fear or face social, professional or actual death. The baby who cannot reach an accommodation with their depressed mother is in very real danger of death by neglect. The teacher who cannot reach an accommodation with their distracted management team is in very real danger of professional burnout.

A relatively benign environment is one that is adaptive and personal. It is generally trustworthy, reliable, collaborative and capable of compromise. These qualities enable enough to and fro between an individual and their environment ((m)other, institution) that the individual can, at times, recognise themselves in their interactions; there is some fit of values, some valuing of efforts, some capacity to 'contribute in' and make a difference. And the judgement about whether there are sufficient opportunities for these things to be experienced to stay alive lies with the one in the position of relative dependence; in the case of an institution, the employee, the department member, the student, and the one 'lower' in the hierarchy at any moment. By contrast, a hostile environment lacks these qualities and forces more compliance making it increasingly difficult for members of an institution to live creatively.

In Chapter 7, I cited Vergaeghe's (in Britzman, 2006, pp.174–175) 'three questions that form the child's curiosity: "What is the difference between me and the other sex, where do children come from, and what is the relation between my mother and my father?"' As discussed earlier, these questions are unanswerable because they ask more than the questions convey. Since they have never been answered, they will later form the basis of the adult's curiosity, perhaps slightly reworded as below:

- What is the difference between you and me? between this and that? (What makes me a woman? What does it mean to be Muslim? What does it mean to be British? Can I be British *and* European?)
- Where do things come from? (How did life start on Earth? When did time begin? What was there before the 'big bang'?)
- What is the relation between the individual and the institution? The institution and the state? The state and the law? Religion and science?

An environment that has become hostile hates curiosity and demands attention be paid to *it*: The early narcissistic demand is that all interest be focussed on *its* knowledge, *its* activities. A relentless demand that our attention be focussed outwards insists that we ignore ourselves and our own questions. Compliance places curbs on our curiosity. We are led to believe that our questions are not the most important and, anyway, there is no time to consider them: We must focus on the knowledge decreed important and at the time and pace demanded; we must focus on the tasks prescribed at the time and pace demanded. The institution's aggressive, narcissistic and omnipotent need to know itself, to end uncertainty, to control outcomes and therefore its future takes over. Once an institution's own interests take over, they constrict the possibilities for experiencing life in that institution and therefore for creative apperception: for thinking and learning across affective responses, perception, experience and 'reality' within the institution and of institutional life. The compliant institution, terrified of its own annihilation, becomes rigid with that fear.

Meanwhile the rigidity and foreclosure of curiosity and thought leave many no longer able to see themselves mirrored in the institution that houses them, where they may have invested much time and effort. Such an outcome – of blind demands for compliance to an institution – may lead to burnout and rejection, to high levels of illness and high staff turnover. If I feel that my values and those of my 'institution' no longer match, if I feel unable to 'contribute in', then my presence here is perhaps an irrelevance. And, of course, an institution can and will go on without me. And notice how, in writing this, 'the institution' as reified object has strengthened under laminated layers of fear, pressure and demand. The paradox that the abjected member is still a member of that institution often fails to survive its own internal contradictions.

So institutions can demand compliance, but they themselves have to be compliant to the larger structures within which they are located: the broader education system, branches of government tasked with accountability and the examination bodies. Within institutions and dependent on those institutions for our wages, also highly invested in the purposes of our institution, its annihilation can also feel like our annihilation: We are it; it is we. To be at the mercy of the capricious winds of government policies at a time when education has been commodified and put beyond the financial reach of many (the rest saddled with debt) is to feel the very real danger of social or professional death, a death of dreams and hopes that education would at other times nourish (see Gill, 2009 for a different and very powerful analysis of this).

Institutional defiance

Chapter 8 considered the defiance offered by learners to the individual teachers, classes and institutions within which they are housed. Now I turn that back on teachers and institutions to consider less thought about nuisance in education lives. To what extent are aggressive and retaliatory acts part of our stock in trade as teachers? How about assessment – the checking of what we have (not) learned, of how we have (not) measured up to expectations? The policies that set out norms of dress and behaviour because we cannot be trusted to behave well if we are not dressed 'well' – or should that be because we cannot be trusted to behave compliantly if we do not demonstrate compliance through our dress? And the retaliation, for daring to ask questions that are presented as the curriculum – the silencing news that 'This is what you need to know to pass your exam'? These are some of the ways teachers and institutions can offer threats that demand compliance to an institution's needs. In this section, I turn back to institutions to look again at nuisance and defiance, aggression and surviving hate.

Nuisance

A nuisance is an irritant, a troublesome matter of annoyance. Unlike aggression the threat of nuisance is perhaps more affective than physical. Institutions can be endlessly irritating! They make small demands on time that feel like intrusions: meetings, exams, deadlines, self-assessment forms, extra supervisions, emails pinging in, letters from managers demanding attention. They are thoughtless: I have to be on time but 'they' take as long as they like; they are inconsiderate, selfish, thoughtless .... In contrast of course, nothing *I* have ever done as a teacher could ever possibly have been irritating to my students or line managers (!) In Chapter 8, the exploration of nuisance suggested that it was an unconscious test of reliability and trustworthiness. To 'pass' this unconscious test, the person being faced with the nuisance needs to remain consistent – to remain steadfastly reliable and not retaliate. This is easier said than done.

Many school and university policies are instigated in the name of consistency and trustworthiness; they can be attempts to formalise procedures to ensure nuisance is managed in the same way each time. Some, like marking or grading criteria, typically require regular moderation meetings to ensure they are being interpreted evenly across an institution. Others, like behaviour policies, are notoriously more difficult to 'police'. And what is more infuriating than an unevenly implemented policy that is supposed to ensure fairness? One policy fantasy is that the mere existence of a policy spelling out steps to control individual responses will ensure that *all* nuisance makers will be treated in the same way: 'fairly'. The trouble with this blanket notion of sameness is that it is not always appropriate. Not all nuisances are the same, and they will not be received in the same way. So, while a marking policy, lists of grade criteria and so on may fulfil a valuable function enabling staff to discuss and compare their reactions and responses to student essays, rigid behaviour policies may not be. The rigid policy that demands precise responses without discussion forestalls thought, prevents discussion, demands compliance, is a nuisance.

The impact of nuisance in relation to a behaviour policy needs considering in more detail. What one individual child is looking for when they present nuisance behaviour – when they test for reliability and trustworthiness – is likely to be different to another. One child's failure to return homework may be a result of a chaotic home life or an unwell parent unable to nag or remind. Another child's failure to return homework may be a sign of contempt, or fear, or their own illness. How in these circumstances can a blanket response be appropriate? Following Winnicott, I suggest that the blanket response is a defence against the time it takes to think about and deal with the nuisance of the late homework. It is a way to circumvent the need to take the time to explore why *this* student's homework might be coming in late; it avoids the 'waste' of time it takes to discuss what is happening. There is a devaluing of the time it takes to deal with nuisance and a simultaneous idealisation of the time given to others. There is an assumption that the time I spend 'teaching' others is time more valuably spent than the time I spend understanding a child in distress when, of course, both need to happen. Rigid policies are also therefore an institutional sign of contempt for individual differences that detract from institutional demands that *everyone* makes steady and even progress at all times so that 'the institution' can be reassured (and reassure others) that it is doing its job. So a blanket response (such as a zero-tolerance behaviour policy) may well be an aggressive and retaliatory act designed to punish nuisance as the thief of time. Such policies, implemented rigidly (without thought), are therefore signals of a hostile environment, a clear signal to the insecure individual, testing trustworthiness with nuisance, that this is *not* a safe environment in which to experiment, think and play. Rigid policies can be a sign of a failing learning environment.

Defiance, aggression and surviving hate

Winnicott understood defiance as the over-valuation of an internal voice (of the True Self). For him it was a position (a quality of adolescence) where the possibility of paying attention to external reality and the voice of the other has been significantly reduced or lost. Some trauma has occurred that has signalled a break in the individual's experience of a continuity of being. Some moment of not being seen or recognised (a moment of annihilation) has tripped an individual up and led to a breakdown in trust and in relating. Typically, people faced with defiance become angry, so it is perhaps unusual that Winnicott understood acts of defiance as signs of hope. He described acts of defiance as a 'reaching back' to the moment before the trauma, as a moment of asking someone to 'try again'. His belief (and experience) was that faced with repeated acts of tolerance (with demonstrable reliability) it was possible for most people (eventually) to rebuild trust and repair their ability to live in relationship with others – to step back from, over or past defiance. The defiance might be offered to the actual relationship within which the break occurred or to a proxy for that relationship. In this way, teachers and other figures in authority can often bear the brunt of challenges to repair relationships tested to destruction elsewhere.

As I explored in Chapters 8 and 9, an individual's responses to defiant behaviour matter hugely. But how about institutions? Can institutions contain creative responses to defiance? Or has curiosity about behaviour been sacrificed on the institutional alter of compliance to consistency? And does it make sense to think of institutions as defiant? Can an institution be thought of as having a 'True Self' and an internal voice it might attend to? Can an institution have a past it might try to reach back into? Institutional nostalgia can certainly exist in the minds of the people who make it up and may be triggered by breaks in relationship with wider education structures. Individual institutions also rely on the responses of key individuals to soften policy interpretation, to show it is possible to think and behave creatively, to stop their (individual and collective) compliance from becoming an act of aggression.

The aggression of an institution is perhaps most clearly seen in its rules and the ways in which it cuts off or otherwise limits and proscribes the activities of its constituents. From education-wide actions by government including (for example) the refusal of ideas: the diminishing of some courses to 'Mickey Mouse' status, to an individual institution's own closure of courses, acts of aggression frequently occur on the institution level. Similarly, the refusal of people, the labelling of individuals as 'uncontrollable' or 'non-compliant' and the exclusion or expulsion of students or colleagues, are also examples of aggressive acts. Discussing the ways in which those teachers who feel resistant to school mores and practices or who feel compelled into 'reluctant compliance', Moore and Clarke (2016) explore teachers' attachments to notions of professionalism. 'Who does not', they ask, 'want to be a professional, when the word is used so very often – in the worlds of education, of business, of politics, of entertainment – to indicate approval and respect?' (p.671). As Moore and Clarke go on to explain, however, the redefinition of 'professionalism' in neo-liberal policy discourses is an aggressive and destabilising policy act. It amounts to a government attack on the 'professions' and a (successful) attempt to bring to heel free-thinking 'experts' who once thwarted politicians' desires. Can the teacher whose planning is too much for the tidy boxes on the *pro forma*, too untidy, too (apparently) chaotic, be given enough free reign to test her ideas? Or must she too be brought to heel immediately? Somewhat surprisingly the metaphors of animal husbandry (here, of the management of horses and dogs) seem to have intruded into institutional space. Must the institution resort to treating its members (its limbs) like 'dumb animals' with no way to respond other than through blind obedience? Or can they be allowed to live as thinking people? Does a professional always and only look like me? Like him? Like her? Or can we find our own professionalisms? Can we be held and handled with love, or do we need a touch of the whip?

And so the doubling back, the turning back of Winnicott's ideas on nuisance, defiance and aggression onto institutions highlights that, although institutions do indeed engage in behaviours that test love and tolerance, their own collective capacities for love and surviving hate are much more limited. Our relationships are not equal or even. As workers in institutions this has implications for us, our professional lives, our professionalisms and the ways we tolerate the group within which we try to hold onto our own humanities.

The wobbly institution in the mind: some final thoughts

Teachers in schools, colleges and universities have a Janus-like status: They look in to the life of the institution and out to the lives of their students; in to their own lives and out to the lives of their colleagues and students; in to their own lives as members of an institution and out to the lives of colleagues and policy beyond their place of work. The difficulty of maintaining access to their own inner voices and a clear vision of the 'reality' of the classroom, staffroom and playground in the clamour for attention is never going to be easy but, at the moment, at this time of austerity and hypervigilance from those who surveille our work and judge it, I think it is particularly hard. Our public institutions are currently treated as neither reliable nor trustworthy (Gill, 2009). Living a professional life in an environment that is not conducive to creativity, to 'going on being', that does not value 'contributions in' unless they map directly onto what is wanted (i.e. are compliant) is very difficult. Not that there are not those who manage it, but it is perhaps harder than it needs to be.

From Winnicott we have perhaps learned why it matters so much where the buck stops; that, from moment to moment, someone or some group must hold the space of responsible adult if lives are to develop enjoyably and creatively. Institutionally, the fluidity of this task is perhaps impossible to tolerate. Rigid management hierarchies artificially solidify responsibility in layers that too often behave omnipotently to survive the impossibility created by their responsibilities. Too often we retreat behind the walls of our silos insulating ourselves from demands that seem to persecute us from beyond the limits of our resilience. The more rigid the hierarchy, the higher the stakes are perceived to be and the harder it becomes for those lower down to 'speak truth to power' and to 'whistle blow'. Institutional policies, put in place to limit the rights of those who would challenge, can be fragile; rights are challenged by 'authority' and its omnipotent certainties and demands. Experiencing the oscillating world between and within our institutional homes, between and within professional and pedagogic relationships, between and within our inner (psyche) and outer (soma) selves is precarious. But education, at its best, is an intensely creative act, an experience of life in vibrant relationships in which we experience being held and holding, offering and receiving. Teachers and students, learning about themselves, others and the world, are engaged in the constant refashioning of themselves and their relationships. Adam Phillips puts it well:

> The child's freedom, the child's self fashioning project, depends on her being able to treat orders and instructions as though they were hints and suggestions; as open invitations rather than prescriptions. Rules are not merely abided by, they are also sounded out; they require that unfounded compliance called guesswork.
>
> *(2007, p.90)*

For 'the child' read also teacher, lecturer, researcher, writer, administrator:

> The [teacher]'s freedom, the [teacher]'s self fashioning project, depends on her being able to treat orders and instructions as though they were hints and suggestions; as open invitations rather than prescriptions. Rules are not merely abided by, they are also sounded out; they require that unfounded compliance called guesswork.
>
> *(Phillips, 2007, p.90)*

In the wobbly institution we move between states of (not) knowing and of relative (in)dependency. While the mandated curriculum aggressively asserts what must be learned (and indeed, as a result, the content of the curriculum is what is assessed and *becomes* what needs to be learned), it is not *all* that will be learned. It may be that the most important learning at any one moment is the manager learning that the administration team has some good suggestions about the way courses are managed, or the teacher learning that a student's apparently odd idea is actually right or the student learning that the teacher does not know everything. Whether we behave as members of a rigid neoliberal coven or as members of a flexible matrix of relationships is perhaps not as 'up to us' as we might like – the stakes are multiple, complex and interdependent. Institutions are both mad *and* maddening. Institutional madness is a form of blindness that comes from a refusal to see. Institutions are maddening when they behave *as if* they were unified and independent entities, *as if* they were the important thing, *as if* their members were there only to serve their needs, *as if* compliance were all that were required. And the actions taken to ensure those *as if*-s become reality are maddening and drive us to madness in their turn.

In the face of such madnesses a 'wellness' industry has sprung up: If you eat this, never do that, practice mindfulness or some other habit. ... Such general advice may be helpful for individuals but, within many institutions there seems to be no *real* care. The individual is left to manage their own needs, desires and disappointments. The relatedness of our lives has been (and remains) under attack. The difficulty of living and working with and within relationships with others is glossed over with thick and cloying layers of 'personal responsibility' and individuality.

If Winnicott's work teaches us anything, it is that living creatively is what can make our lives feel real and satisfying. This does not mean we all need to become artists or writers, nor does it mean we should all throw tradition and rules out and 'let it all hang out'! His understanding of creativity means that apparently unpromising ground can be intensely creative: mathematics, engineering, parenting, teaching, caring. What matters is how we approach our relationships and how we care for ourselves as we care for each other. While we do need to take a measure of responsibility for ourselves, we also need to be able to (in a careful way) reveal our vulnerabilities to others and allow them to be part of our care of self.

Being open to other defended subjects, learning to test trustworthiness and tolerating the limits of our adaptability: These are the tasks of the learning teacher and the learning colleague. Psychoanalysis as a tool for thinking can help us keep a weather eye on our creative selves as we live and work with others trying to do the same. And while psychoanalytic theory and the work of Winnicott can be a comfort and a help, it can also be a nuisance. At best, theory can be an object that may survive the aggression of our curious questions, that may enable us to wobble productively between our internal lives and our experiences of the world beyond our skin, and that can help us to live creatively. At worst, theory can also feel aggressive, like an assault on our rationality and our sense of professionalism.

To many teachers, theory can both seem mad and be experienced as maddening such that at times we may hate it and want to hurl the book across the room. The questions with no answers, the provocations that leave us floundering and lost – these can be hateful. The challenge lies in shuttling our responses to theory from aggression to creativity. Of course, there is the danger that we may come to idealise theory – as we can come to idealise any knowledge – and use it as a defence. My own effort in this book has been to open up a safe space in the middle ground between these two extremes.

The difficult choice, for me and perhaps for readers, is to try to maintain awareness, as far as is possible, of the multiple entwined realities we are embedded in and that shift as our relative resiliences and vulnerabilities ebb and flow. The difficult action may well be the non-action of thought that enables us to sit with and tolerate the paradoxical tightrope-like off-balance balance that apperception requires. Through patience and the (in)action of hard thoughts, we can however keep trying, always imperfectly, to learn and work creatively in relationship with others.

References

Ball, S.J. 1993. Education policy, power relations and teachers' work. *British Journal of Educational Studies*, 41(2), 106–121.

Benjamin, J. 2004. Beyond doer and done-to: an intersubjective view of thirdness. *Psychoanalytic Quarterly*, 73, 5–46.

Bibby, T. 2011. *Education – an 'impossible profession'? Psychoanalytic explorations of learning and classrooms*. London: Routledge.

Bion, W.R. 1961. *Experiences in groups* (2004 edition) Hove: Brunner-Routledge.

Britzman, D.P. 2003. *After-education: Anna Freud, Melanie Klein, and psychoanalytic histories of learning*. Albany: State University of New York Press.

Britzman, D.P. 2006. Sigmund Freud, Melanie Klein, and little Oedipus: on the pleasures and disappointments of sexual enlightenment. In *Love's return: psychoanalytic essays on childhood, teaching, and learning*, edited by G.M. Boldt and P.M. Salvio (pp.165–84). London: Routledge.

Freud, S. 1921. Group psychology and the analysis of the ego. In *The standard edition of the complete psychological works of Sigmund Freud*, edited by J. Strachey (Vol. XVIII, pp.65–143). London: Vintage.

Freud, S. 1930. Civilisation and its discontents. In *The standard edition of the complete psychological works of Sigmund Freud*, edited by J. Strachey (Vol. XXI, pp.59–145). London: Vintage.

Gill, R. 2009. Breaking the silence: the hidden injuries of neo-liberal academia. In *Secrets and silence in the research process: feminist reflections*, edited by R. Flood and R. Gill. London: Routledge.

Menzies-Lyth, L. 1960. Social systems as a defense against anxiety. In *Identity: a reader*, edited by P. du Gay, J. Evans, and P. Redman (2000, pp.163–82). London: Sage in association with the Open University Press.

Moore, A., and M. Clarke. 2016. 'Cruel optimism': teacher attachment to professionalism in an era of performativity. *Journal of Education Policy*, 31(5), 666–77.

Murris, K. 2017. Reading two rhizomatic pedagogies diffractively through one another: a Reggio inspired philosophy with children for the post developmental child. *Pedagogy, Culture and Society*, http://dx.doi.org/10.1080/14681366.2017.1286681.

Phillips, A. 2007. *Winnicott.* London: Penguin.

Stokes, J. 1994. Institutional chaos and personal stress. In *The unconscious at work: individual and organisational stress in the human services*, edited by Anton Obholzer and Vega Zagier Roberts (2004 edition, pp.121–28). London: Routledge.

Williams, R. 1961. *The long revolution*. Harmondsworth: Penguin Books.

Winnicott, D.W. 1960. The theory of the parent-infant relationship. In *The maturational processes and the facilitating environment: studies in the theory of emotional development*, edited by D.W. Winnicott (1965, 2007 edition, pp.37–55). London: Karnac.

Winnicott, D.W. 1971. *Playing and reality* (2008, Routledge Classics edition). London: Tavistock Publications.

INDEX